KT-371-272

LITERACY TECHNIQUES

for Building Successful Readers and Writers

General Editor: DAVID BOOTH

NORWICH CITY COLLEGE LIBRARY

Stock No.	204398	
Class	372.4	Boo
Cat.	Proc.	

Stenhouse Publishers

YORK, MAINE

Pembroke Publishers Limited

MARKHAM, ONTARIO

204 398

Contributing Writers

Ann-Marie Adams
Diana Attar
John Bairos
Helen Belcev
Melanie Brennan
Maria Bruno
Lisa Bunga
Drue Burnstein
Suzanne Ceccato
Eric Chercover
Costa Cristou
Graziella DeLorenzi
Georgia Demakopoulos
Kimberley Erickson
Maxwell Evans
Silvana Febbraro

Frank Galati
Jerry Georgiadis
Shannon Grant
Andrew Hall
Andrea Hastick
Leeanne Hoover
Robert Kay
Waheeda Khan
Sarah Kurita
Sherman Lam
Zita Lapinskas
Loreen Lee
Michael Lee
Martin Lewis
Anria Loubser
John MacMillan

Michele Martin
Kimberley McCallum
Morgan McQuay
Wendy Menzcel
Julie Millan
Vivian Milios
Kally Nastos
Avy Ouaknine
Marilyn Orszulik
William Parsons
Mary Piercey
Deanna Pikkov
Tammy Pochmurski
Wanda Postill
Lilian Pritchard
Rosa Puopolo

Elissa Rodriques
Paula Rosa
Karin Schemeit
Chan Seow
Caroline Simmons
Kathleen Simon Lee
Claire Slater
Walter Teres
Christina Tolone
Efthimia Tsianos
Reinaldo Valverde
Andrea Van Kampen
Denise Westbrook
Melanie Wolfe
Jimmy Yee

©1996 Pembroke Publishers Limited
538 Hood Road
Markham, Ontario L3R 3K9 Canada
www.pembrokepublishers.com

Published in the U.S. by Stenhouse Publishers
P.O. Box 360
York, Maine 03909
ISBN 1-57110-324-4
www.stenhouse.com

All rights reserved. No part of this publication may be reproduced in any form or by any means, electronic or mechanical, including photocopy, recording, or any information or retrieval system, without permission in writing from the publisher.

Every effort has been made to contact copyright holders for permission to reproduce borrowed material. We regret any oversights that may have occurred and will be pleased to rectify them in subsequent reprints of the work.

Canadian Cataloguing in Publication Data

Main entry under title:

Literacy techniques for building successful readers
   and writers

ISBN 1-55138-078-1

1. Reading (Elementary). 2. English language -
Composition and exercises - Study and teaching (Elementary).
I. Booth, David.

LB1573.L58 1996   372'.4   C96-931060-9

Editor: Joanne Close
Design: John Zehethofer
Cover Photography: Ajay Photographics
Typesetting: Jay Tee Graphics Ltd.

Printed and bound in Canada
9 8 7 6 5 4

Contents

Preface

This book is truly a collaborative effort. Over sixty new teachers worked on different aspects of literacy learning, reading books and journals, interviewing mentor teachers, observing and collecting ideas from successful classrooms, sifting and revising their findings with peer groups, and gradually sorting out those strategies that seemed most useful in helping children on the journey towards becoming effective readers and writers. We shared, rearranged, and modified our suggestions and activities to build the components that will help each teacher in designing a literacy program that works. Of course, the art of teaching is knowing what is needed for each child in a particular context, and we offer this book of strategies to help all of us create successful literacy classrooms for today's young people.

It is difficult to attempt to thank those colleagues who helped us create this book, for fear of omitting anyone. However, in our attempts, we are hopeful that those we have missed will include themselves in this general statement of gratitude.

We want to thank the children who shared time with us throughout the year, time they might have preferred to spend with their classmates or their homeroom teacher. They accommodated themselves to our needs and brought both learning and satisfaction to all of us engaged in this literacy project.

We thank the mentor teachers who opened their classroom doors to us, instructors and new teachers, and offered guidance, support, and willing shoulders when the journey grew difficult. We thank our school librarian, Barb Young, for her amazing knowledge of learning resources and her encouragement and permission in allowing us free rein with her superb library.

We thank the principal, Anne Christy, and the vice principals, for their support in offering us Wilkinson School as the base for our explorations in literacy, and for guiding us around the mine fields.

We thank the Wilkinson School Family for its collaborative school culture, for welcoming us to its meetings and potluck dinners, and for making us feel like members of the community.

We thank Dr. Carol Hennessy, coordinator of off-site centers of the Faculty of Education, University of Toronto. She spent hours organizing and supervising the project, bringing her wisdom and patience to solving the "nuts and bolts" problems that surfaced daily.

We thank our colleagues in education who gave us the rich library of resources that we drew upon in our reading and research, authors such as Lucy Calkins, Randy Bomer, Regie Routman, Nancie Atwell, Constance Weaver, Aidan Chambers, Bob Barton, Jan Wells, Jo Phenix, and dozens more. Their writings enabled us to design our literacy project and to strengthen our philosophy and our techniques for helping young readers and writers.

Ten Principles of a Literacy Classroom

1. Parents place their trust in teachers and believe that their children will be encouraged and assisted in their journey toward literacy. This is a complicated task in today's world of changing values and customs, but it must remain a strong mandate for those of us who believe in the child's right to become a reader and writer.

2. Teachers need to set up explicit expectations for their students, and struggle to help them fulfill their independent expectations as learners. The best learning/teaching situations generate a joy and satisfaction in children as they grow toward becoming members of the literacy club.

3. Children need to read and write frequently for authentic reasons as they come to realize that being an efficient reader and an effective writer contributes to their communication success and personal satisfaction, and gives them control over their lives. Teachers need to model their own language development, and support literacy growth for each child with appropriate and involving strategies.

4. Schools need teams of teachers to design and implement programs that support a child's development. Children do not change all at once; learning is developmental and children progress individually, requiring literacy programs for specific phases. Every teacher brings strengths to a classroom, and when teams encourage collaboration and cooperation, teachers and children benefit from the shared knowledge and special competencies. Teachers need to be open and flexible, welcoming new ideas and reflecting on the changes that occur.

5. Teachers know they are not in classrooms only to locate errors and circle mistakes. They need to focus on what children can do, through observation and assessment, and recognize the possibilities that lie ahead for each child. They need to see mistakes as part of the learning process, and to use the knowledge that they have gleaned from the children's attempts to offer support and instruction in literacy techniques.

6. Teachers do not dismiss invented spellings or ignore phonic generalizations; they learn from the child's representation of language and help the child, tapping into his or her knowledge base, to work toward modifying and extending language use toward clear, standard English. Teachers use a variety of strategies to help a child learn how to read and write in developmental steps. They know there must be literacy growth and that they must work toward developing each child's potential in language competency.

7. The chief goal of literacy teaching is independence for each child. If children remain dependent on teachers and texts, they will never take charge and self-monitor their behaviors and progress as learners. Teachers need to celebrate a child's new-found independence at each stage of growth in this lifelong journey into literacy.

8. Children need to negotiate the learning with the teacher, making responsible choices and taking ownership of their decision making. As teachers share the responsibility of developing the content and structure of the program, the children co-plan literacy events, developing a commitment to their learning and to the progress of their classmates. The teacher defines the goals – the children are part of the design team that implements them.

9. Teachers need to organize their classrooms for maximum learning. Efficient systems of managing behavior, of creating workable routines, of ensuring suitable resources and materials promote a classroom atmosphere of cooperative and collaborative learning. Demonstrations and mini-lessons are vital in helping children become independent learners.

10. A classroom is a community of interdependent people who meet daily throughout a year for the betterment of all. Teachers need to take time for classroom meetings to work out problems, to celebrate special events in children's lives, and to help them to work together in a variety of modes, to learn that everyone can contribute to both the work and lives of all who are part of each classroom. Parents (extended members of the class community) are important to the success of the program. They need to be communicated with often, to be welcomed into the class whenever possible, and to be respected by school personnel. When parents participate in their child's learning, the child grows.

Part A: Learning to Read and Write

1: Conditions for Literacy

1. Reading is a meaning-making and meaning-driven activity. A reader requires prior knowledge in order to construct meaning with a text.
2. Reading success can be determined by the context of the print, by the format of the text, by the style of the writer, by the purpose of the text, and especially by the background and life experience of the reader.
3. Writing is a complex act, a symbolic system – a means of representing thoughts, concepts, and feelings – that involves memory and the ordering of symbols to communicate ideas and feelings to others.
4. A child's attitude or disposition to reading and writing may determine his or her success in each act of reading and writing.
5. Individual aspects of writing (phonics, sentence structure, punctuation, format) are important parts of the whole process of writing, and can be focused on and learned through a variety of effective strategies that remain connected to making meaning with print.
6. While reading is much more than pronouncing words on a page, reading text aloud can be a significant part of becoming a reader and writer. Joining in the act of reading with one's own voice while others listen or participate leads to the satisfaction associated with belonging to the literacy club.
7. The context in which a reader finds himself or herself may determine the nature of the literacy event. Reading a science report to a group differs greatly from chanting a big book with the whole community; a teacher listening with interest differs greatly from an observer conducting an assessment.
8. Each child's response will be unique for a variety of reasons – social experience, cultural connections, personal interpretations of words and expressions, relationships with others, and appreciation of the author's message.
9. As part of a community of readers, members talk about personal interpretations and questions related to common themes that, in turn, affect the thoughts of others in the community.
10. Reading and writing are closely connected processes of learning. A child who writes down his or her thoughts thinks and reads while re-composing, revising, rereading, and editing the final product.
11. Literacy learning is developmental. Children proceed at individual rates, and teachers must provide the conditions that allow and enable their literacy learning to take place. Teachers must have high expectations for each child's success, and support development and learning with appropriate and supportive attention that embraces the child's interests and needs.
12. Teachers need to read to young children throughout the day, at times rereading the same text, and provide time for the children to read. It is important to develop the children's familiarity with a great variety of texts, to have them reread passages and texts for the sake of developing fluency, and to reread selected parts of the material in order to develop varied reading responses.
13. Teachers may select books that share a common element: author, form or structure, theme, time, topic, setting, or contrasting views. Such structuring enables the reader to develop a perspective and an increased awareness of literacy resources.
14. For the purpose of developing the child's awareness of the scope of responses available to a text, the teacher may model particular responses.
15. Encouraging a child's personal response remains a priority. The child's individuality of expression and interpretation is supplemented by the guidance, the encouragement, and the knowledge of the enabling adult.
16. Methods and skills for examining the content of literature can be introduced and developed in a variety of ways that will sustain the interest of the child, increase comprehension, and generate variety in expression.

2: Print Awareness

Children need a way into the world of words. They need to hear, talk about, read, reread, write, explore, and experiment with print to develop and internalize literacy strategies. Teachers can surround the children with an environment of interactive print experiences.

1. Make Available a Variety of Materials

The children's reading and writing environments can include a variety of materials that will allow them to pursue interests and discover new information while developing their literacy skills. Classrooms, libraries, and home environments can offer abundant resources that are appealing and relevant to children, such as books, magazines, anthologies, novels, picture books, poetry, newspapers, biographies, folklore, and reference materials. Then children will want to explore and deepen their understanding of the written word. Unlimited access to writing materials – pens, markers, pencils, paper – is also important since they provide a palette and canvas for children's expression. Moreover, the integration of technological aids – typewriters, word processors, computers – helps children to develop skills that are important to their future, and the use of these tools in the classroom, in libraries, and in the home acts as a motivator for further reading and writing.

It is also important to have a large quantity of reading material available to children. The years between eight and thirteen are considered to be the "quantity" years where children gain reading power through in-depth experiences with a profusion of reading materials, including biographies, science books, and novels. Often children of this age group will enjoy reading several books by a favorite author, or a series of books with a familiar set of characters. However, a reader's taste may shift frequently. Moreover, a vast supply of books is necessary to satisfy the range of reading levels within a classroom. In addition to providing books for new learners, children who have become mature and independent readers need to be challenged with materials that present problems and situations of greater complexity, contain subtle characterizations, and provide contexts that challenge their concepts and ideas.

2. Surround Children with Print

Literacy development is a seemingly natural act that requires an unnatural environment. Effective classrooms are those that surround children with print: displays of text demonstrate to children the power of writing and may foster their natural desire to express themselves.

Display Ideas

- Clearly label all material and centers.
- Display children's written work, important notices, newspaper articles on current events, "quotes of the day," and the conventions of writing.
- Monitor the number of books the children read.
- Create and post reviews and ratings of books and authors.

Sample Display Forms

bulletin boards	advertisements	mobiles
posters	flyers	maps
newspapers	filmstrips	surveys
newsletters	banners	murals

---

3. Develop Meaning-Making Strategies

Schools need to provide children with time for independent reading, but that is not enough – they must be given time to reflect and develop responses to what they have read, relating print to their own experience. Children need many opportunities to respond to text in a variety of ways in order to enrich and extend their process of developing meaning. Personal written reflections can demonstrate the power of writing, and can serve as a launch pad for future thought.

Learning through literacy can also be a social act: children can deepen their understanding of texts by discussing their thoughts with peers, family members, teachers, and librarians before or after writing reflections. Other effective literacy strategies include conducting classroom discussions, developing projects that require group research, writing in literature journals, role playing, and retelling stories.

4. Practice Makes Perfect

Children who only read and write periodically often dislike or can't relate to reading and writing.

The process of literacy requires much practice at home and at school. Children need time for reading, choice in the books they read, and what they write about. A child who reads and writes freely at school is more likely to do the same outside the classroom and will utilize literacy to become an independent learner, able to identify his or her needs.

5. Book Talks

A successful classroom reading program incorporates book talks on a regular basis. This strategy enables teachers and children to share their thoughts and feelings about books they have read in group settings. In this way, children can begin to develop an appreciation of genres of literature, promote favorite books to peers, and learn how to summarize a book or retell a story. For the reluctant reader, this is a good way to introduce him or her to new and suitable books.

Book talks can take place in the classroom, library, bookstore, and at book fairs. When introducing book talks, a useful way to stimulate interest is to group and display books under categories, including new books, books with similar themes, books that celebrate an occasion, and books written by a specific author.

When initiating a book talk, avoid questions that can be answered by only one response. Instead, a conversational approach such as, "Tell me..." invites children to share their opinions more freely. Book talks can be done by children, teachers, librarians, or invited performers such as authors and publishers.

6. Reading Displays

Children's written stories can be displayed at a center and others invited to respond to the display. Questions inviting further responses could be posted on cards. As examples: "Write a speech bubble telling what your favorite character is saying" or "Which character would you most want to interview? What would you ask him or her?" Children may write a script for the interview, which can be role played and presented to others.

7. Pen Pals

Children can become highly motivated to build literacy skills when you integrate letter writing into classroom time by arranging for them to correspond with peers at area schools, or in other districts, cities, provinces, or countries. Children can read to their classmates the letters they have created or received. These activities can also include Internet experiences. For more on pen pals and the Internet, see page 99.

8. Incorporating Other Media

The development of children's literacy can integrate resources other than books. Television, for example, is a powerful force that has a tremendous impact on most children. Instead of ignoring it, consider utilizing it as a vehicle for invitation, exploration, and integration of literacy in the home and school.

Children can keep a journal of the television shows they enjoy watching. They can be encouraged to discuss, retell stories of, and write about relevant programs, and to write stories involving some of their favorite characters. Many kinds of shows can be considered, and the class can participate in a rating survey of current popular programs. Similarly, movies, songs, and the Internet can be integrated in the literacy curriculum. Be creative when considering the use of these resources as ways to develop literacy.

3: Environmental Print

Most children begin to notice how print works, at home and in their environment, long before they start school. Most are fascinated with print – some can write a few letters or their name, understand that print carries meaning, or retell favorite stories; others model pretend writing. A few can read favorite books and satisfying stories that provide the background for literacy. Children first learn to read from environmental print, and by talking about and listening to, many times over, the predictable patterns found in favorite stories. Teachers can often identify the children who are read to regularly at home, and they appear to have an educational advantage over those who have not had similar experiences, adding weight to the argument that strong literacy links should exist between home and school from the time a child starts school.

Children need many opportunities to preview books, take part in literary events, and talk about books in order to enter the world of reading. Each child progresses at his or her own level – teachers must recognize and build on these emerging understandings, find practical ways to monitor progress, and record the broad spectrum of observations, ranging from a child's beginning sense of story to his or her expanding awareness of the significance of print. Children must see themselves as successful readers, and teachers must demonstrate a full range of reading strategies in order to build their confidence. When children see a reason to read and write, most will want to become literate. The creation of real-life reading and writing situations, developing from specific needs in order to accomplish goals, results not only in literacy but also in pleasure, joy, and a lifelong love of reading and writing.

Some of the first words children recognize will be found on labels and signs. We do not need to teach these words because we automatically attach meaning and relevance to them and their symbols. In a language-based classroom, the environment is full of print, signs, books, magazines, stories, labels, and lists. These written messages help us communicate and give us information.

Teachers can draw children's attention to print by creating an environment that is full of meaningful texts: signs, books, magazines, stories, pop-up books, pattern books, joke and riddle books, baseball cards, children's names, messages, labels, and the letters of the alphabet. Texts can be displayed on the walls, chalkboard, ceiling, floor, bulletin boards, and hall closet. Boxes, folders, puppets, masks, and mailboxes are more ways in which print, story, drama, and drawing can be integrated. The physical setting (e.g., pillows, carpets) acts to complement and enrich the cognitive setting. Through such means children become aware of written messages on both cognitive and visual levels. Acting as literacy role models, teachers can read aloud to emphasize the power of print and the joy of story. Reading naturally expands to include writing: reading and writing expand language development. Teachers should possess an understanding of the ways in which literacy emerges from a child's perspective both at the theoretical and practical levels.

4: Reading to Children

Reading to children encourages literacy, promotes reading skills, and contributes to the sharing of the joy of literature. As children listen and respond to literature, they predict, make inferences, hypothesize, identify with the characters, respond critically and creatively, and develop a sense of story. Stories read aloud can be above the class's reading level, exposing them to an even greater range of literacy.

A one-on-one school reading activity (based on the home bedtime lap-reading experience) usually occurs between a teacher and child, but it can also occur between an older reading buddy or a parent volunteer and child. As the child listens to the story being read aloud, she or he begins to notice the words on the page. By following the eyes of the reader, the child understands that books are read from top to bottom and left to right. As she or he hears and sees words of a favorite book, the child notices that some words occur repeatedly, leading eventually to recognition of these words. This recognition also stems from familiarity with known words in specific contexts. A whole-class shared reading experience is a natural extension of the one-on-one lap reading activity.

Reading aloud can alter a child's attitudes to and appreciation of the developing journey towards literacy. The teacher models the joy of reading, and the satisfaction that comes from making meaning with print. A child who cannot read well is able to understand orally the stories and articles that are brought to life by a willing teacher, building vocabulary and sentence patterns through the ear, and connecting what she or he hears to printed text. Children benefit from listening to stories and books read aloud, from repeated readings of favorite books in the primary years to book talks, demonstrations, and sharing of excerpts and poems in the senior years. Hearing text read aloud allows children to focus on how various types of text work and how authors work in the writing process. Children who have limited reading ability can still appreciate the text and join in a variety of response activities. Examples include: forming discussion groups, working at thematic centers, taking part in whole-class drama, working from within the book's story frame, and learning how readers seem to function.

When teachers read aloud to children, they act as language role models. A teacher can read aloud a variety of literature forms, including folk tales, stories, poetry, and biographies. Children should have the chance to experience hundreds of books through their teacher's voice to provide opportunities for language and concept development.

Preparing for Reading Aloud

1. Utilize books suited to the children's age level. Often, older children have not considered reading picture books, but enjoy experiencing them when teachers read aloud.
2. Choose books that are appropriate and relevant to the needs and wants of the class.
3. Develop performance strategies that invite children into the story:
   - use dynamic shifts in volume,
   - fluctuate the timbre and tone of your voice,
   - develop character voices that can be used in a number of stories,
   - find places to pause and ask questions or make observations,
   - understand the stories you plan to read.
4. Rehearse the stories you plan to read.
5. Develop a repertoire of practised stories for rereading.

Reading aloud can be integrated into a curriculum in many ways. For example, when working on a unit about exploration, a teacher can include books about the Franklin expedition, space pioneers, or mountaineering in the Himalayas. When involved in a novel study, a teacher can read excerpts from books similar in theme to those being read by the children.

Invite Authors

Local authors can be invited to visit the school and share their reading and writing experiences. Children enjoy these visits where they get to meet a "real" author and can ask him or her questions about writing, being a writer, and favorite stories. They can also submit their writing to a professional author for feedback via WIER (Writers in Electronic Residence) on the Internet (see p. 99).

Sharing Stories

A variety of guests from the community (e.g., hairdressers, doctors, athletes) can be invited to serve as reading role models by preparing a story to read to the class, supporting the idea that all kinds of people are readers – not just teachers and librarians, but people who read because they want to. Older students, parents, teachers, senior citizens, and other members of the community can share stories.

Children can participate as storytellers by creating and completing their own stories and preparing a tape of themselves reading. The final version of the taped story is then made available at the listening center for others to enjoy. Pairing individuals can create some interesting, creative results. Further, some children may be inspired to dramatize or videotape their work.

5: Storytelling

By watching the listeners in a storytelling session, a teacher can come to a new understanding, and share with the children an enriching experience. The pleasure that arises between speaker and listener rests on the teller's interpretation, which may stimulate the listener's imagination to set the scene, visualize the players, and follow the action. The voice, expression, gestures, and imagination of the storyteller are powerful factors in determining whether the audience experiences a story vividly and creatively.

If a teacher is enthusiastic about a story and motivated to tell it, genuine success with storytelling will likely follow. She or he will need to pay attention to selecting, shaping, and presenting a story, but the main thing is to plunge in. Of the hundreds of thousands of stories to choose from, folk tales are an excellent source for storytelling since they possess immediacy, surprise, and support for the children's predictions about story.

Folk tales often offer the teller opportunities for outstanding oral performance. It is essential that the storyteller remain faithful to the core of the tale, but each person's embellishments are what makes storytelling such an exciting art form.

Storyteller Bob Barton's Suggestions

1. Read the story slowly. Make an outline of it in your own words and retell it to yourself. Read the story a second time to check that you have not left out any important details.
2. Read the story a third time and consider the feelings and attitudes of its characters. Tell the story to yourself again.
3. On the fourth reading, pay attention to the language of the story. What words or phrases should be preserved to retain the story's unique sound? Tell the story again to yourself.
4. A fifth reading might be devoted to blocking the story into scenes and considering the sensory details (e.g., lights, sounds, color). Now tell the story to yourself again.
5. During your final reading, concentrate on the beginning and ending. A strong start and a confident finish are important: you may want to memorize the beginning and ending of the story.
6. You can employ various editing techniques (e.g., condensing the story, elaborating on a small point, converting dialogue to narrative or vice versa, rearranging the plot particularly if the story's exposition is long). Insight into the kind of shaping a story requires becomes more apparent after you have told yourself the story a few times.
7. The real test of your telling comes when you face your audience. Storytelling is an audience-valuing situation. The storyteller should feel the audience response throughout and modify the delivery accordingly. The important thing is to start slowly, observe the responses of your listeners, and maintain your concentration. See your story, feel it – make everything happen. Use the voice you use in everyday conversation and respond naturally to your feelings about the story. As for gestures and body language, let them be natural as well. With practice you will learn what is right for your style and delivery.

6: Building Background Experiences

Teachers can provide concrete experiences before reading to broaden the children's background knowledge. Such experiences assist in providing clues for readers: the more we know about a topic, the greater our background experience and the easier it is for us to read about a topic. Children who have visited zoos, for example, will have more background knowledge relevant to reading about animals than those who have not had similar experiences. By sharing and discussing these experiences, a child's knowledge of concepts and related vocabulary is extended. Videos or drama are sometimes a more convenient way to provide necessary background experience.

Semantic cues help readers derive meaning from print by drawing on the reader's personal experiences and prior knowledge of the reading process and subject material. In order to understand a text, a reader needs to identify the meaningful relations among words (context clues) and comprehend facts, ideas, or concepts. If the text contains new information, it needs to be related to and integrated with what a reader already knows by building on prior knowledge. A reader who utilizes semantic cues uses picture clues, rereads the text, skips and reads on, and employs the meaningful substitution of words in order to gain understanding from the material being read.

Teachers can help the children expand their personal experiences by involving them in real situations, such as going on field trips, nature walks, and engaging in hands-on activities and experiments. If this is not possible, the children can be provided with experiences through videotapes, audiotapes, drama, and discussions. Young readers need to relate life experience to print experience.

Children can be helped to relate their background experience to "print materials" to aid their understanding that reading is meaningful on a personal level, and that it is also functional and worthwhile. Reading experiences can be personalized by building on the children's interest with a selection. As an example, if they are reading a story about a musician, the teacher can bring to class books and materials that relate to the topic. Childrens' knowledge and interest can be furthered by sharing with them background information before they meet the story on their own.

Pragmatic cues refer to the characteristics and the organization of different types of print materials. For example, a book and a menu are organized using different types of writing and print styles, vocabulary and language, and grammar and syntax. Prior knowledge about the practical organization of books or materials shapes a reader's thinking before and during reading. A reader that utilizes pragmatic cues uses main heads and subheads, skims for information, uses environmental print to gain meaning, adjusts his or her reading speed to the text's level of difficulty, stops and rethinks what is being read, and is able to move back and forth from print to graphic representations.

7: Shared Reading

Shared reading teaching procedures are based on observations of the way children learn to read during bedtime or lap-story reading experiences in the home. In a shared reading experience at school, reading becomes an enjoyable social activity when an entire class reads collectively. Through cooperative learning, children can tackle texts that are slightly beyond their developmental stage.

The teacher, through the shared reading experience, provides input and a supportive, motivating atmosphere in order to facilitate the construction of knowledge. Children are considered "doers" as readers; the reading experience furthers their lives in the here and now because it is an enjoyable and social activity; and they are free to take risks in a safe, encouraging atmosphere. Young readers, through a shared reading experience, make meaning as story, images, words, sounds, and rhymes combine and complement one another in a collaborative group setting. While shared reading experiences are most commonly associated with the primary grades, big books do exist for older children and the range of associated activities is vast. Shared reading is also a most effective strategy to use with ESL children of all ages.

In shared reading, the teacher uses a text that all children in the class can see. The text can be a commercially published or child- or teacher-authored big book, or it can be printed on chart paper, slides, or overheads. Appropriate texts can also reflect the oral and literacy traditions of the children's community through songs or poetry. Likewise, they can include alternate texts of class routines, rules, labels, and directions, reinforcing for children the concept that reading is relevant for action.

Shared Reading Learning Experiences

1. **Reading Skills and Strategies, Including:**
- using a variety of strategies to get at the meaning of a text
- predicting what will follow
- self-correcting through meaning making

2. **Conventions of Print, Including:**
- pages are read from top to bottom, left to right
- recognizing what a word is, what a letter is
- understanding how punctuation helps make meaning

3. **Sight Vocabulary and Sound-Letter Relationships**
In shared reading experiences, children learn sight words and sound-letter relationships incidentally when the teacher points to them while reading and directly when she or he draws attention to them for the purpose of discussion. Words children already know through speech and hearing are emphasized or noted in print by the teacher so that they will eventually be recognized by the children (sight words). Corresponding letter sounds are easy to remember because of the child's familiarity with the word in context and the known common sounds of several of the letters. By hearing favorite stories over and over again, speaking, singing, or chanting them in unison, and seeing the words and letters pointed to, children synchronize their ears, voices, and eyes with the print, leading eventually to independent reading.

Sequential Shared Reading Activities

1. Introduce a New Story

At least once a week, introduce a new story in big book format. The primary aim of the first reading will be to simply enjoy the story. Begin by displaying the cover and inviting the children to make predictions about it. List their predictions and talk about the author and illustrator before reading. To do a cued reading, cover the text and invite the children to make predictions of what the story is about based solely on the pictures. These predictions can be recorded and later compared to the children's understanding of the story based on hearing the words and looking at the illustrations. Reading the story with enthusiasm helps to engage the children's attention, making for lively post-reading discussions. Then read the story again.

2. Collective Rereading and Discussion

For a period of five to six days, reread and discuss one of the children's favorite rhymes, songs, poems, or stories. Point to words while reading and emphasize aspects of print and reading strategies that you want to reinforce (e.g., predicting, using context cues). Singing, choral speaking, or chanting repeated refrains is another way to involve children in shared reading. Stories with rhyme may encourage children to tap, chant, or dance. Emotion-laden words from the context of the story can be emphasized to generate a discussion and stimulate role playing to explore the words further. When finished, go back to the text and ask the children to find (read) the specific words they have discussed. A favorite activity is to have the children be the words. With your help, they print the words and punctuation marks on cardboard before lining up to tell the story.

After discussions and activities stressing the meaning of the story and words, you may wish to include activities emphasizing the mechanics of language, as illustrated in the following examples. Begin by writing the letters of the alphabet in a row across the chalkboard. Assign one word to each child. Ask them to come up to the board and make a mark under each letter that is found in their word. When everyone has finished, count the marks under each letter and make a graph. The children can identify the most common let-ters. A related activity is to have the children sort the words according to length (number of letters in each word) and then match the appropriate words with corresponding cut-up numerals.

Children can then sort the words according to one letter (preferably a pure initial sound). They can look at words where the letter is in the middle or end and discuss the sound it makes. Select and show two words with clear and different initial consonant sounds (e.g., bear, little). Have the children pronounce the words and notice the placement of their tongues and the shape of their mouths as they say the words and initial letters. What do these letters and words taste like? Brainstorm other words that start with the same letters and have the same sounds to make a key word chart that can be added to during the year. Isolating particular sounds in known words helps children to remember them. With subsequent selections of the text, you may choose to focus on other sound-letter relationships, punctuation marks, or a multitude of other aspects of print.

At every opportunity, help children predict, share feelings, use approximations, rerun/correct miscues, check for meaning, confirm, elaborate, make connections, see likenesses and differences, and draw conclusions about what they are reading and discussing. Conclude with a collective rereading of the story.

3. Rereading the Story Independently

This is the most important follow-up activity to the shared reading experience. Children can have a small version of a big book or individual copies of class-authored big books to read and reread. Often, the selections are available on tape or children can make their own tapes. Listening to the tapes facilitates learning to read. Children may want to read selections from the text aloud to you, a buddy, or a broader audience. (In the case of oral reading to an audience, it is crucial that children want to read to a number of people and that they have taken the time to rehearse the reading.) Children can also participate, in smaller groups, in related arts, crafts, drama, music, and writing activities as additional reading response. Opportunities should be provided for children to share their responses with other groups or the class as a whole.

8: Alphabet Activities

The bright colors and interesting items for each letter in an alphabet book attract and hold children's interest. Listening to the teacher read the books and paging through them on their own are recurring activities that children enjoy. Alphabet books also teach letter form, and most will include upper- and lower-case letters. Once children have grasped basic letter forms or shapes, teachers can help them focus on the style of letters. Teachers can also use alphabet books to help children make the connection between each letter and its sound. Of the many alphabet books available, the following three have proved popular with children.

Antics by Catherine Hepworth
Putnam, New York, 1992
- Challenge children to duplicate the word play and create their own version. They can brainstorm words beginning with the same letter and make up sentences using these words. As well, they can create alliterative poems, graph letter frequency, and create alphabetical lists.

Chicka Chicka Boom Boom by John Archambault and Bill Martin, Jr.
Simon & Schuster, New York, 1991
- Read the book several times, emphasizing its rhythm, and ask the children to chant along. When they need little in the way of prompting, ask them to sit in a circle with their feet crossed. They make a strong beat by alternating a clap on their legs with a clap of their hands. Make a tape of the children chanting and clapping the rhyme. Later, you can place the tape and the book in the listening center for children to use independently. They can build collections of words, phrases, and sentences, which they organize alphabetically (e.g., word charts, word files, alphabet posters, friezes, pictures, big books).

I Spy: An Alphabet in Art by Lucy Micklethwait
Greenwillow, New York, 1992
- The intention of this book is to introduce children to fine art. Objects are presented for each letter of the alphabet in paintings by Magritte, Picasso, Botticelli, and Vermeer, for example. Younger children can use the pictures to play "I Spy" while older children can research the lives of artists. If possible, invite a local artist to share information and take part in an art activity with the children.

1. Twinkle, Twinkle Little Star
Countless numbers of children have learned to sing the alphabet to this age-old tune. Those children who know the verse can teach their classmates the song. To help them, you can point to each letter of the alphabet as it is "sung." An incidental moment for learning can occur when children line up to leave the class. Randomly, give each child a letter – they can order themselves according to the alphabet.

2. Action Alphabet
Write a word on the back of each alphabet card that can be mimed (e.g., a=act, b=bounce, c=cat). Children can work in small or large groups. One child randomly selects a card, reads the word on the back (with or without your help), and performs a mime for the others to guess.

3. Eating from A to Z
Before beginning this activity, ask each child's parents or guardians to submit a written record of any foods to which his or her child is allergic. Over the course of six weeks, hold an alphabet eating activity. Each day, children suggest and decide on the food that will represent a letter (move through the letters in alphabetical order). If they suggest a food to which one or more classmates is allergic, explain the reasons why they will have to make another choice. Depending on your class, you may decide to supply the food, or you can ask children to take turns bringing the various items to class.

4. An Illustrated Alphabet
As a whole-class activity make an illustrated alphabet. The alphabet can be a themed alphabet, such as fairy tales, or it can be a mixture of images. Children draw one or two images for each letter of the alphabet. Work with the children to ensure that the words they choose to illustrate do not begin with consonant blends. Instead, brainstorm for other words that also begin with that letter but provide a pure sound (e.g., cat vs. chair). Display their completed work at children's eye level for easy reference.

5. Letter Alphabet Books

For each letter of the alphabet, children contribute one page that contains a word beginning with that letter and an illustration of the object. Completed books can be displayed for the children to use as a reference. As they discover new words, they can add to the books through the year. A class project that can be completed toward the end of the year is the creation of a class dictionary. Children input, with your help, words they have included in their books. For each word, they compose a brief definition and can include a small illustration. Pages can be copied and compiled so that each child has a copy of the dictionary.

6. "Grandmother Went to Market"

Children can form a large circle. Ask one child to begin by saying, "Grandmother went to market and asked for an apple." The second child repeats this and adds another word that starts with the letter "a." When children can no longer remember all the items, begin with "b," and so on.

9: Sight Words

To read effectively, a reader has to recognize words quickly, accurately, and easily. Readers translate written symbols that are grouped into words into their oral representation, hearing them inside the head during silent reading. In order to focus on making meaning with the text, the reader has to become efficient at word recognition, with as little effort as possible. Familiar words need to be recognized automatically; difficult words need to be recognized using a variety of techniques. Most of the words we learn to recognize almost subconsciously are learned through reading, where the context drives the reader toward making sense of the words if she or he is involved in authentic reading and construction activities. Some readers need to learn to deal with the nature of how words work in the following ways:

- Children need to play with words. Through exploring, constructing, observing specific techniques, and talking about words, they begin to develop an awareness of how words work.
- By seeing difficult or unfamiliar words in a variety of texts, children apply their knowledge of word decoding to make meaning from unknown words. The more children read, the more familiar the words become, and their subsequent recognition of those words becomes more efficient. They begin to see themselves as effective readers.
- Children can use texts that are memorable, such as rhymes and rhythms, predictable patterns, and series like "Toad and Frog" where the same words are repeated, as well as reading their own compositions and teacher-generated texts that highlight or repeat core words.
- Selecting a text in which the reader knows most of the words allows him or her to focus on making sense of the text.
- Children need to develop a sense of ownership of words they are learning to recognize. They recognize and retain words that are meaningful to them, and use elements of known words.
- Children can increase their word power by using words in the context of authentic language events – meaningful talk and real reading and writing.
- Children gain new vocabulary from their experiences with language used in context for real reasons – books, television, games, talking with friends, and overhearing parents.
- A bank of sight words or familiar vocabulary is necessary to make sense of a particular piece of text. When there are too many unfamiliar words to decode, a child loses control over the context. Since sight words are necessary for progress in reading, teaching strategies for inferring meaning is vital for developing readers.
- Children gain new print words through extensive reading and follow-up discussion to ensure that the words become integrated into their personal discourse. Teaching lists of new words out of context has little or no potential for increasing vocabulary.
- Teachers can teach strategies for inferring the meaning of words best through the context of the selection (and seldom through direct instruction).
- In order for a word to enter children's personal vocabulary, they need to generalize its meaning and apply it to a new authentic context.
- Dictionaries help children only if they understand concepts related to the word.
- Children will choose from their reading those words they make part of their own vocabulary.

- Children can often substitute words meaningfully and continue to understand what they are reading.
- Children can return to an unfamiliar word as meaning accrues through their contextual understanding.
- Children can examine text during a demonstration and point out words that the author has chosen because of qualities the words possess and predict meanings as they connect new words to their personal, internalized lists.

Not surprisingly, as children engage in activities that promote fluency (e.g., rereading, partner reading, choral reading) they begin to recognize words quickly and accurately. As children are exposed to words and word chunks that appear often in text, they begin to respond automatically. Good readers know many words, which helps them to focus on concepts and ideas as they read. Encountering a number of difficult words is frustrating for a developing reader, and extra preparation may be required when curriculum materials have specialized or uncommon vocabulary.

A love of reading and a fascination with words, along with activities that cause children to think about and use words in meaningful contexts, will help them to build vocabulary through the years. Fluent reading and writing requires the ability to immediately recognize (and spell) the majority of words needed to make meaning. As well, they require strategies for identifying (or spelling) the occasional unfamiliar or difficult word. High-frequency words, or words specific to a curriculum topic, can be displayed in a variety of ways so that children can refer to them as they read and write.

Developing a Sight Vocabulary

1. Matching Words on a Card
After the children have read a story in a reading group, write some high-frequency words on index cards. Children who have difficulty identifying a word can go back to the text, find the page that has that word, and using the story context and pictures, match the word on the index card to the word on the page.

2. Pattern Books
Try using pattern books to build sight vocabulary and fluency. Write sight words on index cards so that children can look at each word and examine its letters. Having children write an innovation on the story pattern is another way of reinforcing vocabulary.

3. And-Sand-Stand
Show children how familiar patterns and little words that they know can be used to figure out new words. Write a word that you think the children will know and use it to guide them in reading the new word (e.g., and, sand, stand).

4. Word Prompts
Emerging readers tend to have a difficult time with words such as "they," "what," and "when," especially if these words are at the beginning of a sentence. For example, the word is "they." You can prompt the child by asking, "What did they do?" or "What happened to them?"

5. Meaning from Context
Have children follow along in their book as you read the text aloud. When you come to a word that you expect them to know, pause and observe if children make connections to other words they know and use the meaning of the story to read the word.

10: The Cueing Systems

Reading is an interactive process in which the reader uses a variety of strategies for comprehension. In order to make meaning of print, the reader blends four cueing systems: pragmatic, semantic, syntactic, and phonographemic (phonics). In reading, all four cueing systems are used simultaneously to varying degrees. Pragmatic and semantic cues help readers to anticipate the meaning of the print; knowledge of syntax and language patterns is used to predict words and phrases; phonics cues test predictions for unrecognized words in order to confirm meaning. When readers cannot make sense of text, they must reread and examine the print more closely. It is important that teachers help young readers be aware of how the various cueing systems are used in order to gain meaning from text, and support their growth through constructive reading and writing activities.

Phonics

- Phonics is a part of word recognition, where readers use knowledge of how words work to make sense of an unfamiliar word.
- Phonic understanding must grow from what a reader knows about how words make meaning.
- Children begin with a story, then move to an analysis of unfamiliar or patterned words in the story, constructing generalizations about sound-symbol relationships from words in context.
- Young children sometimes think phonics drill sheets represent reading – that sounding out letters is all that readers do.
- Children should come to understand, through a teacher's demonstrations, that word games and phonic instruction help them to focus on words while they continue to read, unlock letter patterns, and decode to make meaning.
- Games and activities can promote an awareness of phonics because the satisfaction of playing with words to gain knowledge is an authentic purpose for learning.
- While teachers need to teach phonics through repeated demonstrations, mini-lessons, and conferences, it should always be done with the goal of helping children to discover and construct words, stressing that they can successfully learn to make meaning with print.
- Phonic instruction should help children to notice letter patterns that occur in a word or a family of words, stressing the larger segments in words, as well as onsets and rhymes.
- To read a word, children need to see it in context to determine its pronunciation.
- Words can be isolated out of context as long as they grow from the context of a story or book and are returned to it so that children can apply their new sound-letter knowledge.
- The better reader notices larger chunks of letters in a word in order to make meaning.
- Readers start with familiar words to unlock parts of unfamiliar words.
- Readers need to discover generalizations about sound-letter relationships, rather than being told them, to discover their use.
- By observing the children's needs through reading and writing, teachers can help children to develop skills of word recognition.
- Children often arrive at phonic awareness in the following order:

  - beginning consonants
  - final consonants
  - consonant digraphs (sh, th, wh, ch)
  - medial consonants
  - consonant blends
  - long vowels
  - short vowels

- As children spell words the way they hear them, teachers can note their experimentation with sound-letter relationships and analyze their application of word knowledge.
- When children use invented spelling to write, they are putting their phonic knowledge into action. From their attempts, teachers can readily see their developmental level and where they may benefit from directed teaching.

Long Words

Efficient readers, on meeting a long, unfamiliar word, tend to break it into recognizable chunks. They look for compound words, prefixes and suffixes, and familiar word clusters. Context then confirms the word recognition strategies they have used. Children learning to read require demonstrations and individual conferences modeling these strategies.

11: Focusing on Phonics

1. Sorting Words According to Length
On a series of index cards, write words that have between two and ten letters. Explain to children that you will call out a number, beginning with "2." All children who have words that contain two letters come up and place their words under the number, which you record on the chalkboard. Continue until all children have placed their cards. Discuss with the children why you didn't start with "1," and ask them to name all the words they know that contain only one letter. Together, identify the smallest and largest words and the number with the most words under it.

2. Filling in the Blank
Record a sentence from a children's book on a long piece of paper. Hold the sentence up and ask the children to read it aloud. Then cut the sentence so that each word is on a separate piece of

paper. One child can be "it." His or her task is to take one word from the sentence, and while the rest of the children turn their backs and close their eyes, hide the word in the room. When the child has hidden the word, ask the other children to turn, open their eyes, and find the hidden word. When a child finds the word, she or he replaces it in the sentence and the class reads it aloud again. The "finder" now becomes "it," and repeats the activity.

3. Names and Other Concrete Words

Print each child's name on a card, laminate it, and put it in a box. Draw one card each day – that child becomes "premier." The rest of the children can ask the premier questions about his or her life, family, pets, and so on. When finished, ask the children to watch as you print the premier's name on the board and show capital and small letters. Together, chant the letters as you spell the name. Cut up the name so that each letter is on a separate piece of paper. Children work to reorder the letters to spell the premier's name correctly, chanting the letters. Continue the activity the next day with a new premier. As the premier's list grows, point out similarities and differences in names, number of letters, first syllables, hard and soft letters (e.g., Cynthia, Connie), and rhyming words. As a class activity, children can create bar graphs of the letters in first and last names, and make up riddles using clues in the children's names.

4. Letter Actions

Laminate cards with a letter on one side and an action on the other (e.g., bounce, dance, gallop, hop, jump, kick, laugh, march, run, sit, talk, vacuum, walk, yawn, paint). Link the actions with letters and practise them until the children are proficient. Ask a child to come up and pick a letter. She or he shows it to the rest of the children who do the action associated with the letter. Continue the activity until children are better acquainted with the game, then pass out a card to each child. Children take turns showing the action while others try to guess the letter.

5. Count Words

Give each child ten counters. Ask the children to place a counter on their table or desk for each word that you say in a sentence. Begin with short sentences that contain simple words before making the activity more complex by including more words, and words that are more difficult.

6. Clap Syllables

Have the children form a circle. Ask one child to step forward and clap the beats (syllables) in his or her name. Model the activity several times before asking the children to join you. Begin with names that have one syllable, building up to names that have two syllables, then three syllables. Extend the activity by asking children to clap the beats in the names of objects in the room. Can they point to an object and tell you the number of beats in its name? When finished, write examples of single-syllable and multisyllable objects. Clap the beats in each word and discuss with the children that longer words usually have more beats than shorter words.

7. Nursery Rhymes

Once children are familiar with a few nursery rhymes, break the class into two groups. The first group can start a rhyme, but leaves out the last word; the second group shouts out the word to fill in the blank. Other activities include:
- making up new verses to rhymes, using the names of children in the class,
- choral reading rhyming books,
- identifying words from rhymes that sound the same and writing them on the board.

8. Little Words

Tongue twisters are a fun way to review consonants. Find one or two simple twisters and repeat them with the children until they can say them on their own. Make a poster of the tongue twisters, underlining the first letter of each word. Add a new poster for each tongue twister you introduce, and encourage children to decorate them.

9. Cross-Checking Meaning and Content

Write a sentence on an overhead, preferably one about a child in the class and which ends in the child's name. Cover the final word so children cannot see it. Display the sentence, and ask the children to work together to guess the word, giving them clues by showing the first letter, second letter, and so on if necessary.

10. Word Families

Begin by discussing with the children the concept that word families contain words that have the same vowel ending and rhyme. On a piece of chart paper, write "cat" on one side; "will" on the other. Children record the words in the same manner on a piece of paper. Next, write "hat" under "cat"; "hill" under "will." Children repeat and chant the words. Ask them to give rhyming words and record them in the appropriate column. Children can chant the words in each list.

11. Reconstructing Text

Cut apart or rearrange the text of a story or selection — the children can arrange the words to reconstruct its meaning. Pocket charts, magnetic boards, charts, and computers can make the re-configuring process easier. The children can sequence pictures, pages, lines, episodes, events, sentences, words, and paragraphs. From folders and envelopes they can sort and order statements, titles, words, webs, charts, books, themes, and nouns and verbs.

12: Word Power

Word Walls

A word wall, a visual display of words children have learned, acts as an immediate, accessible class dictionary and aids in the assimilation of high-frequency words. Word walls should always be used to associate meaning and practice activities: frequently used words should ultimately be automatic, and not phonetically spelled, in order that children can spend their time and energy decoding and understanding less frequently used words. Five words per week can be added to a classroom word wall, usually all on Monday, so that the wall will comprise 200 to 220 words by the end of the year. Words can be displayed alone, with a picture-sentence clue, or with a picture-sentence-poster displayed in the room.

Words selected for a wall are those children commonly misspell, confuse with other words, meet, or need in their reading and writing. Word walls, which are useful from grades 1 to 5 and higher, are arranged alphabetically on different colored pieces of construction paper. In addition to adding new words to the wall, children can read and write the words each day through clapping, chanting, rhyming, and spelling activities. Other word wall activities include: adding endings (e.g., "s," "ing," "ed") to words; handwriting; making sentences using the first letter and cloze to select a word that makes the most sense; making sentences from wall words; mind reading, in which the teacher thinks of a word and then gives five clues to guess the word; ruler tapping, in which the teacher calls out a word and then taps out some of the letters without saying them or finishing the word — the children finish spelling the word aloud; and sorting words based on features (e.g., all words starting with "t," words that end with "b"). Word walls for older children can include words related to current events or topics they are studying in other courses. In this context, word walls can resemble webs as words relating to shared topics are linked.

Classification Suggestions for Word Walls
- double letters (e.g., daddy, mommy)
- letter clusters (e.g., tion, ish)
- compound words (e.g., goldfish, housecoat)
- unusual letter clusters (e.g., aardvark, vacuum)
- prefixes (e.g., in, de)
- suffixes (e.g., tion)
- root words
- two-, three-, eight-, and twelve-letter words
- silent letters (e.g., ghost, knock)
- rhyming words (e.g., hear, fear, near)
- homophones
- plurals – regular and irregular
- contractions
- abbreviations
- synonyms
- functions
- joining words (e.g., and, but, however)
- alphabetical order

Word Banks

Word banks give children ownership and investment in the words they learn, increasing their interest and enthusiasm for learning in general. Children choose key words from their reading, based on a quality (e.g., sound, length), record the words on index cards, and file them in a personal word bank. Because the children own their banks, they recognize their words more easily. The teacher may also add complementary words to the bank to emphasize concepts (e.g., sound-letter relationships), but it is the children who ultimately control their bank and the words in it.

Each child may have two word banks – one for words that are being learned and one for recognized words. Words can be used in a number of ways: practised, matched, used in posters, made into cartoon captions, discussed, sorted, played with, cut and pasted, expanded, used to generate rhyming words, phrases, or sentences, shared, and traded. Through the use of word banks, meaning is made as words are recognized effortlessly and used in both contextualized and decontextualized settings. The growing number of recognized words (50 to 150) enables children to read independently texts of increased complexity, as well as to write their own stories with confidence.

Making Words

Children are given individual letters of a word on separate cards (upper-case on one side, lower-case on the other) in scrambled order. They make as many little and big words as possible before creating one word that contains all of the letters. In addition to a class pocket wall chart containing letter sets and word combinations, an overhead projector is an effective way to manipulate letters and demonstrate patterns.

Children, working collectively, can make words as well as engage in a number of activities, including: making up sentences, exploring sound-letter relationships and letter-vowel-consonant identification, practising capitalization, and transposing letters. Repetition, chanting, rhyming, placing, and writing are effective, fun ways to reinforce learning. Games progress from simple one-letter identification to four- and more letters until children create the final word employing all letters (with clues given by the teacher). The words often come from stories children are reading as part of a shared reading experience.

Word activities help children look for patterns in words that, as emerging readers and writers, they will be increasingly able to recognize as familiar words. Children in higher primary and junior grades can make larger words, demonstrating increased reading and writing fluency.

13: Moving into Literacy

The most critical factor of fluent reading is the ability to recognize letters, spelling patterns, and whole words automatically. The cueing systems coalesce when the child reads familiar texts with confidence and meaning emerges. The teacher can provide a variety of independent reading materials, including resources that address the cultural diversity of the class. Independent reading should be a daily whole-class activity in which every child and the teacher participates – children can choose the material with the teacher's help.

Choosing Books Carefully

Pattern books supply children with repeating words, sentences, and story parts. These books also focus on the rhyme and rhythm of language, which can lead to playing word games (e.g., matching words and word patterns). The predictability of pattern books enables children to join in reading in a risk-free environment, allowing them to feel comfortable and successful.

Illustrations in picture books can be discussed to help children realize that meaning can also be derived from illustrations to help them understand print. Illustrations support print and extend the meaning of the text by providing clues for the reader to discover what the author has written and the ideas she or he is trying to convey.

Reading Groups

Interactive reading in small and large groups should be encouraged. Children can be invited to predict vocabulary and outcomes by answering questions (e.g., "What do you think will happen next?"). During oral reading, children can complete sentences and fill in gaps (oral cloze). Readers and anthologies allow small-group discussions for readers at similar stages or with similar interests. Individual impressions find support and strength through collective sharing and recording of ideas. Examples of recording strategies are group record keeping, chart paper lists, and graphs.

Oral Reading

Oral reading can occur between one child and the teacher, a parent, or a buddy. Buddy reading, being read to by and reading to an older reader, is an effective one-on-one interclass literacy and community-building activity. Collective oral reading, in pairs or in small groups, can also increase comprehension as can activities involving whole-class shared reading of big books and chart paper/overhead reading of stories and poems. When reading for an audience, children should be given the opportunity to decline and time to rehearse. Readers' Theater offers an authentic reason for reading orally.

Reading and Writing

Children should begin to write as early as possible. The reciprocal nature of making meaning becomes evident as children learn that they can receive and send messages in print. Drawing, mapping, tracing, modeling, and constructing are representational activities that foreshadow writing, just as looking at pictures foreshadows reading.

Emerging readers borrow words and language structures from books to make up their own stories or model them after books. Words, stories, structures, and pictures serve as tools for a child's own writing. Complementary reading and writing combinations influence which books children choose to read – they begin to select books for content or author rather than for pictures or ease of reading. As children gain confidence and begin to experiment, patterns emerge from their reading and extend to writing, to language, to play and back to writing and reading. Children read for meaning by reading their own stories and often enjoy reading them aloud. Child-created pattern poems can result in choral reading through the use of chart paper with different colored pens highlighting certain words to make the reading easier. Opportunities and time must be provided for children to take responsibility for what they read by responding in tracking logs and response journals. Their written responses must be as embedded and as authentic as the stories they read.

Language Experience

A written language experience arises out of a collective shared reading experience. It involves the teacher as a scribe, recording children's talk about reading and books. It follows the same principle as shared reading and can occur between one child and the teacher, or the whole class and the teacher. As in shared reading, dictation and overwriting can give children the experience of being fluent language users. These techniques, despite being teacher-directed, help give children ownership over the writing, a sense of accomplishment, and a sense of freedom for those who do not have the working tools at their disposal (e.g., sound-letter associations).

Guided Writing

A guided, group, or shared writing activity arises out of a collective experience, including reading responses, field-trip notes, integrated curricular webs, lists, messages, narratives, nonfiction, and poetry. It is similar to language experience, but broader as it usually stems from a brainstorming session, includes both children and the teacher as scribes, and may culminate in a finished product. From brainstorming, ideas are selected, sentences composed and shaped, and the text reread and edited. Finished products may be displayed, presented, or published.

Modeling Writing

In this instance, the teacher demonstrates the writing process "live" by thinking out loud and composing a real piece, usually on the chalkboard, as the children watch and listen. The activity, which makes them aware of the need to write for real reasons, can include writing the morning message, notes home, and reminders for after-school activities. Children may, in some circumstances, copy what was written. They see the thinking, speaking, writing, and reading processes in action and are aware, either explicitly or implicitly, of the real links between spoken and written words, sound-letter relationships, punctuation, mistakes and corrections, and the use of different writing styles for different purposes.

Retelling

Internalizing a story and retelling it in a child's own words, both orally and in writing, increases the child's comprehension and improves his or her writing as it gives it a purpose. Storytelling centers with tape recorders, where children tell their own stories and perhaps teach them to others, provide effective venues for a number of retelling activities.

Integrating the Curriculum and Other Emerging Literacy-Related Activities

There are any number of activities in various areas that help children to become literate. Among them are drama, song, movement, choral speaking, Readers' Theater, storytelling, drawing and story writing, painting and murals, and computers. The use of print-related equipment as reading resources – overheads, slides, filmstrips, recorded plays, audiotapes, CDs, stencils, pens, puzzles, cards, art materials – also contributes to literacy development.

Guided Reading Strategies

For many children, learning to read does not come automatically, immediately, or easily. A teacher can make the difference between a child who does not develop into a successful reader and writer, and a child who becomes literate.

Guided reading can operate with a whole class sharing the same text, a group thinking critically about a book they are reading, or an individual involved in a one-on-one conference. The teacher supports the children's attempts at understanding the text and at working with the words inside it. A balanced program requires guided reading opportunities where the teacher assists the children in thinking their way through a story or a curriculum text, thereby helping them to think of themselves as readers who are involved in constructing meaning. Focused questions and activities that challenge and encourage children will support their efforts at meaning making with text.

14: The Stages of Reading

Children learn to read just as they learn to talk – by seeing others read, by listening to others read to them, by reading collectively with others, by reading by themselves, and by having someone listen to them read aloud one-on-one or in small groups. While some specific patterns of literacy development do exist, young children follow their own unique pattern of development, and may experience what appears to be temporary regressions on their road to literacy, depending on what they are reading and the context of the reading situation.

Characteristics of Emergent Readers

- understands directionality of print,
- identifies and names most letters,
- understands common words as well as some environmental print,
- exhibits interest in literature read aloud,
- voluntarily selects and shares books,
- uses literature as a framework for dramatic play, exploration of rhythmical language patterns, painting, sculpting, movement, music,
- chooses to hear familiar/unfamiliar stories, rhymes, jingles, songs,
- echoes recognized passages,
- recognizes predictable patterns in print,
- retells past experiences,
- relates sequences of events from personal/heard stories,
- follows a line of print in an enlarged text,
- realizes that print has common meaning,
- relates print to personal experience,
- makes meaningful predictions using context and syntax clues,
- understands function and power of print,
- reads back short experience stories dictated to teacher,
- attempts to write using consonant sounds, familiar patterns, images,
- connects visual images to text,
- experiments with forms,
- engages in pretend writing as a means to experience pretend reading,
- appreciates personal talk written down and read by others,

- role plays reading using oral language, writing, painting, symbols, sounds, movement,
- represents many words with invented spelling (often initial consonants only),
- enjoys text with vivid illustrations,
- likes to verbalize stories when watching videos,
- demonstrates confidence when silently reading along to audiotapes.

Characteristics of a Developing Reader

- comprehends sound-symbol relationships,
- pays attention to print for decoding purposes,
- recognizes phonic generalizations – digraphs, blends, rhyming words,
- often finger points and/or subvocalizes,
- uses all cueing systems – pragmatic, semantic, syntactic, phonographemic,
- periodically self-corrects,
- makes substitutions when text does not make sense,
- exhibits some independent reading, particularly with familiar texts,
- possesses a storehouse of sight words in writing and reading,
- uses invented or standard spelling to represent syllables when writing,
- relies on subvocalizing when reading silently,
- begins to develop a strong sense of story,
- enjoys discussing readings in small groups,
- values the connection of reading and writing,
- uses context clues as a means of predicting and meaning making,
- appreciates opportunities to verbalize stories to adults.

Characteristics of an Independent Reader

- reads without assistance at the appropriate level,
- reads silently with ease,
- uses all cueing systems – pragmatic, semantic, syntactic, phonographemic,
- becomes proficient at predicting unfamiliar words,
- self-corrects when reading becomes unclear,
- tests hypotheses,
- self-monitors for understanding,
- creates mental images to visualize descriptions,
- analyzes for roots, prefixes, suffixes,
- confirms, changes, makes educated guesses,
- absorbs diversity of meanings through discussion and analysis,

- makes meaning through language syntactic patterns, idioms, imagery, multiple word meanings,
- enjoys responding to reading – talking, writing, illustrating, role playing,
- maintains strong listening abilities,
- readily discerns book choices suiting needs, interests, abilities,
- delights in retelling stories to adults and peers,
- recognizes varieties of style,
- enjoys writing "in the style of,"
- has a well-developed sense of narrative and its diverse forms,
- prepares for reading by drawing on prior knowledge and analyzing text to be read,
- builds coherent, personal interpretations of selection and real-world connections,
- seeks important ideas,
- paraphrases, predicts, anticipates, and reads ahead for additional content,
- rereads for clarification purposes or to relate new knowledge to existing knowledge,
- looks for interconnecting details.

15: Parents as Partners

Children learn best when the home and school literacy environment are congruous. Greater parental involvement in education may be the strongest single factor that promotes a child's success. Teachers can help parents recognize the importance of a child's literacy development. When the school's environment is seen as inviting and collaborative, and in need of their support, parents often become involved.

When parents provide relevant information regarding their child's development, teachers have a greater potential to meet his or her needs. Parents can encourage their children to build on the work they are doing at school, play a part in developing curriculum, and help as public relations advocates for the school.

Parents need to be involved in the development of literacy. At the beginning of the school year, teachers can meet with the parents as a group to discuss their plans and goals for the upcoming year. During the school year, parental involvement, with feedback about existing literacy programs, can offer teachers a view as to what parents find most useful for their children.

1. Parent Volunteers

Supportive parents often serve as volunteers. Encourage male role models to participate whenever possible, since they, too, are essential for young children. Parents can:

- listen to children read individually,
- type children's stories so they can be published,
- help children do simple research,
- read to individuals or small groups,
- read stories on tape for the listening center,
- present personal stories,
- work with children on yearbooks, newsletters,
- help children select books at the library.

2. Newsletters/Calendars

A monthly newsletter or calendar can include stories about the school's sports teams, upcoming arts events, after-school programs, and so on. These can be written by children, club members, parents, and staff. This format enables parents to act as literacy role models to their children while becoming informed about school events and the talents of the student population.

3. Home Learning

Learning at home provides an opportunity for a parent, child, and teacher to work cooperatively. Some ideas that cultivate literacy at home are:

Borrow-a-Book: Children choose a book to borrow from school and share it with a parent — reading it aloud, retelling what was read, discussing it, and writing about it.

Share-a-Tape: Children use a tape recorder at home to interview parents, grandparents, and other family members telling stories. They share the stories at home and school by using the tape, a transcription, or an oral retelling of the story.

4. Recognize the Efforts of Parents

Parent letters can be an efficient means of recognizing parental contributions to their child's literacy at the same time that they keep them abreast of class and school events. The following letter was written to parents when one school undertook a home literacy campaign.

Dear Parent or Guardian,

You are your child's greatest learning resource. Recognizing this, our school has developed a "Parents as Partners in Learning" program. Projects within this program encourage learning and reading at home. They also provide an opportunity for me to talk with you about your child's learning throughout the school year.

Classroom Lending Library
Your child can borrow classroom books on a regular basis. This is a simple and efficient system that encourages reading at home. It also helps your son or daughter to develop a sense of responsibility.

Book Bags
Each Friday, your child will receive a tote bag that contains four or five quality children's books that share a similar theme. As well, the bag will contain an index card listing the books in the bag, a letter to you, instructions, activity ideas, and materials your son or daughter will need to respond to the readings (e.g., puppets). Instructions for these book bags will vary from week to week.

Monthly Parent Bag
Each month, your child can select ten books to explore with you. The books, chosen by your child, can cover a range of topics, and can include novels, nonfiction books, poetry books, and anthologies.

Newsletters, Dialogue Journals, Parent-Teacher Meetings
These give us a place to talk about your child's learning. Newsletters will supply information on school and class events and general news. Dialogue journals will be of a more personal nature and will keep you informed of your child's school experiences. Parent-teacher meetings will be held periodically through the year so that we can discuss your child and his or her school program.

Your support of this program is greatly appreciated. Please feel free to call me at any time to discuss your child's learning.

Yours truly,

Part B: Reading for Meaning

16: Comprehension Strategies

Teachers want to help children develop into independent, purposeful readers who think carefully about what they have read. Often, readers in trouble make little sense of what they have been decoding, or they choose to ignore meaning making completely, and give up in frustration. All children need effective comprehension strategies to become independent readers and writers. Teachers will need to promote thoughtful interaction with what is being read so that readers will be able to focus on relevant information in the text, make sense of it, and integrate that learning with what they already know.

Points to Consider in Promoting Deepened Comprehension

1. Real reading experiences will motivate children to explore the ideas in print further because what is being read will be significant to the readers, enabling "deep-structure" meaning making to occur.

2. Teachers need to help young people reveal their thoughts about what they have read so that they can begin to clarify, modify, revise, and extend their frames of reference. If they are afraid to share their understandings, or misunderstandings, how will they begin to grow as readers?

3. Each child must focus on making meaning for himself or herself in becoming a thoughtful reader. Comprehension is about thinking and understanding, and is affected by each person's knowledge, experience, and reason for reading a particular text. Proficient readers are aware of the techniques involved in making the most possible meaning with print; they make predictions, draw conclusions, and revise hypotheses about the text.

4. Proficient readers take risks. They learn to make educated guesses, predicting what the print

will mean, rereading for clues that are missing, confirming or making alternate predictions. By caring about the reactions children have to what they are reading, teachers can encourage them to speculate about the text, to think about its meanings, to reread for clarification, and to recognize difficult words through context clues.

5. The maxim says, "It takes two to read a book." By organizing book clubs, literature circles, and discussion groups, teachers can help children increase their understanding of a text. As members reveal their reflections about what they have read and interact with their group in exploring the meaning, everyone has opportunities to rethink and modify their personal understanding.

6. Teachers can encourage children to respond in a variety of modes to what they have read, helping them to think about the text in personal and meaningful ways. These interpretations, whether they be art, drama, verbal or written, can be shared to increase everyone's understanding of how text can be appreciated and valued in different ways.

7. Rereading or revisiting the text increases understanding. Teachers who use innovative strategies for having children interact with the selection help them to extend their appreciation of the text.

8. Teachers can help children to evaluate their own efforts as readers with activities and frameworks that promote sharing and exploration, and that continue the inquiry process for learning.

Encouraging Comprehension Before Reading

Many things affect how a reader makes sense of a particular text: knowledge of the content of the selection from life experience, familiarity with the author's writing style or other books, and an understanding of the issues or the setting of the selection. When teachers spend time with children before their reading time, especially with material that is unfamiliar or appears to be of little interest, then they will help them ensure that the reading is a more meaningful and satisfactory experience. Teachers help children to build and activate their background knowledge so that they can integrate the print experience with what they know. Prereading activities can arouse the children's curiosity and give them reasons for reading. Teachers may teach vocabulary that may be necessary to understanding the main idea, but only a few words, since children need to learn to identify words from context.

How Children Can Preview a Text

- Brainstorm as a group what issues and events might take place in the story.
- Describe what might happen in the story, based on prior knowledge and past experiences.
- Predict, from a summary or cover blurb, what might happen.
- Formulate questions about the story or selection to be read.
- Engage in a thematic exploration of ideas related to the story – view films, listen to stories, share poems, interview speakers, read extracts, articles, or summaries, conduct surveys.
- Conduct a discussion about ideas and issues related to the text to be read and share personal views.
- Organize a demonstration where you model the importance of prediction in reading. You can read the first part of the selection and then discuss with the children what is happening and what will likely happen. Special formats and print conventions can be explained.
- Examine a few difficult words that will appear in the text and predict what they are and what importance they may hold for the selection.

Encouraging Comprehension During Reading

Teachers now recognize that many children need support while they are reading, not just to be tested after they have completed a passage. Many factors affect the understanding of or the ability to continue reading a text: the context in which the children are reading (peer group pressure, the physical setting), the purpose of the reading (the kinds of interaction, subsequent assignments), supportive assistance (discussing a complex format, clarifying an unfamiliar phrase), sharing predictions to confirm or rethink hypotheses about the text. Teachers can focus a child's attention on particular issues or characters as the story unfolds, and note effective or difficult uses of language. This enables the teacher to monitor the child's developing comprehension.

Teachers can encourage comprehension during the reading in a variety of ways:
- directed reading activities with a small group or the whole class,
- cloze procedures that assist the child in looking at meaning in a text,
- dialogue journals that are incorporated during the reading of a novel, revealing the reader's thinking processes.

Encouraging Comprehension After Reading

Teachers need to help readers to continue reflecting upon what they have read and to help them integrate the text with what they already know and can do. Children need to interact with the text – rereading, revisiting, rethinking, and reflecting on the content and style. By promoting critical thought through activities that require thinking, solving problems, and making decisions, and by encouraging personal responses, teachers help children to construct meaning with the text. Teachers want young readers to make connections with books, authors, and issues, and to realize that reading response is about making more meaning, rather than just completing follow-up activities. Of course, the best extension activities grow naturally from the reader's reactions to what was read.

Teachers want, for good reasons, to promote activities that encourage critical thinking, reading, writing, and discussion, challenge attitudes and ideas, connect literature to life, and integrate reading and response inside the learning spectrum. Unfortunately, many children have spent more time completing follow-up activities than they have spent reading the selection. At one page per minute, a five-page story takes five minutes to read. Since children become fluent by reading, and since making meaning is a cumulative process, they need to read much more than a few minutes a day to develop into literate human beings.

In a print-rich classroom, children have opportunities to read a variety of books for different purposes: stories in anthologies (or readers), novels, curriculum materials, poems, plays, and references. As well, children benefit from reflecting on what they have read, listening to classmates' interpretations, raising their own questions about the text, retelling what they have read, reworking and reformatting ideas (necessitating a careful examination of the text and a thoughtful response to what the author was trying to say), examining the author's style and language choice, and reflecting on ways in which individual class members bring meaning to the printed page.

17: Predicting

How to Encourage Prediction

1. Stress with children the importance of predicting when reading by reading/viewing together and discussing how each child comprehends, demonstrating the importance of prediction to other readers.
2. Invite children to predict a text's vocabulary, language style, structure, and content from its title, cover, table of contents, pictures, photographs, diagrams.
3. Ask questions: "What do you know?" "What do you want to find out?" Encourage children to formulate questions using guiding words – who, where, when, what, why, and how.
4. Have children consider previous experiences related to what they are about to read or view. Questions can focus and extend the child's thinking about a particular aspect related to the material at hand. The discussion itself may also generate new questions.

Strategies for Teaching Predicting Techniques

1. Advertisements
Share with the children a book or movie advertisement. Ask, "What do you see?" "What do you think this book/movie is about?" "What kind of book/movie is this?" "Have you seen this phrase or picture before?" "Where?" Read/view the first part of the material, then ask the children to discuss what is happening using the information they have read/viewed and what they already know to justify their responses and to predict what may follow. Read/view the next part and repeat the process. When finished, children can check for predictions that have been confirmed. As a group, read/view the material a second time, this time predicting meanings. Read/view the material a third and final time, pausing before repetitive parts and inviting children to join in.

2. Short Stories
Divide a short story into three or four episodes. Title each episode and record it on a separate piece of paper. Copy and attach the three or four pages so that each child or pair of children has a booklet. Ask them to read the title of each episode and draw a picture of what they think it is about. When finished, children can compare and discuss their picture sequences. Read aloud the story to the class. How accurate were children's predictions? Discuss with them how the titles helped/didn't help them to predict.

3. New Texts
Before reading an unfamiliar nonfiction text, write its title on the board. Ask the children to brainstorm sentences they think would be in the text. (An alternative is to have children brainstorm on their own or in pairs, and record their sentences before a class list is compiled.) As a large group, classify the sentences and display them where all children can see them. During and after reading, they can note how many of their predicted sentences were included in the text. A variation of this activity is to ask children to brainstorm words that will be in the text.

4. Grouping
Provide pairs of children with a series of pictures, words, sentences, or combinations of these related to, or from, a text. Ask them to determine methods of grouping, classifying, and sequencing the elements. Children can share their work with another pair. Together, the four pool their work and present it to the rest of the class. Make a class list of organizational methods.

5. The Z Was Zapped

Before reading Chris Van Allsburg's popular book, ask the children to list as many verbs as they can. Write their responses on chart paper. Read aloud the first page of the alphabet book and ask the children to predict what will happen to the letter before you turn the page. Make a list of the action words used in each "act," relating them to the children's verb list. As you continue to read aloud, children can pantomime the verbs. They can start to grow like the letter "G" and melt away like the letter "M." Ask the children to think of different verbs to perform a new version of the story, which can be made into a class big book.

6. Brainstorm and Categorize Information

Before children begin to read a piece of text, ask "What do you already know about this topic?" Record all responses. After they have finished brainstorming, ask children to categorize or classify the information to give it a logical structure. Each child can then identify what they want to find out by writing one or two sentences. At the end of reading, take a class poll to find the number of facts that were answered by the book.

7. Before and After Charts

This activity reminds children of what they already know and helps them link this to new information. It also clarifies the purpose of reading. Before reading, ask the children to list all they know about a topic to be studied. After reading, they write all they have learned. Children then find a partner with whom they compare lists, and write questions they still need answered. Together, they research the questions and write a short report that details their findings.

8. Think Sheet

This strategy directs children to set a purpose for their reading. Ask them to list all headings and subheadings of a book. With a partner, they brainstorm the contents of each section of the book and select what they think will be included. Each child reads the book and substantiates or revises the predictions. When finished, the children meet with their partners to revise information, record changes, and add other information.

9. Select a Reading Style

Children need to be aware of reading strategies and how they increase reading efficiency. Two useful strategies are skimming and scanning. To introduce the strategies, ask children to form small groups of four or five members. Give each child in the class a copy of the same text, complete with headings and subheadings. Using these as cues, children quickly skim the text and write predictions for each section. When finished, they compare their predictions with those of fellow group members to determine how well their predictions matched the content. An alternative is to give all children a copy of the same text and a list of questions that can be answered from it. Children read the questions and identify key words. They then scan the text to locate the key word and answer the questions orally in groups.

10. Set a Purpose

Discuss a text to be read by outlining its content and objective. Children establish a purpose for reading the text, for example, reading for enjoyment, skimming for a piece of information, or rereading sections for detail. Encourage children to decide on how they will read each new text.

11. Word Charts

These charts can help children to clarify vocabulary and use context clues to work out word meanings. Each child records new words she or he has met while reading and includes a brief description, based on content. This provides children with practice in paraphrasing, a useful skill in making notes and summarizing. If necessary, model the strategy until children are comfortable recognizing and using context clues.

12. Graphic Outline

A basic knowledge of text layout can help children to comprehend texts. Consequently, a graphic outline, a diagram of information located in the text, can be used by children as a framework for note taking or summarizing information. Ask children to look through a text and list features, in sequence, on the left-hand side of the page (e.g., main heads, subheads, diagrams, maps). On the right-hand side of the page, they record information in boxes, the size of which corresponds to the importance of the information. To help children, give clues as to how many ideas or points may be included under each heading.

13. Signal Words

Authors can organize text using any number of patterns. If children are to use these patterns to help process information, they need to be able to identify them, as well as the attendant strategies for summarizing information. To begin, introduce children, in small groups or as a whole class, to one type of text organization. Discuss signal words to look for in a text and how to record information through the use of diagrams suited to the text's organizational pattern. When children can identify and use one pattern, introduce another. Create reference charts that detail the organizational pattern, signal words, and ways to record information.

18: Guided Reading

An awareness of the development of group reading can help teachers understand how reading instruction in groups has evolved to what it is today and that it will continue to evolve. Directed group reading instruction was first described by Betts in 1946. He hoped to give teachers a format for providing group instruction, to improve children's word recognition and comprehension skills, and to help guide them through a reading selection. The activity was thought to be most beneficial when basal readers were used for small, homogenous group instruction. The benefit of directed reading lessons, or DRL, was that it was one of the first tools that consisted of step-by-step instruction.

Four Steps of DRL

1. Establish the purpose for reading, provide background information to children, and introduce new vocabulary.
2. Follow with silent or guided reading and purpose-setting questions.
3. Use oral reading to clarify or verify a point.
4. Conclude the lesson with follow-up activities.

The directed reading thinking activity (DRTA), an alternative to DRL and designed to develop comprehension and critical thinking, was first described by Russell Stauffer in 1960. In DRTA, children make predictions about what they're reading using information they already know and information in the text. The focus of the activity is to provide arguments that support predictions. One benefit of this strategy is the learning that can occur as children interact with one another to analyze and justify answers to the story in relation to what they know, or think they know, and the information in the text.

Examples of DRTA Activities

- Select an appropriate picture sequence. Give children the title on separate sheets.
- Read the title and ask children to predict what they think the title suggests. Make a list of their predictions.
- Show children the first picture and ask them to make further predictions. Encourage them to explain and justify their answers until they have placed the pictures in sequence.
- Have a discussion about the accuracy of their predictions and how they may have changed as each new picture was introduced.
- Follow the same guidelines as DRTA and ask children to draw what they think the story is about. The story should be short so that the activity will not be too long.
- On completion, provide time for children to discuss and compare their picture sequences.
- Staple picture sequences together to make a book.
- At the end of each "stop point" and discussion, ask children to record their predictions, reasons for the predictions, evidence from the text, and what they already know. This activity will allow them to examine how their thinking may have changed through the reading of the text.

Teachers control the rate and flow of information and decide on the amount of text to read between "stop points." It is important to accept children's predictions and not judge their correctness, and allow the children to explain and justify their answers. Only questions that will elicit as much information as possible should be asked. Two types of questions are standard to the DRTA: speculation and prediction (e.g., "With a title like that, what do you think the story is about?") and questions that require drawing conclusions and/or providing support (e.g., "What makes you say that?" "How do you know that?"). Literal questions are asked only to clarify a misunderstanding. Short stories selected for this activity should be unfamiliar to the children and have the ability to promote thinking. The teacher usually begins by giving children small amounts of information (e.g., the title) before supplying increasingly larger amounts (e.g., one line, one paragraph). The first "stop point" follows the title of the story. When reading is completed, a discussion or assignment may follow.

Directed Reading/Guided Reading Lessons – Moving On in Reading Instruction

Most children benefit from some guided reading instruction. In early primary, the guided reading lesson focuses on developing confidence, fluency, independence, and early reading strategies. Teachers need to be aware of each child's competencies, experiences, and interests. Guided reading instruction may involve the whole class or a small group.

During whole-class guided reading instruction, children read and discuss the same book at the same time. The way this is done varies: teachers may read aloud while children follow along, or teachers may ask children to read a part of the text silently for a specific purpose.

Children who are quick readers may be asked to "find the sentence that tells us... ." Individual silent reading, paired reading, or a class discussion may all be part of whole-class guided reading. Whole-class guided reading is an effective way to observe children's strategies and attitudes while building a reading community.

Small-group guided reading focuses on high-level discussion in which children react to all or part of a text, and is especially effective for teaching specific skills that require close supervision and interaction. Small-group guided reading allows the teacher to observe strategies that the children are using and to get to know each child as a reader. In early primary, the main purpose of small-group guided reading lessons is to develop confidence, fluency, and early reading strategies, and to promote independence.

19: Semantic Mapping

Semantic mapping is a prereading graphic display of categorized information written in chart form. Typically the activity, which involves the whole class, is based on material from teacher-directed discussions and/or whole-group brainstorming sessions. The technique activates and draws on the existing background knowledge and personal experiences of the children. This knowledge, when illustrated through a semantic map, is acknowledged, respected, and grounded, and thereby acts as the firm base and pivot point on which new concepts, revealed through the reading of texts, are understood.

In one method of building a semantic map, the teacher writes a term central to the reading selection, for example "whales," in the center of the paper. She or he then generates categories related to this concept, such as "life span," "types/size," "location," "habits," and "other whale stories." Each term is circled and lines are drawn to the central term to indicate relationships and adjacencies. The children then expand the categories to include specific details, examples, or related ideas. They may list "Waiting for the Whales," "Free Willie," and "The Whales' Song" in the category "other whale stories." The ensuing teacher-led discussion about the terms and their relationships is key to the effectiveness of the technique.

Another way of generating a story map is through child-initiated brainstorming and recording of details, ideas, and examples after being told the central concept. These secondary ideas or puzzle pieces could then be arranged and grouped in labeled categories. The organization of ideas flowing from a semantic map assists in the recall of additional related concepts. In both methods, circles do not have to be restricted to known facts – they can also include associations, concepts, and memories. Semantic maps should be seen as fluid and dynamic reference tools to be used throughout the reading process.

Semantic maps stimulate interest and confidence in reading, build vocabulary, and can serve as a teaching guide. They help children recall material they have read, and have been found to be a particularly effective strategy to help children who are reading below level in recalling text. Semantic maps help readers tap into existing networks of knowledge easily and integrate new information with previous understandings, resulting in restructured information networks. A slight deviation from traditional mapping occurs when the teacher gives, or generates with children, specific instructions or summaries regarding a text. This information can be given to the children before or during the course of reading, or it can be combined with related activities such as drama.

As a post-reading activity, children can create their own story maps. These maps, somewhat more similar to plot organizers than semantic maps, tend to detail the structural elements of a story – its characters, settings, events, problems, solutions, themes, and so on, and are arranged in story order. While the primary use of a story map lies in its usefulness as an aid to comprehension, some children may want to apply its strategies as an organizing structure for stories they want to write.

20: Responding to Reading

Responding

- Some books require no formal response.
- Children may need to explore a text in their own way.
- Some books require guided reflection.
- Children may need to share and listen to others' responses:
  - to develop insights into other worlds,
  - to notice and accumulate new words and language patterns,
  - to learn to discuss a range of texts with confidence,
  - to analyze and form generalizations from text,
  - to apply new learning to their own lives,
  - to become members of a literacy community.

Reasons for Responding

The teacher can take these opportunities to extend the child's response to the selection by offering a variety of activities. Limited readers, in particular, need to see the richness of literature response, and to recognize that a story is only a beginning point for expanding ideas and increasing language strengths. A good story provides a powerful context for looking at how words work. What children do after reading should relate directly to what they have read and to what they need or want to do.

- Establish a core set of resources for the classroom;
  - sets of books to be shared (e.g., novels, anthologies, collections),
  - a collection of books for independent reading (e.g., novels, biographies),
  - curriculum resources (e.g., texts, kits, media).
- In the beginning, teachers can use prepared resources (e.g., book guides, manuals, idea booklets) that accompany selections in anthologies or readers. These offer starting points for literature exploration, and free the teacher to observe and work with each child to personalize the activities.
- Teachers can create folders of follow-up activities for each selection (e.g., question guides, author information booklets, documents).
- Generic response activities promote interpretation and word play.
- Teachers want to encourage children to engage in "grand conversations," to think and feel and respond to the issues, the characters, the events, and the language of the selection. The focus is on topics of interest to the participants, and everyone's opinions are valid when supported by the text. Teachers can encourage children to share their thoughts and experiences with their classmates, extending the meaning making for everyone.
- Teachers need to provide experiences that help children to access relevant knowledge before reading a text, to think about experiences they have had, or to organize their thoughts and opinions about what they are going to read.
- Teachers need to integrate the language processes by ensuring that response activities provide opportunities for further reading, writing, speaking, and listening for thoughtful reactions that further language growth. Children need to use language to articulate ideas and to interact with the thoughts and feelings of others.

- At-risk readers require group members who will listen to one another, help activate background knowledge and build upon it, each learning from the other as they share and contribute ideas. By using a variety of grouping patterns, teachers can offer each child flexible settings for growth, ensuring that the purpose will determine the groupings. Heterogeneous groups, whole-class, and sometimes ability groups offer children opportunities to grow in particular skills and to engage in discussion and activities with a variety of children who offer different strengths. For example, ESL children need to read, write, and talk in meaningful contexts in cooperative and collaborative settings that encourage interaction. They require a modeling of language by participants engaged in using English for authentic purposes.

- Literature instills a love of reading, but not when it is accompanied by fragmented activities. Instead, activities need to be integrated, significant, and thoughtful sets of response modes that encourage children to think about what they have read long after the book has been closed.

- The development of independent readers is best accomplished by an enabling adult through the purposeful structuring of literacy experiences. It remains valuable to read to children throughout the day, to reread the same texts, and to provide time for the children to read. It is important for them to develop familiarity with a great variety of texts, to reread passages and texts for the sake of developing fluency, and to read selected parts of material in order to develop varied reading responses to the text. In providing structure, books may be selected that share a common element: author, structure, theme, time, different versions of the same book, setting, or contrasting views. Such structuring enables the developing independent reader to build a perspective and thus increased awareness of reading sources.

- There are many ways in which children can describe and thus express their thoughts and opinions about a book they have read. In choosing words to describe a particular story or passage, the child's ability to think critically and make judgments is challenged and expanded. As the child is directed to important words within a text, focus on meaning is stimulated.

For example, the construction of a word collage in a response encourages the child to make multifaceted connections to the material. In considering a single, appropriate statement for a book, the child is engaged in making the meaning relevant and particular to a point of view.

- The development of writing skills in conjunction with reading response also assists the child to focus on literacy values and skills. Encouraging the child's response, however, remains a priority. The child's individuality of expression and interpretation is supplemented by the guidance, the encouragement, and the knowledge of the enabling adult. Methods and skills in examining the content of literature are introduced and developed in a variety of ways to sustain the child's interest, and to increase comprehension in thinking and variety in expression.

- Responses to literature may be personal within a group context. Sharing informal gossip broadens the opportunity for children to express their opinions and perceptions about what they have read. The opportunity for discussion can be formal as well as informal, and the teacher may facilitate the opportunity for different kinds of discussion by directing attention to specific aspects of the literature. What is of interest to each child, however, is a prime factor that extends the child's interest in literature through his or her response to the form and content.

Teaching Tips

1. Provide a variety of response modes from which children can select.
2. Model and demonstrate examples of various response strategies.
3. Share, display, and discuss reading responses with the class.
4. Display examples of effective responses from previous classes.
5. Organize a class chart or schedule of reading activities each week.
6. Design activities surrounding a specific author or illustrator.
7. Make a reading response folder for each child. Children can record books read, those they want to read, and the time spent reading.
8. Establish reading contracts and schedules for conferences and group activities.
9. Encourage and negotiate with children to undertake a variety of response activities.

21: Cloze Procedures

Despite its appearance, cloze is not a typo! In 1953, Wilson Taylor derived "cloze" from the Gestalt psychology term, "closure."

What Is Cloze Procedure?

Cloze procedure involves oral or written deletions of parts of words, whole words, or phrases in a passage of text. "Clozing," or restoring these gaps, requires children to scan the text, recognize and process contextual cues, and then choose the most appropriate word. The reader learns to use context to help figure out unfamiliar words. It's an active, constructive language process.

A Cloze Passage

The cabin was buried deep (in) the woods. The water came from a (well) dug into the earth. Old trees were cut into (logs), and bushes were full (of) juicy berries. The birds sang each (morning) and the brown squirrels (gathered) acorns.

Cloze activities are suitable for use at all grade levels and help to build a number of skills exhibited by strong, fluent readers. They

- focus on contextual cueing systems, strengthening the readers' abilities to anticipate the text to make the most sense.
- have children interact with text – searching, scanning, and thinking – which may result in making meaning with print. Cloze can help expand the readers' reper'oires of thinking strategies.
- increase the readers' confidence – as they experience success with cloze, readers realize that they can predict in order to recognize words.
- are useful for assessing children's reading ability, comprehension, and vocabulary awareness.

Using Cloze Activities

Before teachers prepare a cloze activity, they will need to identify objectives. Teachers can consider the following points.

1. Cloze activities should have a collaborative component where children can brainstorm, discuss, and debate responses, focus on problem-solving skills, and share and value contributions.

2. Cloze activities can help emergent readers develop reading fluency by encouraging them to move from letter recognition to word recognition as they interact with text, focusing on context and meaning, predicting and confirming as they meet new words.

3. Cloze activities encourage readers who rely on memory to focus more on print. Teachers can sometimes help them predict a word by supplying its initial letter.

4. Cloze activities encourage readers who rely on print to focus on meaning when content words such as nouns and verbs are deleted.

5. Oral cloze activities encourage the development of listening and comprehension skills, focusing on semantic and syntactic cues.

6. Cloze activities can focus on language structure (i.e., syntactic cues) when structure words such as articles and pronouns are deleted.

7. Cloze activities explore elements of genre when they focus on genre-specific forms (e.g., rhythm and rhyme in lyrics or poems).

8. Cloze activities expand or review vocabulary when the children are provided with a definition of the missing word.

9. Cloze activities strengthen sight vocabulary, pronunciation, and spelling when they focus on patterns in words and word families.

10. Cloze activities stimulate children's creative writing when they involve deleted sentences or paragraphs.

Selecting a Text

Cloze procedure helps teachers assess the appropriate level of reading material, and can help reveal the child's understanding of what is being read. While any type of text can be used for a cloze exercise (e.g., familiar and unfamiliar stories, letters, instructions, comic strips, poems, riddles, songs, articles, diary entries, recipes, advertisements, interviews), it is important that the text be well written. In this way, children are predicting using quality writing as context.

- Teachers choose a text their children can read independently when intact.
- Teachers choose a familiar text to introduce young children to cloze.
- Teachers motivate children by using a text that interests them.
- Teachers choose a text that reflects their objectives (e.g., recalling a story, reviewing a specific form of text).
- Teachers consider their teaching strategy (e.g., rhyming text is effective as oral cloze).

Designing a Cloze Activity

1. Deletions can target particular words or can be made arbitrarily by formula (e.g., every fifth word). Teachers can also tailor cloze exercises by:
- deleting parts of words, whole words, or phrases,
- retaining words that are structurally interdependent,
- providing visual aids (e.g., the first letter of each deleted word) when introducing written cloze to young children,
- using dashes, boxes, or numbers in brackets to indicate the number of letters deleted.

2. Along with the teacher's choice of text and children's knowledge and literacy levels, the deletions they make will strongly influence the difficulty of a cloze activity. Teachers need to consider that:
- content words such as nouns and verbs are more difficult to predict than structure words such as articles.
- deletions at the beginning of a sentence are more difficult to predict than those made at its middle or end.
- difficulty increases with the number of deletions made.

3. To maximize the learning benefits of cloze activities, teachers can structure a lesson to focus on the process of restoring deletions, as opposed to the end product. In pairs, small groups, or as a class, children generate, discuss, debate, justify, compare, and select possible solutions for each deletion. The author's original choice is only use-ful when presented as a focus for discussion: Why might the author have chosen this word or phrase?

4. Independent activities (e.g., worksheets) may not capitalize on the potential for learning. Given the range of experience and literacy skills of a group of children, individual cloze will be boring for some and frustrating for others. Teachers can combine independent cloze work with group discussion, and pair or group children with varying abilities.

5. Written cloze can be presented in a variety of ways. An enlarged reproduction can be prepared for a whole-class activity. Pairs or groups can use worksheets before gathering as a class to share, compare, and discuss selections. (When designing worksheets, teachers need to leave room for multiple suggestions at each deletion.)

6. For oral cloze, teachers read aloud and pause at deletions so children can brainstorm, record, and discuss predictions. Illustrations can be used as visual cues. (Many of us present oral cloze regularly – predicting what will happen next in a story is cloze!)

7. Children can ask themselves these questions when attempting to select words:
- What is this text about?
- What kind of text is this?
- What is the author trying to say?
- How is the author trying to say it?
- Why does this make sense?
- Is that the way we would say it?
- Why would that word work?
- What other words could we use?

Twenty Ways to Cloze

1. Create a rhyme cloze by deleting rhyming words in a passage of text.

2. Help children by performing rhythm clozes (clap the syllables of suggested words).

3. Prepare a homophone cloze, for example: "I was ___ tired ___ read the last ___ pages.

4. An example of a grammar cloze would show all adjectives deleted; another, all adverbs.

5. Replace deletions with pictures in a rebus cloze.

6. Leave one or more letters of a word intact to create a letter cloze.

7. Create a "Wheel of Fortune" cloze to illustrate to children how consonants, vowels, and first, last, and middle letters help us identify words.

8. Prepare an enlarged reproduction of a cloze passage. Mask the deleted letters of each word with cards, flaps, or tape so that you can reveal the word one letter at a time. An alternative is to number each deletion and attach an envelope to it. Children, in groups, suggest words for each deletion, which they record and place in the appropriate envelopes. Discuss the suggestions as a large group.

9. Prepare a vowel hunt by deleting the same vowel throughout the text. You can also do this with a consonant, prefix, suffix, phoneme, syllable, letter string, or word.

10. In a synonym or antonym cloze, provide children with several synonyms or antonyms as clues to deletions.

11. Replace each deletion with its definition.

12. To make a partner-sentence cloze, select a word from one sentence to complete another.

13. Provide alternatives for each deletion or a general word selection list.

14. Children can play word detective by detecting superfluous insertions or deletions you made in an unmarked text.

15. Replace deletions with nonsensical words to make nonsense clozes.

16. Use a familiar passage to make a missing cloze. Provide the first letter of every word. Successively add one letter at a time to each word until the text is decipherable.

17. A ghost cloze asks you to do the opposite of a missing cloze. Present a well-known text on a piece of chart paper. Read through the text and delete one letter from each word. Continue reading and deleting until only one letter of each word remains.

18. In an acronym cloze, provide the first letters of a familiar word sequence (e.g., Ouat - Once upon a time).

19. To make a story or factual ladder, summarize a story or content information, but provide only the first half of each sentence of your summary. Children, in small or large groups, discuss possible endings for each sentence.

20. To make a paragraph cloze, provide the lead-in to each paragraph. Children, in small or large groups, discuss possible sentences that would complete each paragraph.

22: Venn Diagrams

A Venn diagram is an effective and concise graphic tool employed in post-reading contexts. It can represent comparisons and contrasting information within one story or book (e.g., settings) or between two or more books. A Venn diagram consists of two or more overlapping circles: the parts of the circles that do not intersect represent unique or contrasting attributes while the intersected sections depict shared or common characteristics that can be compared.

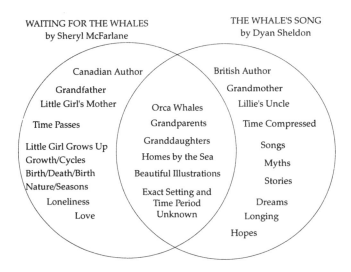

23: Plot Organizers

Plot organizers, an example of a post-reading activity, provide a visual means for organizing and analyzing plots and can often be geared directly to specific types of texts. These organizers help children summarize a plot and understand its organization, and they act as models for children writing their own stories. While there are at least four types of graphic plot organizers, pictures tend to take too much space and some are too challenging to depict in words. Instead it is easier for the reader to refer directly to the text. Notwithstanding the lack of visual aids, specific plot organizers (circular, stair-step) directly complement, represent, and heighten particular recurring plot patterns (e.g., circular, cumulative, count down) found in children's books. Plot profile line graphs and cut and paste grids are examples of organizers where children rate events on books using horizontal and vertical axes (events – horizontal; rating – vertical). Children's illustrations often accompany these organizers.

Sample Plot Organizer

Name: _____ Story Outline For: _____

Author: _____ Publisher: _____ Date: _____

Setting/Main Characters   +   Story Theme

The Problem

Story Sequence:

1.   2.   3.

24: Questions that Matter

In past decades, children were often required to prove their mastery of curriculum content by answering teacher-generated questions, most of which demanded brief, factual responses. This method of teaching often encouraged children to memorize answers, but did little to foster in-depth inquiry, a necessary component of deep-structured learning.

As educators extended their understanding of how children learn, they modified their questioning techniques. They know that open-ended questions can serve a variety of functions:

• introduce reading tasks by stimulating interest and curiosity,
• set up problems that require reading,
• identify important ideas to look for when reading,
• reinforce and organize ideas gained from reading, and
• help readers construct meaning by using questions that initiate dialogue.

Teachers ask questions that help children to develop higher-order thinking skills and that require them to draw on personal knowledge and experience. They foster environments that are conducive to sharing ideas and opinions, realizing that the environment in which questions are asked is as important as the questions. For many teachers, a natural outgrowth of this approach is the development of child-generated questions as an integral part of the classroom climate.

Children as Questioners

Teachers now know that for true learning to occur, children need to be able to pose questions to themselves. When children ask questions about a story, they require a detailed knowledge of the text and need to have thought deeply about what they've read. The ability to pose questions has application in all areas of life, and has particular relevance to tasks such as problem solving.

Children can increase their questioning powers by drawing from the models that teachers present, but teachers can also teach questioning as a process. The following activities allow children to learn about questioning and may help

them to overcome any discomfort they may experience when asking questions.

Tips for Asking Good Questions

1. Avoid asking yes/no questions. Instead, ask open-ended questions.
2. Avoid repeating children's responses since this encourages them to listen to you and not to one another. Arrange the children so that they can hear and see one another.
3. Use probing techniques to help children move beyond their original response (e.g., "How does that relate to...?").
4. Be prepared to change the order of questions if a discussion takes an unexpected, fruitful turn.
5. Be aware of the intent of your questions. Questions can elicit information, shape understanding, or press for reflection. It is important to ask a variety of questions as all have value.
6. Questions require a wait time – the time a respondent needs to consider a question and formulate an answer. As well, it is important to pause after the response is given. This provides an opportunity for the respondent to modify or elaborate on his or her response and for others to react and add their ideas.

Activities that Promote Effective Questioning

1. Question/Question
Children find a partner. In pairs, they practise asking questions by answering each question with another question. For example:
A: Are we going together?
B: Do you want me to come with you?
A: Isn't it necessary for both of us to go?
B: How much do we have to carry?

2. Answer/Question
Present children with an answer (statements from a familiar text) and have them provide the question. This is an effective means of testing children's knowledge and understanding.

3. Re-Quest
In Re-Quest, or Reciprocal Questioning, you and the children take turns asking one another questions about a small segment of a text. Begin by reading a sentence from the text. Close the book and answer questions the children ask about the sentence. Reverse roles. Children read a sentence,

close their books, and answer questions you ask. The activity can also include silent reading of a short passage. Children ask you questions about the reading; you answer and then pose questions to them. This is a good opportunity to model how to ask and answer questions by drawing on information in the text and your knowledge.

4. Role Playing

Role playing offers children another way to question curriculum content. As an example, a child in the role of a novel character can be questioned by another child in the role of a reporter.

5. Brainstorming

Select an informational text and give the class a brief overview of one topic outlined in it. Children then find a partner and generate, within a ten- to fifteen-minute time period, questions that may be answered about the topic in the text. When the time limit is up, children take turns calling out their questions. You can record their responses on chart paper then read the section of the text that pertains to the topic. Children compare the information in the text with the questions they generated: which questions were/were not answered in the text? What aspects were not addressed by questions? List any new questions that result – these can lead to further reading and research.

6. Devising Test Questions

At the end of a unit of study, ask the children to form small groups of four or five members. Each group develops a series of questions based on a topic they have studied. Group members discuss and then defend their questions to the rest of the class. An extension of this activity is to ask children to identify the types of thinking the questions produce. They will discover that questions can do more than elicit information.

7. Conducting an Inquiry

Ask children to select a research topic. They can list their questions under the following headings:
• What Do I Know About the Topic?
• What Do I Need to Know?
• Where Can I Find Answers?
• Who Might Help Me?

The children can conduct research in response to the questions. When finished, they summarize verbally or on paper what they have learned and what new questions have arisen as a result of their research.

8. Three-Step Interviews

These interviews provide a structure for practising active listening and the use of open-ended questions. Three teammates take turns role playing an interviewer, an interviewee, and a recorder. Partner "A" interviews Partner "B" while Partner "C" summarizes the session.

9. Developing Discussion Questions

To help children construct meaning, they can develop questions about a piece of literature they are studying. Questions should not be easily answered and should be genuine. When finished, children can form small groups of four or five and pool their questions. One question from each child can be selected and discussed as a group, with each member offering his or her response to the question.

Good Questions...
• allow discussion and the give and take of ideas.
• can be followed by prompts that make us aware of our metacognitive skills (e.g., "How can you tell?").
• provide a purpose for our reading, and help to spur motivation and interest in reading and comprehension.
• improve our experience with a book.
• challenge our existing thinking and encourage reflection.

25: Talking About Books

The reading experiences of children can be extended by what other people reveal to them about their reading and what they reveal to others about their reading. Text-based discussions in the classroom give children the opportunity to construct meaning from the text by returning to it to clarify and support their ideas, ultimately directing their learning. Giving children the means to engage in discussion about a text gives them the power to edit and reform their perceptions, as well as to expand personal meaning and deepen comprehension.

How to Get Children to Talk About Their Reading

Before children can start talking, they may need a goal or point for discussion. Teachers can provide them with these points by implementing the following steps.

1. Letting Individuals Prepare for Discussion

Children need time to reflect on a text and formulate their own ideas before they discuss them with others. Teachers can encourage them to record their responses to a text as a preparatory step to discussing them in peer and group situations. The act of recording a response may increase children's comfort level at later stages.

2. Discussing with a Partner

Children can share their thoughts and ideas about a text with a partner. They can use their recorded responses from the previous step to support the discussion if they wish.

3. Discussing as Part of a Small Group

In groups of four, children can discuss and reassess their original ideas and possibly modify their thinking. This modification is the essence of extending comprehension.

4. Sharing as Part of a Large Group

Depending on the nature of the discussion, ideas stemming from small-group discussions can be shared among classmates. This form of sharing can be done by jigsaw grouping whereby each child, in his or her small group, takes a number from one to four. Children from other groups who also took that number form a second group. New group members take turns sharing their previous group's discussion.

Talking About Text

1. Book Clubs

Have the children meet on a regular basis (e.g., weekly, monthly) in groups to discuss books they have read. The book clubs can be organized according to various genres; for example, fiction, nonfiction, poetry, science fiction, and mystery.

2. Book Recommendations

Children take turns to recommend a book to the rest of the class or other classes in the school. A class poster can be created that displays their recommendations and ratings. Children can decide and vote on rating categories.

3. A One-Minute Book Talk

Children can select a book they have read. In a one-minute time period, they share their opinion of the book in a small- or large-group situation.

4. Share Time

Provide a daily time for children to share thoughts about a book they have read with the rest of the class. Keep a record of sharing times in order to ensure that each child has an opportunity to share his or her reading at least one time a week.

5. Reflect/Pair Share/Group Share/Reflect

Provide a block of time for the children to engage in this discussion sequence (outlined previously) about a book they have all read.

6. Debates

Select a book that the class has read and make a statement about it. Divide the class into two, or select volunteers to form two debating groups. One group argues for the statement while the other group argues against it. Prior to beginning the debate, you can brief the children on rules to follow when participating in a debate. Choose one child to be the chairperson. At the end of the debate, children can vote for the team who provided the soundest argument by scoring a prepared checklist. The criteria for the checklist can include: planned as a team, team effort, kept to time limit, clear voice, and good summary.

7. A Thirty-Second Radio Spot

The children can prepare and tape record a thirty-second advertisement that recommends a book they have read and that they think others would enjoy. These advertisements can be prepared for other classes in the school, based on individual and class responses to books. Advertisements could be taped and played over the school's public-address system.

8. Story Mapping

Provide the children with a sheet of paper that shows a pictorial theme from the text. Using a story map, ask them to create and discuss story making references to the book they have read.

9. Comic Strip

Children can work in small groups to create a comic strip of events from a text, using published comic strips as a model. Groups determine how they will paraphrase text and dialogue to reflect the genre. Groups can trade their comic strips with others before posting them in class.

10. Story Grammar

A story grammar activity can take the form of a chart or web that describes a book's setting, characters, plot, problem, and resolution. Children can share their story grammars in small groups. Story grammars, because of their visual nature, help to increase children's comprehension.

11. Story Representation

Prior to children reading a story, you might prepare a visual display of one scene from the story, preferably a scene that involves major characters and that hints at the plot. Have the children predict the story's plot based on the picture and list their predictions. After reading the story, children can compare and discuss their predictions with events they read in the book.

12. Story Objects

Have the children bring an object to class that represents the theme of a story they have read or heard. In groups, they take turns outlining the relevance of their object to the story.

13. Summarizing a Passage

The children can write or review verbally the events of a passage. This can help you to check for comprehension and solidifies the events and meaning of the passage in the reader's mind.

14. Building Vocabulary

Review key story vocabulary for its contextual meaning, as well as for more formal definitions. Depending on the class, this activity can be done in large or small groups, or independently.

26: Literature Circles

A literature circle typically comprises three to five children who are reading the same book and who come together in small heterogeneous groups to discuss, react, and share responses. The purpose of the circle is to promote reading and responses to literature through discussions and to provide opportunities for children to work in child-directed small groups. When first starting literature groups, the teacher may choose the same book for everyone to read. As time progresses, children should be encouraged to choose from among three or four books, giving them some control over their own learning.

When organizing literature circles for the first time, teachers may want to assign children to a group. However, once children become familiar with literature circles, they can form their own groups. The teacher's role is now that of observer and evaluator, problem solver and facilitator. She or he monitors the groups and may join a group to add to the discussion. When there are more than five children who want to read the same book, several groups may be formed. With chapter books, children usually meet following each reading session. Literature groups meet three times per week for a period of fifteen to thirty minutes, and can last from one day to six weeks, depending on the length of a book. Of course, the entire class does not have to be engaged in a literature group at the same time.

Literature circles may take time to establish. Introduction, explanation, and demonstration of the concept of a literature circle and good questioning and discussion behavior provide the appropriate atmosphere for success. A literature circle discussion chart can prompt and spark discussion, and may include some of the following:
- talk about the book's title and author,
- discuss what has been read,
- identify favorite parts of a book, and reasons for this choices,
- list topics for the next discussion.

Before beginning to read, the children may do an introductory activity. This can include answering a survey or questions, completing a cloze activity, or a "What I know about... ." Children come to the group with their reading and journal entries completed. Reading goals and other information for the following meeting should be recorded in the journals. Oral reading occurs only when a concept needs to be clarified or when beginning readers or other children need assistance – the teacher may need to read aloud to this group. As well, a tape of the book can be placed in the listening center for those who need it.

There are many benefits of using literature circles. Children take charge of their learning, all children improve listening and comprehension skills, and children who are reading below level gain in self-esteem through participating equally with their peers. Generally, literature circles give children the opportunity to appreciate that everyone has different points of view while all have the opportunity to speak and be heard.

To help children become accustomed to participating fully in literature groups, some teachers assign roles, vary the duties, and eliminate them when they are no longer needed. Roles include: reteller (briefly recounts book), questioner (presents puzzling issues), instigator (comments, adds questions), and summarizer (concludes session). Children can do their silent reading in class, and discussions can follow after they have completed a small chunk of the text. Group members can decide on what to read next and how much they will cover. (Some readers-at-risk may need to listen to a taped version as they read to prepare for the discussion.)

Journals can be used as both follow-up to the discussion and as preparation and guiding statements during the next discussion. Taping a session can help the teacher to observe the dynamics of the group and the literacy behavior of its members. As well, the group can view the film after completing discussions on the book and reflect on their contributions and the process. An assessment meeting can be held to consider modifying the mode of working, and each member can self-reflect using his or her journal. This process models future shared literacy events, from discussions on work-related issues to participating in political action groups. Children talk, read, write, and think for real purposes. Such self-regulating management takes time to establish. Periodic whole-class discussions can generate guidelines to help children function and grow from the process.

27: Response Journals

A response journal is a notebook or folder in which children record their personal reactions to, questions about, and reflections on what they have read, viewed, listened to, and discussed. As well, they reflect on the strategies they use when taking part in these activities.

Journals serve a number of purposes:
- they help to connect reading and writing, enabling children to see literacy as a whole,
- they promote critical thinking and affective response,
- they help children develop interpretive skills as well as organize simple recountings,
- they offer children a record of their reactions to a literature selection or to a group discussion to be reflected on at a later time,
- they encourage a range of responses beyond literal questions and answers,
- they facilitate thoughtful and personal responses to what has been read,
- they offer a means of reacting during the reading of a selection, and not just at its completion,
- they support follow-up discussion activities,
- they present opportunities for examining words and language patterns used by authors – slang, idioms, unusual or unknown words,
- they invite open-ended questions that promote further discussion,
- they offer opportunities for assessment, weekly and throughout the year, as children reread and reflect on their entries,
- they establish opportunities for independent work while the teacher assists other groups of children.

Using Response Journals

Teachers can set aside twenty minutes of reading time, and ten minutes for journal writing. They can display a list of possible starters that children have formulated previously; for example:

I was surprised when _____ .
I predict that _____ will happen next because _____.
The story reminds me of the time I _____ .

Typically, children summarize the plot of the story they have read when they are unfamiliar with the format and purpose of response journals. As they become more familiar with the concept, their entries gain in insight, particularly those written in response to whole-class readings.

Dialogue Journals

In dialogue journals, the teacher and children participate in weekly open, written conversations about a book the children are reading, in order to share interpretations and viewpoints. The teacher must be sensitive to the beginning efforts of the children, and think of the entries as conversations around books. Because the teacher is part of the dialogue, the children are often highly motivated to participate. She or he responds to what the children have written, elaborating or extending their entries, answering their questions, and asking questions the children might consider. In some instances, the teacher may have to establish a minimum or maximum number of sentences to develop the rhythm of dialogue journals. Both partners are free to choose what to write about and whether or not to respond, and are considered equal in the exchange. Dialogue journals provide a good opportunity for teachers to model writing skills. By working with three or four children a day, the teacher can quickly dialogue with the whole class within a few days.

Response Journals Help the Teacher to:

- support individual progress
- explore personal responses
- develop small-group discussions
- guide the student-teacher conference
- connect with other books and authors
- track independent reading
- maintain personal dialogue
- track understandings
- encourage writing in any form
- identify themes

Response Journals Allow the Learner to:

- record likes, dislikes, and preferences
- explore feelings stories elicit
- associate with previous experience
- predict and validate predictions
- develop literary analysis skill (plot, setting)
- foster awareness and appreciation of an author's style

Tips for Teachers

- Support the child's message. Connect with what the children have said in some way, whether by acknowledging, agreeing, or sharing similar ideas.
- Provide information. This is important when an entry indicates that a child misunderstands or lacks facts.
- Clarify and extend thinking. When an entry is unclear, ask for clarification. Challenge children to rethink, reflect, and stretch their minds.
- Provide questions to answer as prompts.
- Write about your reading and share your responses with the children. Let them know that you have favorite writers and genres.
- Respond in writing to children. Since journals are not assignments, they should not be given a mark or grade. Children must feel free to write their true responses to their readings.
- Ask children to share entries with one another and with you. The response journal is a good source for discussion in child-teacher conferences and in peer reading groups.
- Ask children to keep track of what they have read and to evaluate the books and their entries. They can also fill in graphs to show how much time they spend reading.

- Books I Have Read

  Date: Title: Comments:

- My Top Ten (My Bottom Ten):

  My Favorite Quotes:

  My Favorite Illustrators:

  Topics I Want to Read About:

  My Favorite Characters:

Questions to Choose from to Motivate Literature Responses

1. When you first chose your book (before you had read it), what kind of book did you think it would be?
2. Now that you have finished it, how did it fit your expectations?
3. What did you like best about the book?
4. What will you tell your friends about the book?
5. What puzzles grew from reading this book?
6. Have you read any other books like this one?
7. What surprises happened during the book?
8. Did you read this book a chapter at a time? Did you read it all the way through? Did you leave it for a while?
9. Do you think you will read it again?
10. If there were a film made about this book, would you want to see it?
11. Whose voice speaks to you most strongly in this book? Was that person the book's main character?
12. Who was telling the story?
13. When did the story take place? Did it matter where it took place?
14. How long did it take for the whole story to happen?
15. Were there any flashbacks, flashforwards, or time warps?
16. What places were described in the story?
17. Would you like to have been inside this story as it was happening?
18. When did you feel as if you were actually inside the story?
19. When did you feel you were staring at the characters as an observer?
20. Did you hope that an event would not happen, but it happened anyway?
21. Did anything ever happen to you just as it happened in this story?
22. If a time warp occurred and you found yourself in the book, which character would you choose to become?
23. When you are reading, do you see pictures in your mind?
24. What would you like to do now to help you think about your book?
25. Which friend would you give this book to for a birthday present?
26. Do you like to sketch as you read – drawing the pictures that play in your mind?
27. How would you have handled the problems characters faced in your book?
28. What do you think the author was trying to tell you about life in this book?
29. Do you agree with the way the author thinks about life as described in this book?
30. What would you ask the author of this book?
31. When were you "hooked" by this book and realized you would read it all the way through?
32. Go back and look at the cover. How accurate is it now that you know the story?
33. Reread the blurb on the back cover. Is it fair?
34. What kind of music could you play for a friend to get him or her into the right mood to read this book?
35. What did you learn from reading this book that you hadn't thought about before?
36. What was special about the way the author used language in this book?
37. Was there anything unusual about the style of the book?
38. What quotations would you choose from this book to put on the wall of your classroom?
39. What special words do you remember?
40. When did you have your strongest feeling while reading this book?

28: Retelling the Stories

Retelling helps children to construct meaning from a text. Children, in preparation for retelling, can revisit the text after an initial reading. This increased exposure to the text may clarify and confirm for children their initial perceptions. In other cases, it might lead children to discover that they need to modify or change these perceptions – perhaps they overlooked the importance of one element or failed to see a connection between points in the text. Once children are satisfied that they understand the text – that their perceptions are accurate – they are ready to retell what they have read to others.

Retelling allows children to explore the language of literacy and reinforces their oral communication skills as they interpret tales to create personal meaning. The urge to share through telling empowers exceptional children to overcome language barriers. Through retelling, children can travel the world to meet and understand other cultures. Its sources are many – nursery rhymes, riddles, chants, show and tell...

1. A Teacher Model Is Important
Begin by sharing your experiences of "home stories." You could hold a teacher show and tell – who you are, where you came from, what you like – and share a favorite photo of yourself.

2. Participation Stories
Engage the children in tales that invite participation through cumulative, sequential, and recurring patterns where they join in a chorus or a refrain.

3. Cooperative Retelling
Children share a story and then retell it, staying close to the plot of the original story. When finished, they add twists to the retelling to create a new story. (They can unravel a ball of wool with knots throughout it to indicate a new twist.)

4. Fortunately/Unfortunately
This activity is most effective when completed by children in small, odd-numbered groups. The first person in the group begins a story with "fortunately," the next person adds on to the story beginning with "unfortunately," and so on until each child has contributed. They then repeat the story chorally and chart it for others to read.

5. Round-Robin Storytelling
Begin the activity by dividing the class into small groups and asking each person in a group to read the same story silently. When children have finished, number them off. On a prearranged signal, #1 from each group begins to retell until the signal sounds. Children #2 take over, then #3 and so on (in this way the story is retold with no one responsible). Children can explore first-person narrations by retelling from various points of view: "Tell the story through _____'s eyes," or they can try multipart narration where one narrator shapes the tale while others retell from their chosen point of view. Finally, children can get inside the story by exploring a challenging or magical part, creating a chant or rhyme to "help" the characters out of difficulty.

6. Learning a Story
Children can read a story several times to familiarize themselves with its plot and characters (they can tape and listen to themselves as they practise). Ask them to consider voice, expression, tempo, pitch, emphasis, gesture, and audience participation. They practise with friends or in front of a mirror before presenting to the group.

7. Telling with a Prop
Children can use a physical aid to help trigger recall, perhaps a prop that has a symbolic link to story.

8. Puppets
Children can use a felt background scene with puppets to relive the story action.

9. Story Maker Game
Create four groups of cards: setting, characters, events, dialogue. In small groups, children draw a card from each stack and begin telling a story in their group.

10. Storytelling Chair
Storytelling chairs are special places for telling stories. Here children share what they've read or written, and tell of stories in progress.

11. Retelling a Story as Part of a Small Group

Children form groups of five or six members. Provide each group with a copy of the same story. Members read the story and then develop a retelling. Each group presents their retelling. When all groups have finished, children can evaluate the retellings and decide which was most effective, and why.

12. Retelling a Story as Part of a Large Group

Read the title of a text to the children. Ask them to predict the genre of the text based on its title, as well as the type of writing (factual, narrative) and possible words and phrases that may be included in the text. List their predictions. Read the text to the children, or have the children read the text. Children can check for predictions you listed earlier. When all children have finished, ask them to suggest how they can retell the text orally as a large group. Record their suggestions on the board before holding a class vote to decide on the method of retelling. Children retell the text and reread the original text before comparing the two. Discuss, as a large group, any details they omitted or changed in the retelling and the reasons for these differences.

13. Retelling a Story to a Group

Find a story that is unfamiliar to the class and share it with one child. She or he prepares and presents a retelling of the story to the rest of the class. Children then read the story. When everyone has finished, children can discuss the content and accuracy of the retelling and how it helped/did not help them read the story.

14. Retelling a Story to Younger Children

Provide opportunities for children to prepare retellings of stories for younger children. The stories they retell should be at the younger child's interest and age level. Retellings could be incorporated as part of a buddy program or story circle time.

15. Left, Right, and Left Again

Following directions after an encounter with text helps children learn to maintain details. Reinterpreting instructions from a picture to a text or vice versa is an excellent way to restructure information into meaningful chunks.

16. Retelling Favorite Stories

Ask each child to retell in writing his or her favorite story. (For children who prefer to express themselves through art, they can retell the story through illustrations.) Collect the stories and compile them to make a book of class favorites.

17. Story Mapping

Select a word representing the key concept related to a text and write it on a large chart. Ask children to brainstorm all the words they can think of in relation to the key concept. Children, in pairs, categorize the words to form clusters or a map of words. They label each cluster before sharing their map with other children.

18. Picture Sequencing

Provide a series of pictures that retell a familiar story. Children can order the pictures to retell the story in sequence. An extension of this activity is to supply children with cardboard cutouts that represent characters and objects from the text. Children use the cutouts to retell the story.

19. Picture Retelling

Following the reading of a story, provide each child (or pairs of children) with a long strip of paper. Ask them to draw a series of pictures that retell the story, and to include captions, labels, and signs where possible. Picture retelling can be used with a variety of texts, including nursery rhymes, biographies, poems, and chapter books. Children can compare their retellings with those completed by their classmates. Did they choose to illustrate the same events? If not, how did this affect the retelling?

20. Taped Retellings

Provide children with a tape recorder. Ask them to read through a text one time and then tape their retelling of the text. Children reread the text before listening to their retelling. How similar was their retelling to the original text? Ask them to explain any differences. Similarly, you can videotape some of the children's retellings and replay them so they can evaluate themselves.

21. Films vs. Books

If the film version for a text is available, present it to children after they have read the text. They can compare the two versions.

22. Retelling in Role

After reading a story, ask children to prepare retellings from various characters' points of view. One way this can be done is to have children divide into groups. Each group chooses or is assigned one character. Members work together to develop this character's retelling of the story. In turn, one member from each group retells the story from his or her point of view to the other groups.

23. And One Step Further...

Provide opportunities for children to rehearse a retelling in costume before presenting it to an audience. Encourage the inclusion of sound effects through the use of instruments or noisemakers.

24. Readers' Theater

Prepare dialogue cards for the characters of a narrative or a poem. (Some factual texts could also be used.) Children can present a reading of the dialogue cards to their classmates prior to reading the complete text.

25. Mask Making

Children can revisit the text and make note of physical descriptions of each of the characters. Each child can make a hand-held mask based on the descriptions. When finished, children find classmates who have completed masks for other major characters. They can form a group to re-enact a part of the text that involves these characters.

29: Oral Reading

Oral reading of a selection by the children brings context and words to life. To read orally, children need opportunities to prepare, practise, and rehearse their reading. When they are comfortable with the text, they can participate in the oral reading of it.

The benefits of oral reading are numerous. It improves comprehension skills, leads to revelation, strengthens reading abilities, and enhances interpretation skills. When used as a diagnostic tool with young readers, it allows teachers to assess pronunciation, fluency, and reading habits.

Oral reading should not be confused with round robin reading, which involves one child reading, then another, and so on. This form of reading is fruitless since it seldom improves reading skills nor does it lead to a deeper understanding/interpretation of print. As well, round robin reading may even decrease a child's understanding and appreciation of the story. A child may decode beautifully yet understand little.

Teachers can model purposeful oral reading by sharing enjoyable excerpts of a book, by making stories personal for listeners, by reading good stories each day, by reading poetry and plays, and by encouraging children to read only when there is a wanting and waiting audience (after an opportunity to rehearse, of course). Teachers can provide a variety of models in the classroom through the inclusion of radio plays, news broadcasts, poetry readings, taped stories, teacher/parent readings, videotapes, and so on.

When children read aloud, the teacher has an opportunity to monitor reading progress by analyzing the miscues they make. Listeners need to listen for meaning rather than to correct the reader and interfere with fluency. Sometimes, only the reader will have a copy of the material; if those listening have copies, they can celebrate the selection together by reading chorally or creating a dialogue from the text. The teacher can resist correcting a child reading aloud until she or he has sufficient opportunity and information to self-correct through monitoring for understanding – children need to develop their own strategies for handling print. If help is necessary, the teacher can give feedback that assists the reader in self-correcting: "Did that make sense?" "What word looks like that?"

Reasons for Oral Reading

1. Reading Together (Belonging)

- Choral readings (e.g., poems, rhythmic stories)
- Big book stories, chart stories, and poems
- Chants (select rhymes, parts of stories suitable for chanting)
- Tongue twisters
- Singing (present song lyrics so all children can follow)
- Line/word-a-child poems (different children read different lines and words)

2. Reading to Share an Enjoyable Passage or Information
- Personal writings
- Findings from research
- Instructions
- Schedule for the day, announcements

3. Reading to Recreate Dialogue or Dramatize Parts
- Scripts (read silently first)
- Dramatize poems
- Readers' Theater (dramatizing narration from a novel or short story)
- Story Theater (interpreting dialogue and narration with action and movement using, for example, fables and legends)
- Plays (prepare and perform scripted plays)
- Action rhymes and poems (devise or follow actions to accompany favorite rhymes and poems)
- Action songs (select songs where actions can be devised)
- Read and act (one or more children read a story while a group acts out the actions)
- Sound effects reading (create effects using music, voice, and percussion instruments)

4. Reading to Prove a Point or Verify an Answer
- Reading select sentences and phrases to support personal views and ideas
- Taking quotes and passages directly from a story

5. Reading to Go Deeply into Context and Share with a Friend
- Reading buddies

6. Reading Their Own Writing
- Class books
- Chart stories
- Jokes
- Stories
- Journals
- Plays

30: Readers' Theater

Readers' Theater, related to both oral reading and story drama, occurs when two or more people read the dialogue of a story in role. Often a narrator reads the narration or the group chooses to read it together as a chorus. There are many creative ways in which narration can be done as long as the script is read with expression, since little or no body movement is used in a Readers' Theater. Instead, emphasis is placed on vocal performance. The use of props, if any, is also kept to a minimum. However, because young children are less inhibited, the use of some actions and props such as a hat, book, or purse may be encouraged. Their use will make the presentation enjoyable for both readers and their audience. When appropriate, the audience can be invited to participate in the performance in some way, perhaps by providing necessary sound effects. Although Readers' Theater requires less practice than a play, children still require rehearsal time. Teachers may want to read the script aloud to the children and then have them read through it and practise it several times before the presentation. Once children are familiar and comfortable with the use of prepared scripts, they can write their own! Readers' Theater also strengthens and improves oral reading and active listening skills.

31: Choral Reading

Choral reading is group recitation of poetry or prose that allows children to explore together the depth and various meanings of the literature in nonthreatening ways. Choral reading allows children to experiment with words and phrases to achieve new and deeper meanings.

It is a useful tool for the classroom, allowing children to explore language without fear, especially shy, withdrawn children or children with speech problems. As a group, children work together to develop appreciation and make meaning of the literature. Choral reading allows opportunities for children to interpret and respond in pleasurable and safe ways.

Children can derive many benefits:

- development of concentration skills,
- development of memory skills,
- sense of security and unity,
- group solidarity,
- social skills,
- encouragement of trust in groups,
- modeling of intonation, rhythm, and beat,
- development of visual and auditory memory,
- improved reading fluency.

Getting Started

Younger children need to be taught choral reading using a simple rote process. Short, lively nursery rhymes work well.

1. The teacher reads the selection to the children.

2. She or he rereads the poem and discusses its words with the children. Is the poem funny? spooky?, and so on.

3. The teacher reads it again and asks children to join in on specific parts or words of the poem.

4. The children join in as much as they can every time the teacher reads the poem.

5. The teacher lessens the amount she or he reads aloud until the children are reading alone.

Even young children can handle relatively sophisticated material. The success of the activity depends on the interests and skills of the teacher.

As children begin to read, the teacher can start working from a script, which can be written on the board, an overhead, or on chart paper. She or he can encourage children to mark up the script. Choral reading is easily integrated into the daily routine of class activities. For example, children can read from overheads, charts, chalkboards, big books, and songs. The teacher may want to prepare a daily message that the children choral read.

Methods of Arranging Poems for Choral Reading

1. *Two-Part Arrangement:* One group of voices balances with another, with each group speaking alternately.
2. *Soloist and Chorus:* One child reads a specific stanza or lines – the rest join in on other lines.
3. *Line a Child:* One pair of children reads a line or couplet, the next pair reads the next lines, and so on. The reading ends with all children speaking the last line or couplet.
4. *Increasing/Decreasing Volume:* Take away or add voices to build up or move away from the climax of the poem.
5. *Increasing/Decreasing Tempo:* Increase or decrease the speed as the poem is recited.
6. *Unison:* The whole group speaks as one.
7. *Effects:* Accompany the choral reading with music, movement, and sound effects.
8. *Divide into Groups:* Each group comes up with its own interpretation of the poem.

Methods of Presenting Poems for Choral Reading

For Younger Children
1. Write the text on chart paper.
2. Divide the poem into parts.
3. Discuss different ways the poem may be read. Discuss the author's intent, and the mood, language, rhythm, meter, rhyme, and use of alliteration.
4. Provide time for the children to rehearse.
5. Place children in groups. They may be positioned so that different voices come from different places within the group.
6. Rehearse the reading of the poem as a whole.
7. Perform the choral reading for other classes, parents, community groups, and so on.

For Older Children
1. Introduce the poem, talk about the subject, then read it to class.
2. Reread the poem. Discuss important points.
3. Begin by reciting the first few lines.
4. Encourage children to mark up the scripts by underlining key words, pauses, and so on.
5. Read the first two lines together, then the next two, then the four together.
6. Increase this amount until the whole poem is finished.
7. Over the next few days, continue to recite the poem until the children have mastered it. Introduce movement, costume, and art.

32: Buddy Reading

Buddy reading is a form of shared reading where one partner reads aloud and another follows along. One partner reads while the other asks questions and retells, or both partners read together. Buddy reading situations may include a teacher and a child, two children with similar reading abilities, or two children with different reading abilities. These pages look at the last form – two children with different abilities.

This form of partnering often comprises a primary student and an older, junior-level reading buddy. Once a week, the two get together. The younger child reads to his or her buddy; the buddy helps out where necessary. Following each session, the pair may complete journal writing and reading activities.

Buddy reading can develop language and literacy in both younger and older children, enhance interpersonal and interaction skills, and improve self-esteem. These programs also benefit teachers, helping them to become more reflective as they examine teaching and learning processes shared by pairs of children. Implementing buddy reading programs also allows teachers to witness and observe children in new, exciting contexts.

Preparing for a Buddy Reading Program

Teachers can begin by observing children in their class, deciding who among them might benefit by participating in a buddy reading program. For each candidate, teachers draw up a short profile that outlines his or her literacy level and interpersonal skills. At the end of September, the teacher meets with the team teacher to pair up buddies.

Older buddies can prepare for their upcoming role by becoming reacquainted with children's literature. The teacher can ask them to read and evaluate several children's books with an aim to establishing a list of recommendations for paired reading sessions. The buddies can work together as a group to discuss quality children's books, and can compare favorite books and authors. Remaining in their group, the teacher can hold mini-lessons on topics relevant to buddy programs, for example, reading aloud, questioning strategies, and child development stages.

> ### Benefits for Older Buddies
> - more skilled, versatile readers
> - enhanced social and interpersonal skills
> - use of English in natural settings (especially beneficial for ESL students)
> - reflection on teaching and skills
>
> ### Benefits for Younger Buddies
> - learn to use a range of reading strategies
> - more confident writers and conversationalists
> - practise in reading to others
> - more skilled at book selection

Younger buddies can prepare for their sessions by practising reading with an adult one or two times a week, and participating in mini-lessons (e.g., listening skills, selecting books).

Pairing Children: What to Consider

Team teachers can discuss each child who is slated to become a part of the buddy reading program and review his or her profile. Younger children who are easily excited or active may require a more patient, mature buddy than a child who is quiet. Teachers can keep in mind that beginning students of English work well with a native speaker of their first language so these children should be matched whenever possible.

Steps to Implement a Buddy Reading Program

1. Teachers can draw up a thorough plan for the initial meeting of the two sets of children. They determine where and when the buddies will meet, and detail activities that will help them get to know each other. (Buddies will need a quiet, private area where they may interact and read.)

2. Teachers set aside a weekly time of at least one hour's duration. This time should remain consistent through the year.

3. Younger buddies read to their older buddies, who help out where needed. The two take time to discuss what they are reading or have read.

4. Teachers circulate and make anecdotal notes of their students.

5. Younger buddies, with the help of their older buddies, may write or draw in their reading journals. The two can discuss what has been read, and their ideas, feelings, and thoughts that have been recorded in the journals.

6. Children return to their own classroom to discuss their buddy experience that week. They can write or draw about their time together – accomplishments, positive aspects, problems encountered, and so on. This allows children to celebrate their achievements, share with their peers, and learn from one another. Older children often notice changes in their younger buddy and take pleasure and pride in their development.

Points to Consider
1. Attentiveness.
2. Shows respect for his or her buddy.
3. Makes good book choices.
4. Creates a healthy dynamic.
5. Takes part in discussions.
6. Refers to specific incidents from the text in discussions.

33: Taped Books

Tapes provide an alternative way for children to experience repeated readings of favorite stories, songs, chants, and poems. Their low cost and simple operation make them an ideal resource for every classroom, and they can be considered both educational and entertaining. Many community libraries and bookstores carry a wide assortment of book tapes for people of all ages.

Tapes may be stored in plastic bags with the accompanying text or multiple copies of the text. Teachers can explain to the children that they will listen to the tape at the same time that they read along in the text. In some instances, the children may then try to read the text, or parts of the text, without the aid of the tape.

The auditory reinforcement of tapes, when combined with the visual image of print, is extremely successful in breaking down barriers for intimidated beginning readers, ESL readers, and readers who are experiencing difficulties. While the focus of this activity is on reading for pleasure, repeated listening and rereading of favorite stories aids fluency, develops sight word vocabulary, and story comprehension. For instance, to demonstrate growth in oral reading skills, the teacher can record a child's oral reading at the beginning, middle, and end of the year. She or he can use the tapes to determine progress, and share them with the child and/or parent if desired.

The tape recorder is a powerful, nonthreatening tool for struggling middle grade or older students. By having a volunteer tape book chapters, children can follow the text at their own pace to work on phrasing, fluency, and comprehension. Some teachers find time to tape a single page of a text for a poor reader to build fluency and self-esteem – rereading a page she or he already comprehends helps the individual to become a better reader. Children can also listen to an assigned short section of the book on tape, following along in their copy. The next day, they read the section orally to others in a small group. Hearing themselves read fluently is a tremendous confidence booster for all children.

Five Ways to Use Tapes

1. Transcribing
Children can tape a casual conversation between friends, listen to the tape, and transcribe the conversation. When finished, they read aloud the recorded conversation, preferably to the friends who took part in the conversation. The activity highlights for children differences in our spoken and written language.

2. Writing an Ending
Tape a mystery or suspense, but only to the story's climax. Children listen to the tape and then write a story ending. When finished, read the rest of the story aloud. The children can share their endings and decide on the ending they most liked.

3. Tapes as a Transcription Aid
Older children who cannot copy from the board or take notes quickly might benefit from taping content-area discussions. On their own, or with teacher assistance, they can listen to the tape, playing it back when necessary, and make notes of important points.

4. Take Home Tapes

A system to enable children to borrow tapes may be put into place. As an example, children could sign out a tape for a period of one week. When they return the tape, they enter the date returned. During this one-week period, children can complete a response activity related to the tape. (This also provides an excellent opportunity for home-school connections when parents help their child complete the response activity.)

5. Making Taped Books

Fluent readers can make tapes of books they have read and would like to share with their class-mates. Given that they will need a quiet time for this activity, they can make their tape at home, using a cassette supplied by the school and, if necessary, the class tape recorder. These tapes can also be used in a tutoring or buddy program. Children may keep records of the taped stories they have made, listened to, and read.

34: Responding with Art

Having children respond to readings with art-work is good for checking comprehension and interest among ESL, kindergarten, and early primary children, children who are shy, or children with poorly developed language skills. However, drawing is not just for those who can't write fluently, and creating pictures is not just part of rehearsal for real writing. Images at any age are part of the serious business of making meaning – partners with words for communicating our inner designs.

Children of all ages can draw along with their writing and their responses to stories. Linking visual with verbal modes of expression will result in better description and detail. There are many ways to see – teachers can capitalize on children's multiple intelligences. Making pictures gives children a sense of freedom of expression because they feel less restricted by rules and convention than when they write without pictures. Making pictures, along with writing, leads to poetic, complex, expressive, imaginative, reflective writing.

> e.e. cummings, when asked if his daily drawing interfered with his writing: "Quite the contrary: they love each other dearly."

Twenty Ways to Link Art and Literacy

1. An Artists' Workshop

Use the workshop approach by asking children to write journals about their artwork, not only to show meaning in their pictures, but to express their thinking, observations, ideas on assessments and revisions, description of process, future plans, and reflections on their learning.

2. Show *not* Tell

Discuss with the children an author's method of handling images. An amateur writer tells a story while a professional shows the story, in essence creating a picture to look at instead of words to read. An amateur writes: "Bill was nervous. " The professional writes: "Bill sat in the waiting room. He couldn't keep his fingers from his mouth, peeling and biting the skin around his thumbnail until the blood came, warm and sweet."

3. Guided Imagery

Visualization improves comprehension. Guided imagery as a prereading activity stimulates children's prior knowledge about a topic, and provides a bridge between the new and the known. Guided imagery requires a script that contains words that appeal to each of the senses, repeating key words and phrases, and frequent pauses so children have time to visualize. For example:

> Relax... close your eyes... tell all your muscles to relax. You are riding in a dogsled south across the tundra to a town you have never seen. You hear the wind moan, see the steam from the dogs' panting breath. Your face burns from the cold, but you are warm under the furs your father has wrapped around you. Your hands, in their thick mittens, grip the side of the careening sled. There is nothing to see but whiteness – snow covers everything – your eyelashes, your clothes. The snow goes on and on forever. You close

your eyes and think of the town you have heard so much about, where big buildings are lit up like giant lamps and contain summer within them. Finally, you drift off to sleep... you are back in your classroom... tell your muscles to move... open your eyes.

Children reflect on their feelings, then read or listen to the book that inspired the visualization. Finally, they compare their visualized images with the book's illustrations.

4. Learn to See

As a class, hold group discussions and brainstorm aspects of slides: colors, contrasts between cool and warm colors, background and foreground, media, mood, character, plot, how each picture tells a story, time of day, light source, weather, associations and comparisons between painting and artistic styles. Let children choose a favorite painting and write about it in detail. Have them tell the story of the painting from any of these viewpoints: third-person accounts, thought tracks of painter or subject, dialogues between depicted figures, or a viewer's interior monologue. Where appropriate, have children dramatize beforehand to deepen their understanding. Publish this illustrated volume of art criticism.

> "This is a picture of a man riding as fast as he can on his horse on a very hot day. He's very tired. He is hitting his horse with all his fears."
>
> Daniel, Grade 2

5. Art Stimulates More Writing

Cut and laminate quality art work from calendars, magazines, catalogues, and journals. Cover the classroom with these prints before children arrive. When they enter the class, ask them to pretend they are in an art gallery. The purpose of their visit is to choose four pictures that they will incorporate into a story. Suggest that they select one or two character pictures, one setting picture, and one event picture. To all their questions, answer "You decide." Have them write narratives including characters, setting, problem, and solution to problem. Their narratives will be rich and complex, with tension created by "disturbing" pictures that lift their stories.

6. Choice Implies Commitment

A scrapbook-style anthology of favorite paintings (in the form of gallery postcards), poems, factual information, and the children's writings can quickly become a valuable resource for the individual and the class as a whole. This is a simple, personal, and effective way to encourage a lively and developing interest in the arts.

7. Learning to Read Through the Arts

Art projects include specialized vocabulary and important sequences of action. "Learning to Read through the Arts" is a nonprofit organization operating in conjunction with the Guggenheim Museum in New York. Artist-instructors develop a series of two- to four-week art/reading/writing theme lessons. Equal time is spent on art and language – lessons are planned to develop cognitive skills such as identification, discrimination, sequencing, memory, and comprehension. Children keep journals that include original stories, vocabulary lists, and detailed directions for various art projects. The program has been particularly successful with children who are reading several grades below grade level, the perceptually handicapped, and the gifted.

8. Art Cards

Have children decorate boxes that house 3 x 5 index cards. On each card they can record steps involved in making an art project (e.g., matchbox furniture for dioramas, papier mâché pinatas). Children can write instructions to help others try something they have enjoyed.

> When a lady visiting Matisse's studio said, "But surely, the arm of this woman is much too long," the artist replied politely, "Madam, you are mistaken. This is not a woman, this is a picture." Children who learn to "read" between and beyond the brush strokes of a painting become more aware of the need to look for meaning beyond the surface meaning of printed words.

9. Explore Picture Books

What relationship exists between the visual and verbal in picture books? Could one stand without the other? Do they tell the same story? Do they interpret the story creatively? Have the children provide alternate illustrations for a favorite story book, or write an alternate text for favorite illustrations in a picture book. They can also create picture books for younger readers.

10. Ways to Respond and Retell

Children can respond to and retell stories using masks, silhouettes, puppets, collages, quilts, student-made costumes, weavings, dolls, mobiles, posters, and dioramas. They can create a photo essay or home video version of the story, perhaps asking fellow students to act out key scenes. As teachers, we need to strive to provide a variety of artistic media and encourage a variety of artistic techniques.

11. Visual Perception

Children can display their familiarity with a story through graphic organizers, including plot relationship charts, story maps, prediction charts, story pyramids, character maps, comic strips, film strips, murals, friezes, shadow boxes, relief maps, story trees, and story ladders.

12. Making Books

Display for children a range of books – big, small, miniature, shape, pop-up, fold-out, see-through, flip, cloth, rebus, and code books. Children can use one or more as a model to create their own book using a story they have written as its base.

13. Place Slogan Here

Children can promote their favorite book by designing stamps, stickers, bookmarks, calendars, badges, place mats, sandwich boards, postcards, plaques, and playing cards that tell others of its merits.

14. Vacation Souvenirs

Set up a display table and ask children to bring in objects from holidays. They write a paragraph that gives some insight into their souvenir's use or significance. They display their souvenir with their paragraph for viewing.

15. Book Motivators

Each child fills a container (e.g., a large yogurt container) with six or seven objects that were mentioned in a book she or he read. They write the title of the book and a teasing paragraph on how these objects figured into the book, without giving away the plot. Classmates read the paragraph and view the objects before predicting what they think the book is about. They can share their predictions with the student who filled the container before they find out, by asking or by reading the book, the plot of the novel.

16. Playing with Words

Children can select novel words they met while reading a book. They play with the words and their shape, illustrating them, writing them in calligraphy, or creating three-dimensional effects.

17. Sketch to Stretch

Children use drawing as an intermediary step between reading a text and discussion. They share their sketches in small groups where other members can speculate on the artist's intent before listening to his or her interpretation. Finally one child can elect to share his or her sketch with the entire class in the same manner that all children shared their work in the small groups. When finished, discuss with children reasons for varying interpretations of text. Emphasize that these differences are to be expected.

18. Sketch a Paragraph

Descriptive paragraphs, whether taken from a newspaper, novel, magazine, or nonfiction book, can be sketched. Children can read the paragraph and interpret its content, mood, and characters by drawing or painting them.

19. Draw as You Read

Draw a straight line on the board or on a large sheet of paper. As the text is being read, have a child draw its ideas along the line, moving from left to right. At the end of the reading, the rest of the children can retell the text using the illustrations as a guide.

20. Listen and Sketch

Select a text and divide it into sections. Provide each child with a grid (as in a cartoon sequence). They can use the first box for the title. Explain to the children that a text is going to be read in sections and that they are to draw a picture to illustrate each section. You can use almost any type of text for this activity.

Suggestions for Teachers

- Make lots of art books, magazines, and book illustrations available so that children may glance through them during free time.
- Share bits of books like Gladys S. Blizzard's *Come Look with Me – Enjoying Art with Children* and *Come Look with Me – Exploring Landscape Art with Children* (1992).
- Learn how to look at art by reading David N. Perkin's *The Intelligent Eye – Learning to Think by Looking at Art* (1994).
- Learn to look persistently and intelligently: give looking and thinking time, make looking and thinking broad and adventurous, clear, deep, and organized.

35: Drama and Literacy

Setting the Stage

Drama is an outgrowth of pretend play and comes naturally to children. With very young children, their play can be guided and encouraged in a variety of ways. Play centers can be transformed into settings that provoke role playing around a chosen theme or issue. Props (e.g., capes, boxes, hats) can be used in a variety of ways to stimulate role play. Teachers can observe the children at spontaneous play and learn about their concerns, interests, and anxieties. Games, particularly cooperative games, can help to promote a positive classroom climate and strong community among children. Teachers need to recognize the importance of negotiation and can make their classroom a place where children expect to be listened to and where their contributions are valued by the teacher and by their peers.

Teachers new to drama can begin by eliciting simple dialogue and questions and answers in role. They can ask children to respond as if they are a character from a story being read aloud. Gradually, children can move into "what if" – speculations based on what they've imagined – tried and true storybooks are sure to elicit imaginative response. Keeping the children in a circle is a good management technique that provides perimeters for the activity and allows all children to be equal participants. The teacher may want to devise a signal to indicate when the work will begin and end. Children can work in pairs, in small groups, or as a large group; the more children can be actively involved at any one time, the better. When possible, role playing can begin with a whole-group activity, move into small and individual work situations, and end with a whole-group situation.

Time Considerations

A drama can last for one session or extend in a unit through many, depending on the interest of the children and the possibilities inherent in the themes or materials with which the group or class is working. A teacher may extend a unit through a number of interlocking dramatizations that take place in different times and places or under different conditions, researching or reflecting in various ways between these events. Children's thinking will deepen over time.

A teacher will collectively decide when the drama is over, based on his or her satisfaction with the outcome of events. Often, a teacher will try to keep the children from rushing to a resolution of the problem in the drama by challenging superficial responses, pressing for elaboration, and extending thoughtless or sloppy contributions. Belief and commitment in drama on the teacher's part passes on to children the importance and power of words and language.

Drama is a shared learning experience and collaborative group effort – the threads of individual response are woven together to build an improvised world in which all the children share. Drama reveals and provides skills for negotiating problems of classroom dynamics and interpersonal relationships. It can enhance individual and group self-esteem – children with learning exceptionalities often experience great success with drama. As we make sense of others' stories, we come closer to understanding our own.

Methods for Integrating Drama

Teachers need not rush into playing too many drama ideas at once or playing them too quickly – ideas need time to develop. Children may be percolating with thought even if nothing much seems to be happening.

55

Where to start with the work? Teachers can look for something in the story relevant to children's experience and with the potential to open up the major themes of the story. They can ask themselves, "Is there a situation I can use to involve the children in the story?"

As a Teacher's Confidence Grows

Situations, characters, problems, relationships, mood, atmosphere, texture, and concepts of a story can be explored extensively. Teachers think deeply about the story, trying to understand and consider its broadest themes and ideas. Questions they ask children must prod them toward these elements, and move from the particular experience of the story to a more general understanding of the nature of what is being explored.

When a teacher puts himself or herself in role, children understand that the focus is not on the individual's response or contribution, but on the problem before the class and the process of resolving it. This is a powerful technique teachers have at their disposal to guide the drama. There are six role categories teachers can enter: teacher as narrator, teacher as leader, teacher as opposer, teacher in lowest status role, teacher as messenger, and teacher in shadow role.

Structures allow children to find new insights and understanding. They will feel most committed if they understand and accept the plan for the drama, and ideally they should eventually contribute to the planning. Teachers must listen, watch, and set up situations that provide lots of room for exploration in a specific direction. Teachers need to know when to:
- intervene,
- introduce strategies to open discussion,
- move into action or provide pause,
- stand back so that they do not determine learning, content, or result,
- use surprise and tension to provoke thoughtful response,
- reveal to children material that will throw an unexpected twist to the story,
- place demands on role players – a task to complete, a condition to accept,
- slow the drama with rehearsals of events planned by participants,
- initiate planning exercises and choices that encourage reflection and enrich context.

1. Familiar Stories
One of the easiest ways to begin story dramatization is to have the children, in small groups, dramatize familiar stories using their own words and movements. They include all major aspects of the plot, but supply their own details and dialogue. Space must always be made for extrapolation and interpretation to allow for learning. (A limitation of retellings, in their true form, is that they ask children to focus on details and sequence, in effect the surface of the story.) When children have dramatized the story, they can explore events that might have occurred before or after it, or change its locale, time, and mood.

2. Shared Reading
Shared reading of poems, songs, scripts, skipping games, and nursery rhymes help children to use their imaginations to interpret what is meant by the text, how it is spoken, and what effect it might create. Choral reading of poems and rhymes can be practised in many arrangements – unison, rounds, line-a-child, and line-a-group, with rhythmic activity or descriptive motion, children joining in on refrains (easily memorized), in two parts, or in a cumulative arrangement (where speakers are added as the poem proceeds, creating a crescendo effect). Children's ideas should be explored as to who might be speaking and how a text might be read – fast, slow, high voice, low voice, expressively, angrily, happily, sadly, like a radio personality, like a robot. This can be a good warm-up for role play activities.

3. Special Effects
Integrate the visual arts and music with drama. Children can make masks and puppets of all kinds to be used in dramatizations, as props, or as part of a costume. Simple, improvised orchestration or sound effects can be created by the children to accompany or punctuate drama. The playing of evocative recorded music can set the tone or mood for their work.

4. Movement
Mime and movement can help children build a repertoire of body movements. Using literature that has an action orientation, children can take turns reading or narrating the selection and miming the actions described in it. Another idea is to divide the class into groups and have each group

mime the actions of the character they represent. Children can recite their parts as they move, or create a simple chant to accompany their movements that indicates the character's feelings.

5. Tableaux

Tableaux or sculptures can be used to develop the context of drama. Have the children act out an activity. On a prearranged signal, they freeze. Creating tableaux or asking the children to move in slow motion is also a good way to control the action in more extended dramas – you can slow children or get them moving if a discussion has gone on too long. You can introduce tableaux work by having children work together in small groups to form a single shape, such as a geometric shape or a symbol (e.g., a letter, a number, the answer to an addition or subtraction problem). Tableaux work can be extended by allowing each child to speak one word, later speaking phrases or sentences that best express their, or their character's, feelings.

6. Extended Role Plays

If you feel you and the class might be ready for more extended role play, it may be useful to carefully explain what you will be attempting before starting. "Going into role" can become a familiar phrase. You might want to set the situation and scene clearly. At first, the children might be more comfortable staying themselves and questioning you in role. You might want to give them some time to think about the characters they will become. Tell them to close their eyes and silently decide the answers to questions such as: How old are you? Where do you live? What are you wearing? Are you kind/angry/miserable/frightened?

7. Interviews

Interviews provide an opportunity to plan questions related to a text's author and/or illustrator, or a character from a text. Prior to planning and role playing interviews, you can introduce children to the topic of interview structure and the types of questioning techniques that elicit desired responses.

- *Character interviews:* These interviews allow children to respond creatively to narrative, factual, and poetic text. They can explore character and make meaning by role playing a character from a text. This activity is most effective when children work in pairs, with each child taking turns to role play a character and his or her interviewer. When finished, each pair decides on the most effective role play and presents it to the rest of the class.
- *Character panel interviews:* Following the reading of a text, children decide to be reporters or characters from the story. Each interviewer prepares a series of questions related to one of the characters; each character prepares a series of responses in relation to possible questions from the interviewer. After the role playing, children can compare their lists of questions to determine similarities and differences.
- *Interview the author or illustrator:* Select a text or a range of texts, and ask the children to find a partner. In pairs, they plan a series of questions they would like to ask the text's author and/or illustrator. As a class, children can pool their questions, draw up a list of the five most commonly asked questions, and submit them to the author or illustrator, care of the publisher.

8. Monologues

Provide the opportunity for children to prepare a monologue about one of their favorite books. Encourage them to make posters and other visual aids that can be displayed while they deliver their monologue.

After the Drama

After the drama, children have the chance to explain and analyze the actions and decisions they made. This form of thought, discussion, and writing makes conscious the learning that occurred during the drama.

After drama work, it is useful to have a large-group discussion about involvement where the teacher can explain that an individual's commitment and level of activity within the drama can vary, for different reasons, and that everyone must consider how their behavior has, or had, the potential to affect the result.

36: Word Play as Literacy

Early childhood is full of playful and adventurous experiences with words and language. From babbling sounds and discovering new words to creative imitation and manipulation of language, children enjoy participating in word play. By the school years, teachers can use children's inherent love of language to strengthen a language arts program and create a climate in which children enjoy acquiring language competence. Word play extends vocabulary, contributes to an understanding of the technical aspects of language, and gives insight into language complexities – spellings, sounds, rhythms, and incongruities. Using word games in class should be guided by these principles:

• games should help to achieve classroom goals,
• the most important reason for using a game is that it will help children to learn more efficiently,
• games should promote full participation.

Jokes, Riddles, and Puns

These are often underused by teachers, but they allow children of all ages to use words playfully and enjoyably. Books based on these word plays provide the enjoyable and often brief reading experiences that children crave, and laughter is the payoff for reading. Children often want to share these readings with others.

The irregularities between letters and sounds in English are often confusing. Many jokes and riddles hinge on those irregularities and therefore draw the child into careful readings to discriminate between discrepancies. A number of jokes and riddles involve homographs (words that are spelled the same, but differ in meaning, origin, and often pronunciation). Others involve homophones (words that sound alike but differ in meaning, origin, and sometimes spelling).

Tongue Twisters

Encouraging the use of tongue twisters in the classroom actively involves children in playing with words and enjoying the sounds of the language. Like joke, riddle, and pun books, collections of tongue twisters provide enjoyable reading. At the same time, they encourage auditory and visual discrimination and physical articulation. Many tongue twisters involve the children in alliteration, an important poetic device.

Rhymes and Verses

Using rhymes and verses in the classroom brings the link between language, poetry, and music to light. Jumprope chants and clapping out the rhythm of words or names in time to the syllables and meter of language provide a natural link to poetry. Songs are one way to bring literacy into the classroom in a fascinating yet meaningful manner. Children enjoy music and singing, and there are many songs that one could teach. Folk songs are especially useful.

Crossword Puzzles

Crossword puzzles are available from many sources for a variety of levels. Children enjoy doing crossword puzzles that are challenging but manageable. The words could be listed at the bottom to make the activity easier for children in lower grades. A crossword could also be designed by a teacher or a group of children in response to a story, novel, or nonfiction book experienced in class. Finally, computer programs allow teachers to employ their own word lists and clues to make crossword puzzles that children can work on during free time, simplifying the activity a great deal.

Board Games

Board games, which involve reading, spelling, and cooperative skills, motivate children and encourage learning. Given their popularity, board games should work well in the classroom. They can also be used in cooperative learning lessons to encourage working in a group with limited conflict, or they can be used in a whole-class activity. Teachers can collect a variety of board games that are popular with children and discuss how each works before making them available to the children.

Children's Literature

Last but by no means least, children's literature provides many opportunities for word play, which can lead to children sharing orally with one another and making new reading discoveries. Word play strengthens reading skills, oral language skills, and listening skills, an important component of effective communication. As well, word play can involve children in the writing process in a fun and loosely structured manner that leads to improved writing skills.

37: Word Games

Reading

1. Character-Title Matching
Give children a series of shapes that represent characters from familiar stories, as well as story titles. Children place the titles in front of them. Under each title, they arrange characters taken from that story.

2. What's the Order?
Cut up a sentence from a text children know well. With a partner, they reorganize the sentence to show its original order. Partners can then challenge each other by recording and cutting sentences from stories or books they have experienced. The partner must try to reorder the sentence correctly.

3. What's Missing?
This activity is similar to What's the Order? but instead of working with words in a sentence, children work with sentences in a passage. As in the previous activity, they can challenge each other using texts both partners have experienced. An alternative is to take one sentence out. Can the partner spot its absence?

4. Mixed-Up Texts
Cut sentences from two texts and mix them together. Ask a child to first sort the sentences according to the text they were taken from, and then arrange them in order. Children can also do this activity with a partner who has experienced the same books and stories.

5. Fishing for Words
Cut fish shapes from a large piece of poster board. Give each child a fish and ask him or her to write a favorite word. When finished, children paste a paper clip to their fish. While they are working, make a fishing pole using a stick (should not have sharp ends), a piece of string, and a magnet. Tie the string securely around the magnet and attach to the stick. Place the completed cards in a large cardboard box that will serve as a pond. Children can work with a partner to fish. One partner puts the stick into the pond of words and fishes for a word. She or he detaches the word, reads it silently, says it aloud to the partner, and gives a brief definition. If correct, the child fishes for another word. If incorrect, the partner child takes his or her turn to fish.

Sound/Oral

1. Tongue Twisters
Children can hold a tongue-twisting contest. Challenge each child to record and submit a tongue twister (delete repetitions). Volunteers for the contest can pick a number to determine who will go first, second, and so on. The point of the contest is to read the tongue twister correctly in as short a time as possible. It is unlikely that the first round of contestants will need to be timed — if they make it through the tongue twister without making a mistake, they qualify for round two. As the field narrows, a timer may be used to help determine the winner.

2. Rhymes and Verses (Chants, Cheers, Song)
Teach a song by rote (sing one line, the children echo). Repeat this process until the entire song is learned. Once the words of the song are learned by the children, they can be incorporated into language activities. Write the words on the overhead and ask the children to read along while you sing. Leave out certain words of a song, and ask the children to fill in the missing words. Talk about the meaning of the song, where it came from, its cultural background, and when it was written. Geography and some social studies activities can be based on information from or about a song.

Spelling/Writing

1. Invented Words

These are common in children's literature, and children enjoy creating their own words as well. Discuss with the children how new words are added to our language. Here are some examples.

- acronyms: scuba (self-contained underwater breathing apparatus),
- abbreviations: ad = advertisement,
- portmanteau words: words created by blending two words together (smoke and fog = smog),
- words that came from names, such as sandwich (named after the fourth Earl of Sandwich, who liked to eat his food between two slices of bread so that he could continue to gamble).

Ask the children to keep lists of new words. For each, they decide what type of word it is (e.g., portmanteau) and, if possible, research and write its history. This type of word study provides children with knowledge about word development and how words are added to our lexicon.

2. Vocabulary-Punctuation

Record the following words on separate pieces of poster board: parentheses, apostrophe, ellipses, question mark, quotation marks, semicolon, dash, comma, colon, period. Record the corresponding punctuation marks on separate pieces of poster board. Children match the two sets of cards.

3. Avoid-a-Word

This game, which works best with two or three players, can be played orally or on paper. The game begins with each player being assigned a random letter. In turn, players must add a letter to their random letter, all the while trying to avoid making a word. (They must have a possible word in mind, and may be challenged to reveal it.) As soon as a word is made, the other player(s) makes one point. Play begins again with the assignment of new random letters.

4. Forbidden Letters

Players, in small groups of two to four, take turns deciding on one letter that cannot be used in answers to any questions. As an example, players decide that the forbidden letter will be "p."
Question: What do you like to do at recess?
Answer: I like to go out to the yard and enjoy a game of hockey.

The player avoids using words like "playground" and "play." When a player uses a forbidden letter, the other player(s) makes one point. Play begins again with the assignment of a new letter.

5. Palindromes

Challenge children to find palindromes (words that read the same way forward and backward). They can find and list palindromes in names (Anna), common words (pop), and even phrases (not Lima Hamilton). As well, children can incorporate their new-found palindromes in guessing games (e.g., What time is lunch? noon).

6. Anagrams and Other Puzzlers

Challenge children to make anagrams by transposing letters in existing words or phrases to make new ones. Beginners could turn "ant" into "tan" and "meat" into "tame" while more advanced players could turn "kitchen" into "thicken." Similarly, children could look for small words in larger words like "read" in "bread." A third type of game might consist of unscrambling nonsense words to form words, such as "tendust" to "student."

7. I Sentence You

This game can be played in small groups of four. Players take turns giving one another short words. The player who receives the word must then make a sentence that uses the letters of the received word in order (e.g., cat = Cathy ate treats). When a player misses or mistakes a letter, other players make a point.

8. Beheadings and Cappings

Beheadings are words that are made by cutting letters from the front of other words (e.g., stowed – towed – owed – wed). In cappings, the action is the opposite because players must add a letter to create new words (e.g., able – table – stable – unstable).

Part C: Becoming a Writer

38: Real Reasons for Writing

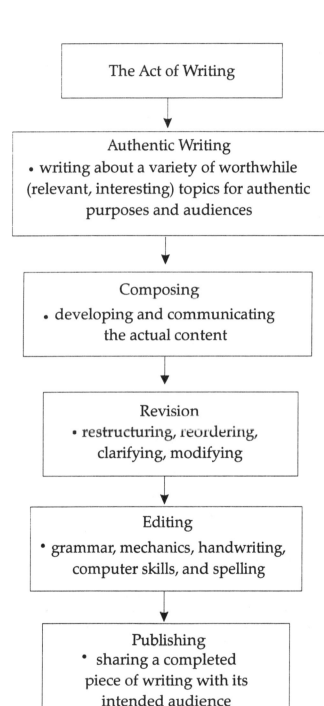

The Act of Writing

↓

Authentic Writing
• writing about a variety of worthwhile (relevant, interesting) topics for authentic purposes and audiences

↓

Composing
• developing and communicating the actual content

↓

Revision
• restructuring, reordering, clarifying, modifying

↓

Editing
• grammar, mechanics, handwriting, computer skills, and spelling

↓

Publishing
• sharing a completed piece of writing with its intended audience

Authentic Writing Purposes
• to entertain (stories, poems, skits, plays)
• to inform (reports, ads, labels, invitations)
• to direct/teach/learn (dialogue, directions, notes)
• to persuade (letters, speeches, ads, stories)
• to express personal feelings (journals, poetry, stories)

Authentic Audiences
• self (diary, journal)
• friends (reports, e-mail)
• classmates (reviews, recollections)
• parents (letters, invitations)
• teachers (reports, dialogue journals)
• known and unknown audiences (computer networks)

Children need to use writing for purposes they feel are significant. Teachers can ensure that they have access to a range of writing materials and tools, including: special notepads, clipboards, graph paper, poster board, stationery, pens, markers, pencils, and computers. An important component of a successful writing program is the inclusion and maintenance of predictable, regular writing times. Teachers need to familiarize children with elements of the writing process and the inherent time commitment for each stage – drafting, revising, rethinking, redrafting, editing, and publishing.

Teachers need to share their stories with children, and encourage children to author their life histories as readers and writers. An open and accepting writing environment will offer a range of writing experiences and products, including: diaries, journals, letters, surveys, how-to books, games, knitting/sewing patterns, job applications, résumés, bibliographies, autobiographies, lyrics, rhymes, riddles, headlines, articles, editorials, essays, memos, advertisements, commercials, brochures, questionnaires, petitions, dialogues, screenplays, and legends.

Teachers can encourage children to:

- write about things they know about,
- write about topics that matter most to them,
- be experts on a topic and teach others (helps children to know what they know),
- share topic ideas (good topics are contagious),
- engage in confidence-building events for continued success as a writer.

Children can choose a project they would like to work on, and can decide if they want to work alone, with a partner, or as part of a small group. Examples of projects they could complete are:

- writing and illustrating a story to be read to younger classes,
- composing and performing a song or making a music video,
- writing and producing a commercial or television episode,
- writing and producing a play,
- publishing a magazine or a class newspaper,
- writing a speech,
- preparing and conducting an interview,
- creating a poetry anthology,
- preparing a job application in role.

In real-world writing, children begin with what they know. Their writing can be one of any number of modes – personal, anecdotal, experiential, research-related, fantastical, dream-like, questioning. Similarly, what they choose to write can range from list making, event planning, and letter writing through interviews, songs, and interest surveys.

Writing Across the Curriculum

1. Record data.
2. Report information.
3. Keep a math/science journal.
4. Dramatize an event.
5. Record scores in gym.
6. Make maps for geography and history.
7. Self-evaluate, group evaluate.

Authentic writing...

- develops decision-making skills:
- learners are involved in choosing their topic, their audience, and their genre.
- gives people voices in the world:
- writing gives an opportunity for the historian, the ecologist, the dreamer, the child to share opinions and ideas with the world.
- helps us rehearse our thoughts:
- it allows time for reflection and refining before we share our ideas with others.
- seeks and elicits response:
- written language is for reading, singing, mailing, exchanging, cooking – when writers imagine the response of their audience, it compels them to revise and improve their writing to obtain the response they seek.
- aids us in finding significance, direction, and beauty in our lives:
- helping children to write well can help them to live well, but to accomplish this the writing must be significant in scope and sequence.
- is self-affirming:
- learners need to know that what they have to say about their lives, their ideas, and their experiences is valued and worthwhile exploring and expressing. Using their experiences and memories can result in a deeper understanding of themselves and their environment. When taken beyond the classroom, this understanding can help them lead more thoughtful lives.

Print has power. Children deserve to know this, to develop the skills to exert this power, and to experience its effects.

39: The Writing Process

Following the steps of the "writing" process will not ensure that children learn about writing or that children write. Teachers may know and implement the stages of writing, drafting, revising, rethinking, redrafting, editing, and publishing, but writing never occurs in such neat phases. Often a piece that will eventually be published has to be set aside and developed at a future date.

Teachers need to engage the children in their writing so that they will want to continue the writing process, which means the children rethinking and revisiting their writing to develop strength or clarity, to alter its organization, or to select effective words and language structure.

Teachers need to model their own writing, sharing copies of notes and memos, demonstrating a writing event (such as creating a parent newsletter), showing that writing remains a significant aspect of adult life. Children need to see teachers revising, struggling, crossing out, adding, moving text, referencing, and publishing.

Children need regular and frequent time to draft if they are to learn the art and the craft of writing. Children should revise and edit to invite readers to their writing. The following exercises help children with the drafting process.

Generating and Collecting Ideas for Writing

In this stage, children should be aware of the purpose and audience for their writing assignment. This awareness will help them to generate ideas. It is equally important that they have the opportunity to discuss their ideas with one another and that they have a chance to view the teacher modeling this writing form. During brainstorming, children can write down all of their ideas so they have something concrete to work from. Some will select writings from their notebooks to use as inspiration for a longer piece.

Draft 1: Piecing Together

Children begin to compose during this second stage of the writing process. The principal purpose of this stage is to set down their thoughts and feelings. Until they have written what they want to say, exactly as they wish to say it, children do not place much emphasis on editorial issues.

Draft 2: Self-Edit

In order to clarify and extend meaning, children self-edit their first draft.

Strong Point Check
Children place a checkmark (√) beside strong points of their writing and then try to build on them by adding additional details and information. They star (*) weaker points, and try to make them stronger by changing words and/or sentences.

Distance
Writers benefit from leaving their writing for a day or two. When they pick it up again, they are better able to "re-see" their writing.

Captive Audience
Writers can read a draft aloud to themselves. This enables them to read while simultaneously listening to their work. After the writers have employed at least two methods of self-editing, they are ready for draft three.

Draft 3: Peer Edit

Group Share
Writers are encouraged to share their work with the whole class or with a group. They can reflect on their work and ask specific questions of their listeners. Feedback can take the form of suggestions as well as questions for clarification. Teachers can facilitate group share by reserving time for it during literacy classes. Listening to the writing of their peers not only gives children fresh ideas, but is also a strong motivator.

Partner Trade-Ins
Partners can trade journals and enter written feedback on each other's writing. As well, writers can read their own compositions to a partner. The partner's job is to offer courteous and helpful feedback.

Draft 4: Teacher Edit

Regular child-teacher conferencing is necessary during the drafting process. However, the teacher should edit only after the child has finalized the text, ensuring that content takes priority over editorial issues. It will be helpful for the teacher to keep a list of all the skills the child has used correctly, as well as skills she or he needs to be taught based on recurring errors in the writing. This editing list should be available to the child as it will encourage him or her to take responsibility for using each newly acquired skill in subsequent pieces of writing.

Draft 5: Published Copy

Children choose an appropriate format for their writing. They incorporate all revisions and recopy or input their final version of the text, adding illustrations if desired. When finished, they can share their work with their peers.

40: Authors' Circles

An Authors' Circle is formed after children have worked on individual pieces of writing and want to meet as a small group to receive feedback on their work prior to another phase of self-editing. Participation is voluntary, but each person, including the teacher if she or he sits in on the circle, is expected to bring a piece of draft writing and share it with the others. Each author reads his or her piece aloud and receives peer input.

In an Authors' Circle, children explore meaning and think critically about their work, while other conventions (e.g., spelling, punctuation) are left for later rounds of editing. An Authors' Circle promotes risk taking in a nonthreatening setting in which writers receive clarification based on the audience's questions and comments. Writers are not obliged to incorporate all suggestions but only to consider them in a nondefensive manner, taking notes and later deciding what to do with advice they have received.

An Authors' Circle helps children to define and see themselves not only as distinctive, singular authors but also as authors from the perspective of readers and as responsible, constructive, critical responders and supporters of one another's writing. Through such real and social means of learning and authoring, literacy is facilitated as children's individual roles are expanded and the reciprocal nature of communication within the broader and cross-curricular contexts of reading, listening, and writing is both heightened and celebrated.

41: Revising and Editing

Teachers need to help children understand that revising and editing are important and essential processes to undertake when preparing a piece of writing for publication. Many children realize the need for editing, but have difficulty revising their ideas and spotting mistakes and omissions. They require strategies to help them recognize problems and make revisions in their own work.

Revising – The Big Picture

The editing process has two elements. The first concerns content and begins when a writer has completed a first draft. The writer checks his or her work and asks questions, such as:
- Is all necessary information included?
- Are there sections that are repetitive, or that stray from the topic?
- Is the information ordered logically?

Invariably the first draft of any writer – child, adult, professional – will have areas that need revision. Perhaps an important point has not been addressed or a "bridge" needs to be included to link facts. The writer can note these changes and incorporate them in the next draft.

At the second-draft stage, writers may find it helpful to have a partner read their work. Unlike the writer, the partner is not "close" to the writing and may see areas that need to be improved more readily than the writer. Depending on the partner's assessment and the writer's own assessment of the work, she or he can then proceed to a third draft, or make small adjustments and consider the revised second draft ready for the next stage of publishing – editing for style.

Ideas to Promote Editing in the Classroom

1. Have a variety of writing resources available in the classroom. Dictionaries, thesauruses, word games, and writings of famous authors and poets can be housed in a writing center that children can use throughout the day.
2. Stress the aspect of an audience for published work. Children are motivated to refine and polish their work to the best of their abilities when they are preparing it for the public.
3. Make children aware that what most interests you about their writing is what they have to say, not their errors.
4. All children need to see themselves as writers. Showcasing a published piece by each child in the classroom at various points in the year is a positive reinforcement for their hard work.
5. Write a letter home to parents about their child's progress in spelling, punctuation, and editing. Set up a parents' meeting to explain strategies they can use at home to help their child in this area.

Style – The Little Picture

Editing for style includes a number of elements, notably, spelling, punctuation, and syntax. Children can be assisted in spotting these errors through the use of group mini-lessons and individual conferences. Using their own writing makes the task of correcting more immediate, given that the piece that is to be edited is intended for an audience. Encourage older children to use the proofreaders' marks shown in the box below since marking up a draft, rather than erasing, keeps it intact and helps them to see where they need to make corrections.

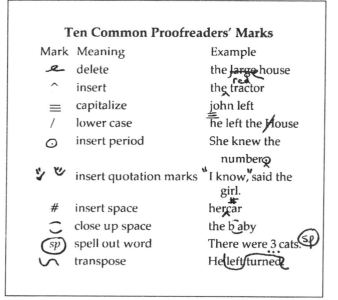

Ten Common Proofreaders' Marks

Mark	Meaning	Example
ℓ	delete	the large house
^	insert	the tractor
=	capitalize	john left
/	lower case	he left the House
⊙	insert period	She knew the number
❮ ❯	insert quotation marks	"I know," said the girl.
#	insert space	her car
⌒	close up space	the b aby
sp	spell out word	There were 3 cats.
⌢	transpose	He left turned

Suggestions for Promoting Revision and Editing

1. A Group Edit

Select a piece of draft writing that needs moderate to extensive revising. The piece can be from a child's portfolio from a previous year, or a piece of writing you have created. In small groups, children read the piece and indicate where revision is needed. When finished, groups compare their notes. Did they spot the same errors or omissions? Were their suggestions similar? If not, ask groups to take turns explaining their suggested revisions.

2. A Look at the Editing Process

Monitor children's work for an example that illustrates the various stages of the editing process.

With the author's permission, display his or her drafts to illustrate the revision process to others. Children can examine the drafts and use them as a model for their own writing.

3. The Editor's Desk

This concept is based on the same idea as a newspaper office. The teacher selects one editor for every four children. The five children (four, plus the editor) sit at a table and discuss the pieces of work. Each child listens to the editor and has a dialogue with him or her as the work is edited. The teacher is available to answer any questions and circulates to assure that everyone cooperates.

4. Pair-Work Editing or Peer Editing

Children choose a partner. Each child takes a turn to have their own work edited by the partner; both children discuss the reasons for the changes. This activity reinforces proper grammatical structures because looking for errors in a partner's work makes children more aware of errors in their own work.

5. Editing the Teacher

Share a selection of your draft writing with the children, and ask them to make suggestions for improvement. Having the chance to see that you – the teacher – need to revise your writing is beneficial for children, and helps them to feel less pressure to "get it right" the first time.

6. Word Doctors

This idea involves treating needy pieces of writing. Children can place their work in a cardboard box at anytime; word doctors (children in the class) are always on call. More than one child can work on a piece of writing that may need editing. Word doctors write their diagnosis (comments) on the work.

7. Ordering Paragraphs

Select a well-written, short nonfiction text of four or five paragraphs. Cut and mix the paragraphs before giving them to a pair of children to order. This activity helps them to read for content, and reinforces the concept that paragraphs contain discrete chunks of information that relate to one topic. When finished, children can compare their work with the original text.

8. Run-on Paragraphs

Find a text that is approximately one page long. Type the text and run the paragraphs together. Ask children to form small groups, and give each group a copy of the run-on text. Children read the text and decide where the paragraphs should be. They cut the text to make paragraphs and tape them to a piece of paper. When finished, groups can share and compare their work.

9. What Sentence?

Discuss with the children how all sentences express a complete thought. Ask them to find sentences that range in length from two words to two lines, and to record one of these sentences on the board. When everyone has recorded a sentence, discuss their common aspects – sentences express a complete thought, they begin with a capital letter, and they end with a form of punctuation, whether it be an exclamation mark, a question mark, or a period.

10. Sentence Weight Reduction

Write several run-on sentences on the board to model to children the art of tightening in writing. Ask them to imagine that a publisher has asked them to tighten these sentences, but not to lose any of the meaning. Children need sufficient time to work on the sentences before taking up the revisions in small groups. In their groups, they can explain the rationale behind their editing.

11. Where Do I Begin?

Copy a piece of text that is familiar to the children. Do not include capital letters or any form of punctuation. Children, on their own or with a partner, read the text and then write it as they think it originally appeared. When everyone has finished, children can compare their work with the original text. An extension of this activity is to have them punctuate an unfamiliar text.

12. Alot or A Lot

Take two pieces of your writing that contain grammar and spelling errors and write them on transparencies. Display the pieces on an overhead and ask the children to identify errors and make constructive suggestions for corrections. To model the editing process, incorporate their suggestions by crossing out, adding, and deleting information.

13. Letter Editing

This activity entails having the children write letters to someone for whom the letters must be perfect (e.g., pen pals, company president). The benefit of letter editing is that the reason for editing is connected to a real person. For some children, this may be what they need to see the relevance of editing.

14. Keeping a Journal

Encourage children to reflect on their writing in a journal. They can make two lists, one noting problems they have solved, and one noting what they have to work on. Children can write briefly about strategies they used to tackle former errors and hypothesize strategies to deal with new errors. Ask them to submit their journals prior to conferences as they will provide you with content and background information for the meeting.

15. A New Reason to Read Aloud

Have the children read orally a piece of writing they wish to publish. They can read their work to you, their parents, a partner, or as part of a small group. Since reading aloud is a slower process than reading silently, it helps children to spot errors in grammar and structure that they might otherwise miss.

An Editing Guideline for Students

1. Some writing does not need to be revised. To help you decide if a piece of writing should be revised, think about its purpose. A list of "things to do" doesn't need revision; a letter to a friend or relative sometimes does. A project for sharing always requires editing.
2. Never expect a first draft to be perfect. Most professional authors revise their writing several times before they are satisfied with their work.
3. As you write, keep all your drafts. When you have finished, review your drafts. This will help you to see your progress as a writer.
4. Recopy your work *only* when you are satisfied with your final draft.
5. Start small. Focus on one aspect of your writing at a time.

42: Notebooks

Encouraging the Use of Notebooks

1. Allow children to choose and design their own notebooks.
2. Have children carry their notebook throughout the day so they can jot down ideas that occur to them wherever they are. If they cannot carry their notebook, encourage them to keep a slip of paper and a pencil handy.
3. Encourage children to look for writing moments during the regular school day (e.g., they can write about an event in gym class rather than waiting for a momentous event to occur).
4. Share examples of other people's notebooks (e.g., excerpts from *The Diary of Anne Frank*) to show the variety of styles a notebook may take. Remember that the children will also have a variety of ways in which they keep notes (e.g., word lists, shorthand, sketches, charts).
5. Show children, through the work of others, how notebooks can serve as the source of a larger piece (e.g., original note compared with a final poem, essay, song, short story).
6. Have children look for recurring themes in their notes that they would like to develop further, perhaps in the form of a research project or paper, or in a fictional form such as a short story.
7. Children can form small groups to share and discuss what they have written. Once they have developed their own work, they can become classroom tutors.
8. Children can lead a discussion or give a short talk on a topic that interests them using notes they made previously.

From Notebooks to Projects

In a one-on-one individual conference, the teacher can ask these kinds of questions:
- How did you decide to write on this topic?
- What drew you to this entry in your notebook?
- Was it a hard decision?
- Do other entries relate to this subject?

Such questions help children to make connections with their writing that will take them beyond a simple retelling of an event to meaning making in a larger framework that is central to their lives. Children can check sections of their writing that they may want to develop further, and star those that hold less appeal. What a child checks or stars provides clues as to what topics or themes she or he is captured by, and can be used in a discussion of criteria the child will use to judge the work.

The teacher can hold a sample group conference with one writer in order to demonstrate the process of conferring. Children can then form small groups to hold similar conferences in which they look for themes in their own and one another's notebooks, connections between entries, and modes of writing and repeating themes that are evident in a writer's work.

Children can be asked to record what they have learned in the process of writing that could help them in future efforts, keeping track of what they decide to do as they progress with their writing. Hold a conference where children talk about the process behind their writing. If necessary, ask leading questions, including "What did all of us do? " "What did some of us do?" and "What can we learn from hearing about one another's processes?"

43: Ideas for Writing

Teachers are all too familiar with the child who takes out his or her writing journal and has a hard time writing anything more than the date. There are many areas from which to draw ideas for writing. The following tips and ideas can help to promote purposeful writing in the classroom.

Motivating Writing

1. A Passion for Writing
Many authors get their ideas from their passions (e.g., a picture book on dinosaurs might come from a paleontologist's passion for these ancient beasts). Have children write about their passions. For some, it may be sports; for others, the love of a favorite holiday spot.

Tips for Encouraging Writing

- Have children write in journals (on a daily or weekly basis) about questions they have, books or articles they've read, items they've watched or heard on the news, and reflections they have on personal growth and events in their lives. Go over some of the entries from time to time with the children, asking them to elaborate where necessary.

- Have children define a topic. Some children will list events (e.g., "What I did on March break"). Focusing on one aspect of the list (e.g., an afternoon spent skiing) allows them to expand the event and makes for a more manageable writing topic.

- Writing needs a predictable place in the weekly schedule so that children can anticipate and plan for it. During this time (five to fifteen minutes per day), children can write, brainstorm, cooperative write, illustrate, proofread, discuss, edit, and practise spelling, punctuation, and grammar skills.

- In addition to writing activities, games, and journals, be flexible and allow time for children to write about something when it occurs to them and while it matters.

2. Writing About Family Members

Ask children to write about family members. This may involve interviewing them or others who knew them. Children can prepare questions and, if possible, tape record the interviews. Transcribing the interviews provides children with text and the voices of others that they can use as dialogue or quotes in future pieces of writing.

3. Writing from a Photograph

Ask children to bring in photographs, which can be old family snapshots (an opportunity to ask questions about family history) or recent photographs. They can write about each photo and the memories or feelings it evokes.

4. Focus on a Picture

Cut out pictures from magazines or newspapers that show detail, and model writing a description of a picture for the class. Children can then choose one picture and write what they see in it. Later, in small groups, they can share the thoughts they had of their picture.

5. Instructions

Each child can write a set of instructions (e.g., how to do long division, how to make an ice cream sundae). She or he asks a partner to check the work. Can the partner follow the instructions easily, or do steps need to be added or clarified? Children can write a revised set of instructions, which they trade with another pair of children. The two pairs repeat the reviewing process and report their findings to each other.

6. Writing in Role

Children have the opportunity to retell a story, justifying a character's actions by giving the audience insight into his or her thoughts. They can put themselves in the character's position and continue the story in the first person.

7. Pass It On

One child starts a story by writing one line on a piece of paper. This is passed to the next child who writes a line and folds the paper so that only the last line is visible. Each child writes a line, but is only able to see the previous line written. At the end, the story is read to the class.

8. Historical Fiction

Bring history to life by allowing children to compose historical scripts. They can write dialogues between DaCosta and Champlain, Donacona and Cartier. They can also write dialogues between historical figures who have never met, but who might have had an interesting conversation.

9. Publish a Cookbook

Each child in the class can contribute to a class cookbook a recipe from home and a story about the recipe's country of origin. If possible, they can include a photograph of the dish, and include a brief caption.

10. Letter Writing

Children can utilize this exercise to write to their school custodian (requesting that paper towel holders be fixed), the principal (school policy), television producers and editors (their reaction to a show, article, or commercial). Children can also write a letter of advice to another child facing a dilemma, or to a character advising them what to do next.

11. Pen Pals

Arrange for children to write to peers in another classroom, school, or country. Each child will have his or her "pen pal" to write to and receive letters from. This process can span the entire year or a shorter period of time. Writing letters is also a good opportunity to teach the structure of a letter, as well as the need to have a finished product that is free of grammar, punctuation, and spelling errors.

12. Report Writing

Following field trips or other special events, children may write about what they have experienced and learned. They can select one aspect of the trip to detail, or provide classmates and others in the school with a report that provides a basic outline of their experience.

13. What If Stories

As part of fictional writing, children begin stories with lines like:
• If I were famous...
• If I were tall...
• If the world was flat...
• If the school day was eight hours long...

14. Job Applications

All classrooms require daily/weekly maintenance. Children can write job applications for sweeping the floor or cleaning the boards on a weekly basis. Conversely, if they do not want a specific job, they can write a rationale for why they should be excluded from this task.

15. Pairing Up

In groups of two, one child begins a story and the other finishes it. Partners can also take turns to write alternate paragraphs to write a collaborative story.

16. Class Classifieds

Each child can place an advertisement relating to his or her expertise (e.g., computers, making friendship bracelets, spelling, model cars, drawing) in a class edition of classified advertisements. Aside from being an interesting writing assignment, this exercise allows children to be more independent by consulting one another.

17. Critiques

Children can critique movies, newspaper articles, books, and so on that they think their classmates might like to see or read. Critiques can be organized according to genre (e.g., a book of movie critiques, video games) and recorded on index card with the title in the left-hand corner and stars (from one to four) in the right-hand corner to indicate rating.

18. Drawing a Description

Each child receives a picture that she or he must describe in writing so that someone who hasn't seen the picture can recreate it. Before starting, brainstorm what the description needs to contain (e.g., placement of objects, perspective, size, color). After fifteen to twenty minutes, children can exchange descriptions and draw pictures. They compare their results with the original pictures and discuss aspects of communication that come into play during the activity.

19. Free Writing

Free writing (also known as automatic writing) is a technique used to help children who have trouble writing, whether it is beginning to write or writing about personal experiences. A free write topic can be assigned to the children or they can write about their thoughts. Before writing, children have a chance to close their eyes and relax. When ready, they are given a time limit (e.g., ten to twenty minutes). On the command, "Go," they write continuously about anything that comes to mind. The one stipulation is that they must not stop writing until the time limit is up. If nothing comes to mind, they must write that nothing comes to mind. Children must also disregard spelling, punctuation, and handwriting, concentrating instead on thoughts and feelings. When the time limit is up, children put down their pens or pencils. They can share their writing with a partner or develop a theme or topic from their free write to explore in depth.

20. Sounds of Music

Play different types of sounds or music for the children. After each track is played, they can write about whatever comes to mind. Have them use these entries to compare and contrast the sounds of music they heard.

21. Read and Write
Set aside quiet reading times. After the children have read, have them write about their reading experience. They can concentrate on summarizing what they read, whether they enjoyed the reading, the characters they met, and so on.

22. Critical Writing
Choose a day out of the week to discuss current affairs. After having a class discussion, allow the children time to write what they felt about the topic. They can also discuss lighter fare, such as movies or plays, and write reviews of what they have seen.

23. Introduction
Introduce any theme to the class. Before discussing it in depth, give the children time to write all that they know about the theme. They can share their knowledge in small groups before reforming as a large group to continue the discussion.

44: Cooperative Writing

Ten Stages of Cooperative Writing

Stage One: Put Groups Together
- set group size (number will depend on group writing task)
- groups can be heterogeneous or mixed
- members assume roles so that each has a responsibility
- members are accountable both as individuals and as part of the group
- get-acquainted activities can focus on shared interests, strengths, weaknesses, likes, dislikes

Stage Two: Brainstorm
- group takes part in brainstorming activities
- creates an idea/concept web
- members create individual writing folders as well as group writing folder

Stage Three: Focus and Planning
- establish common rules (e.g., responsibilities)
- create a time line
- divide tasks and responsibilities
- share and negotiate ideas with group members
- work together toward a common goal

Stage Four: Research
- decide on what to research and where to research (e.g., school, local library)
- divide research tasks
- conduct research
- regroup to share information and materials

Stage Five: Prewrite
- consider topic and main theme
- identify audience
- develop a set of questions that will be answered by the research

- discuss ideas with classmates and teacher for feedback
- plan how to present work

Stage Six: Draft
- organize group ideas and pick those that are most effective
- break up writing tasks to write a first draft
- regroup to read draft together and to others not in the group for feedback
- listen to suggestions with an open mind

Stage Seven: Revise
- consider feedback
- revise writing by adding, deleting, changing

Stage Eight: Proofread
- proofread and peer edit within group
- read to others for feedback
- incorporate suggestions
- complete style edit (e.g., capitalization, punctuation, spelling, word use)
- ask for secondary opinion (e.g., teacher, educational assistant, student teacher, parent)

Stage Nine: Rewrite
- recopy work, incorporating all corrections

Stage Ten: Final Product
- complete finishing touches
- share final product with others

Post-Writing Activity: Reflect
- group reflection
- audience feedback – reflect on in journal
- group wrap-up, group and whole-class discussion
- final journal reflections

There are many benefits that accrue to children when they work in groups, including learning and practising cooperative skills as they study and explore topics together and proofread their own work as well as that of their peers. As well, children:

- increase their self-confidence when they work cooperatively as a group and independently of the teacher,
- assume responsibility for their learning by taking control of the topic they wish to explore (with only marginal teacher input),
- learn to work with peers,
- consider and evaluate the input of others,
- capitalize on one another's strengths.

The Program

In order to benefit from cooperative writing endeavors, children should have a valid reason for working in a group rather than on their own or with a partner. Typically, reasons will include breadth of topic, or the need for a variety of opinions and approaches to tackle an issue.

Group members can write letters to the teacher at different stages of the work to describe the growth and development of their group. This activity helps the group to define its personality and gives the teacher a window into its dynamics. Children need to understand that each group member is accountable for the group's success and that everyone must work toward a common goal – the analogy of a sports team might be appropriate and useful for some – in order to achieve the maximum benefit.

Types of resource materials children will use include books, cassettes, videos, film, and libraries, as well as librarians, teachers, friends, parents, and guardians. Time required for cooperative projects will vary, but it is unlikely that any project would be of a shorter duration than several days since children need time to brainstorm, discuss, research, share, and publish or present.

Ideas for Cooperative Writing Experiences

1. Create an Advertising Campaign for a School Function

Children, as a group, decide on a function to be advertised. Drawing on all members' creativity and experiences, the group selects a medium (e.g., print, radio ad) and produces a presentation for the school's staff and students.

2. Design a School Safety Handbook

A group can decide on safety issues that have relevance to their school. Group members research the issues using community, library, and municipal office libraries and resources. They write a handbook and work with school administrators to publish and distribute it throughout the school.

3. Publish a School Newspaper

A group can publish a class or school newspaper. They begin by deciding on its length and the sections to be included. Group members assign or volunteer for roles of writers, editors, designers, proofreaders, and so on. They prepare their pieces and compile them to make a newspaper. Depending on the scope of the paper, the group may make a copy for each person in the class, or make a copy for each class in the school.

4. Write a Script for a Small Play

Children in a group can create characters based on group personalities. They select a genre (e.g., comedy, mystery, suspense) and develop a script incorporating all of the characters. After rehearsing their script, they present their work to another group or the rest of the class.

5. Prepare for an Informative Debate

Two groups select a topic they would like to debate (e.g., smoking in public places, school uniforms vs. casual dress). Each group picks a side (for, against). If they have difficulty picking a side, a representative from each group can participate in a coin toss to determine who will have first selection. The two groups research their topic before engaging in a debate. If they like, they can appoint a judge to keep order and determine the most successful team.

6. Consumer Research Report

Children in a group can investigate how garbage leaves their home and school, and how it leaves the community. They research local recycling practices and prepare a consumer research report, which they present to another group.

7. Movie Reviews

Children in a group can interview teachers and peers to discover favorite movies. They regroup to compare and contrast findings, developing a ranking of favorites. The group shares its findings by posting a graph in the class or in the hallway.

Group Writing Tips

1. In addition to a group writing folder, each member should also have a personal writing folder.
2. Members keep a log of the group's progress.
3. Members brainstorm and record an idea web.
4. Members record ideas on index cards so they can be regrouped easily.

45: Publishing

A writer needs to know that different audiences require different styles of writing. Publishing provides one kind of purpose and audience for the children's writing and a valid reason for revising and editing. Teachers can publish and display one piece of writing per month per child. Publishing should be viewed as something one does only with his or her best work, as it is in the real world.

Ten Steps to Publishing

1. Decide why and how to publish the work.
2. Determine the audience for the work.
3. Ensure that it is polished (no spelling, grammar, or punctuation errors).
4. Decide on the number and size of pages.
5. Select a font.
6. Determine if illustrations will be included.
7. Include a title page, a dedication, and an "About the Author" section.
8. Design the cover and back cover.
9. Create an illustration or logo for the front cover.
10. Decide how the book will be bound (e.g., string, staples, rings).

Sharing Published Works

1. Publishing for Parents and Friends

Collect the best of each child's poetry and create a "Best of..." collection. Hold an evening of poetry reading that parents and friends may attend. Children can set up the room for a reading by arranging chairs, a stool for the reader, and serving refreshments. Each child can read his or her contribution. An extension of this activity is to contact a nursing home to arrange a reading.

Publishing Ideas

accordion books	rebus books	see-through books
pop-up books	push & pull books	shape books
fold-out books	lift-up books	atlases
diaries	instructions	jokes (tongue
albums	observations	twisters)
recipe books	photographs	dioramas
mobiles	cubes	author books
comic strips	silhouettes	dictionaries
reillustrated books	calendars	cartoons
record books	wordless books	letters & envelopes
cards	paperdoll books	directories
advertisements & flyers	brochures	miniature books
file cards	question & answer	pocket charts
surveys	murals	scrolls
word-shape books	flip books	flap books
long books (landscape)	tall books	alphabet books
	box books	scripts
		time lines

---

2. Publishing for Younger Children

The class can create its own book of short stories, fables, or tales for young children. As a large group, they plan the book – order of material, illustrations, chapters, cover illustration, and design. They produce the book and invite grade one children to attend a reading. Each child reads a section or one of the tales from the book.

3. Publishing for Peers

Children can write mystery short stories. They illustrate and bind their stories and display them at a "Publishers' Corner." During silent reading, children can read one another's short stories. When finished, the display can be moved to the library where other children can read the stories.

4. Publishing for the Computer

Children can share their writing on e-mail or join networks of young writers on the Internet.

46: Patterns for Writing

Patterns for writing present creative structures that order or arrange ideas into specific formats that provide signals for the reader. Here is a glimpse of some forms of writing:

ABC books	advertisements
banners	brochures
chants	commercials
debates	detective stories
emblems	epitaphs
fables	for sale ads
greeting cards	graffiti
haiku	horoscopes
interviews	invoices
jingles	job applications
legends	memos
movie scripts	novels
nursery rhymes	odes
opinions	palindromes
posters	questionnaires
quotations	raps
real estate notices	string writing
subtitles	tabloids
trilogies	verses
visitor books	wills
yarns	yearbooks

Providing children with many opportunities to hear and experiment with a potpourri of formats that are meaningful to their lives, to discuss both the distinctive and similar linguistic and structural features of certain modes, and to share their own pieces of writing are signficant to young writers. When teachers read aloud strong examples of genres of writing, children are inspired to create their own works and may develop an understanding of how to write like a reader and read like a writer.

47: Journals

The reasons for asking children to keep journals are many. Journals provide opportunities for children to reflect and make connections between new and prior knowledge; they serve as a connection between reading and writing; they place children at the center of their learning; and they demonstrate a writer's ownership of ideas.

Journals, as part of a child's writing portfolio, also serve other functions. They act as a connector between home and school; they warehouse bits and pieces of thoughts and writing as well as lists of books children have read; they chart the child's development in language, spelling, dialogue, and sentence structure; they can be used for self-evaluation; they keep children and teachers in touch with a child's feelings and thoughts; and they are viewed as safe places to try out expressive voices without fear of evaluation.

Types of Journals

Reading Response Journal
• thoughts about books, materials children have read

Reflection Journal
• thoughts on any subject or activity

Dialogue Journal
• conversational journey between child and teacher

Personal Journal
• personal writing that is not to be shared

Work Journal
• summaries of project work, activity assignments

Writer's Journal
• records of potential writing ideas

Project Journal
• lists of work done on projects

Listening Journal
- responses to text heard read aloud

Family Journal
- parents' and child's thoughts on reading and writing

Fictitious Journal
- entries written in role

Reading Journal
- lists of and responses to books read

Field Journal
- records, descriptions of trips taken by the class

Ideas Journal
- notes on miscellaneous topics

Cooperative Journal
- entries composed and written by all members of a class

Learning Journal
- new facts, reflections on learning as a class

Contents of Journals

pictures	puzzles
feedback	lists
portfolios	observations
brainstorming	posing, solving problems
memoirs	free writing
retelling stories	special words
reviews	poems
dreams	phone numbers

48: Memoirs

Pre-Writing Warm Ups that Lead to Action

- sharing memories
- two-week detailed diary
- questionnaire
- photos
- sharing hobbies
- personal time line
- family tree
- magazine montage
- conversations

From a young age, children begin to share their experiences through illustration and print. When personal stories are developed and shared, young authors become aware that writing is a natural process. By linking personal experiences with developing language skills, children find that their lives hold the potential for starting points of significant writing.

A Place to Start

1. Spontaneous Memory Writing – Free Association
Children look around until they see something that reminds them of a person or event. They write down what they were reminded of, letting that memory lead them to another, and so on. (This technique can be helpful in clearing writer's block.) Children choose one memory from their list to explore further, digging for details to flesh out the memory and including material they think others might like to read.

2. Reflections
Children relax in a quiet spot, focus on something they want to clarify or think through, and let the topic fill their mind until ideas come to them (ideas can be recorded). Alternately, children can form a small-group focus session where all concentrate on the same object. Children, who do not talk through the activity, pass a piece of paper on which each child contributes a thought.

3. Sharing Personal Revelation
Ask children to reread several memoir pieces to look for recurring themes or issues in their life. For some children, a writing conference can help to

shape their focus and increase awareness of important personal issues. As they read, children can jot ideas, moments, and realizations central to the theme or issue to help them during the composition phase. After children have composed their first draft, they can read their work to check that it reveals the theme or issue. Peer editors can help during this phase by telling the writer what they believe is the theme of the piece. Children can incorporate revisions in their next draft. Polished pieces can be displayed in the class.

4. Exploring a Period of Time

Encourage children to explore a phase of personal growth, moving away from focusing on a single incident. This writing differs slightly from exploring a single incident since the children will need to organize their writing thematically rather than chronologically.

Fictional Memoirs

Fictional memoir creates a first-hand view of a person or group as witnessed by an outsider. This form of writing allows children to adopt a voice and a point of view while focusing their center of attention elsewhere.

1. Telling About Someone Else

Children can write of an incident they witnessed or were a part of that centered on another person. They can give an "insider view" of the event, their thoughts at the time of the incident and what they think now, given a period of reflection.

2. Telling as Someone Else

Writing in role integrates curriculum and extends learning as children witness life through another's eyes:

Nature Observation: Children can write in role of an eyewitness to a natural incident or disaster, for example, reporting on a hurricane or an event involving an animal.

Current Events: Ask children to take a side on a global issue. Writing in role, they defend their position as an interested party.

Historical Events: Children research a historical personality involved in a contentious issue and write about the event from the personality's point of view.

49: Scripts

Writing a script involves bringing written words to life. It is literature that speaks the words aloud. Examples of writing that incorporate scripts are:

- plays
- television and radio scripts
- comic strips
- dialogue
- lyrics
- news reports
- monologues
- sermons
- conversations
- characterizations
- morning announcements

Writing Scripts

1. Interviewing Friends and Family

Have children interview friends, parents, and relatives about events they have experienced. They will need a tape recorder and a list of questions that they generate. After the interview, they can transcribe the most relevant material, leaving out the questions. Children can continue to work on their transcription until their story flows smoothly. An extension of this activity is to ask children to form small groups and dramatize the stories.

2. Creating a Comic Strip

Ask children to form groups of five or six. Each group member creates one character who could be in a comic strip, drawing and naming his or her character. As a group, children make a comic strip following this plan:

- make up a story using all of the characters,
- decide what each character will do and say,
- decide what will occur in each frame,
- cooperatively draw the comic strip,
- print and draw bubbles around dialogue.

3. Interviewing Figures from the Past

In groups of eight to ten, children can choose several famous people from history. Some members will be in role as one of the famous people (they will need to read as much information as possible on the characters), while other group members will act as reporters or members of the community who might have been alive at that particular time period. They role play a press conference where the reporters ask questions of each famous character and his or her views of issues at the time. Reporters can write an article based on one or more of the interviews.

4. Reliving an Important Moment
Ask children to describe a situation they observed that made a lasting impression on them. In their descriptions, they include specifics such as setting, character, action, mood, and the role of the characters. They can work with as many classmates as needed to improvise a scene that brings this incident to life.

5. Advertising a Product
In groups of four or five, children prepare a script for a thirty-second television commercial advertising a pair of shoes. The commercial has one spokesperson, for instance a pro athlete or a high school basketball player. Children write their commercial, detailing camera angles and shots. They could videotape their dramatized commercial.

6. Role Playing a Scene in a Restaurant
With a partner, children create dialogue based on a scene in a restaurant that centers on an unhappy customer and the waiter. The customer wants to speak to the restaurant owner – the waiter is afraid of losing his or her job if the owner becomes involved. When they have scripted the scene, partners take on a role and practise it before presenting to another pair of children.

50: Writing in Role

Writing in role allows learners to work in a new way, fostering the development of writing in more complex modes. It offers children the chance to view themselves as writers who can control the communication medium. Examples of writing in role opportunities are:
- proclamations
- speeches
- diaries
- lyrics/songs
- first-person accounts
- spy stories
- petitions
- detective stories
- monologues
- novel characters
- travelogues
- advertisements
- interviews
- biographies
- cartoons
- commentaries
- newspaper articles
- announcements
- comedy scripts

Medieval Times

The following examples of writing in role activities are structured around the theme of medieval times. In order to write in role, the children will need to research this period of history – its achievements, people, dangers, growth, and development. Artistic license, a part of any writing in role activity, will come into play here as children put themselves in the place of inhabitants of the Middle Ages, or those who are revisiting it.

1. Diaries
Children imagine that they have traveled back in time to the year 1300 and have landed in a medieval town. They write an entry in their diary detailing experiences they faced that day, incorporating their research findings.

2. Detective in Role
Ask children to form groups of three or four. As a group, they must try and solve a mystery that took place in 1200. The children take on the role of detectives who find the answer to the mystery, retaining the time period as much as possible.

3. Travelogues
Allow the children to assume the role of travel agents who have been asked to plan a tour of the medieval castles of Europe. They are responsible for choosing at least ten famous castles representative of the age. In addition, children must prepare detailed itineraries for their clients.

4. In Memory of...

The children research medieval times to find a person of note, for example, a politician or a legendary figure. Writing in role as a court biographer, they tell of the person's contribution to the society of the time.

5. Reporting on the Black Death

As a newspaper reporter for a large, medieval paper, children write of the plague and its impact on cities in Asia and Europe. They can base their story around 1350, when the Black Death was at its most virulent.

6. Fashion Times

Children, in small groups, imagine themselves as clothes designers who have been asked to design outfits for both women and men that will be worn at a huge feast. They can base their designs on fashions of the time. They sketch and color their designs, and list at the bottom of each sketch the materials used to make the clothes. (The materials should be consistent with fabrics available at the time.) The work of each group can be posted so that children can share their designs.

7. Minstrel Music

Working alone or with a partner, the children take on the role of a minstrel. Minstrels, who were singers or musicians, sang or recited poetry that they wrote themselves. In some instances, they would incorporate news and gossip into the lyrics so that isolated townspeople could learn of life outside their immediate area. The children can make their lyrics serious or light-hearted, mysterious or informative.

8. Serfs' Petition

In groups of four or five, children meet as serfs on a medieval fiefdom. They draw up a petition that demands better treatment for serfs, and that outlines the extent of their duties and the lacking compensation offered by the owner of the land.

51: Letters

Writing letters helps children to develop skills in a number of areas: sharing information and ideas, practising cursive writing or computer skills, writing collaboratively, talking, planning, and negotiating, spelling, and structuring sentences. Letters connect reading and writing and home and school communities, and help teachers to be aware of children's thoughts and feelings. Letter formats can be demonstrated and placed on a helping chart.

Types of Letters	
Cards:	thank you, sympathy, get well, invitations, postcards, birthday, holiday
Business:	for information (e.g., company products); for service (e.g., complaints)
Casual:	informal letters sent to friends
Internet:	electronic mail to anyone in the world
E-Mail:	brief memos, typically sent by and for work cohorts
Response:	answer questions posed in a letter or conversation

Audiences for Letters	
celebrities	musical groups
authors	illustrators
editorials	time capsule
friends	parents
relatives	pen pals
companies	employers

Writing Persuasively

Persuasion is a form of communication that attempts to change the attitudes or behaviors of others by appealing to their reasons and emotions. To speak, write, and think logically, to analyze skillfully, and to reason effectively are lifelong processes. Key elements of persuasive writing include: arguments, assertiveness, critical thinking, convincing writing, the inclusion of facts, details, and logic, and well-developed opinions.

Examples of Persuasive Writing	
advertisements	slogans
commercials	announcements
invitations	dedications
reviews	letters
advice columns	speeches
editorials	debates

Persuade Me

1. Formal Letter
In role as members of a small community, children can brainstorm and record reasons to save an old playground. Once the list is complete, they write a group letter to the mayor explaining the playground's importance to the community.

2. Proposal
Have the children write to you about a field trip that they want to take. Their letters must persuade you that the field trip would be a beneficial experience for the children.

3. Write a Contract
Working and writing in role, children want to play on a school team, but their parents refuse the request because they don't do their homework. In role, children must persuade their parents that they can be responsible. To win back their parents' trust, they write a contract stating that they will do homework every day after supper, in exchange for being allowed to play on the team.

52: Information and Research

Writing to inform provides the opportunity for children to work from the familiar in their lives as they communicate information and give short narrative accounts about what they have learned. They can write about topics of interest, exploring and expanding their knowledge by asking questions, investigating, gathering information from resources, and recording ideas. In turn, they can describe, explain, and state opinions and arguments as they interpret data to reveal a critical level of cognitive development.

xpository writing:	thinking with pen and paper, or computer
xpose topic:	objects, interests, hobbies
xplore:	provide foundations
xperience:	ask questions and investigate brainstorm (active processes), write details, capture essentials
xpand:	write about the topic incorporating other areas of the curriculum
xplain:	opinions, points of view, problem solving
motion:	write about the topic with feeling and commitment
mphasis:	strive for a balance between fact and emotion

Informing Activities

1. Labels
Children can label photos and drawings. In addition, they can write a response or ask questions to which others respond on a notice board.

Forms of Informational Text		
definitions	directories	instructions
recipes	manuals	atlases
dictionaries	explanations	reports
alphabet books	memos	articles
newspapers	letters	announcements
summaries	reviews	journals
television guides		

2. Webs
With the children, brainstorm a topic. Children can offer information they know about the topic to create a web or a chart.

3. Diagrams
Children can label diagrams and drawings. They expand the labels by recording information on use, purpose, or characteristics to give the reader additional information.

4. Calendars

Children can record facts about the weather and make predictions.

5. Lists

After discussing a topic, ask the children to write a one-sentence opinion of an aspect of the topic that is supported by several facts. Place their responses under headings according to categories.

6. Process Writing

Children can write directions telling how to do something — "This is how I learned to... ."

7. Poetry

Children work with a research topic, and turn the information into a poem.

8. Comic Strips

Collect, display, and explore with the children a variety of comics. Have them interpret the message they believe each cartoonist is trying to convey. Children then use a comic strip to demonstrate their findings about a topic.

9. Storyboards

After reading a nonfiction book, children can draw a series of pictures accompanied by writing that describes the events in the book and ends with a prediction of what might happen if the book were to be continued. As well, children can describe how they will apply the knowledge they gained from reading the book.

10. Storybooks

Encourage children to write "All About" stories documenting experiences they have had or people they have known.

11. Maps

Children can map out an area of land that was described in a nonfiction book. They can include a key to forested areas, and mark lakes, rivers, and other topographical information.

12. Interviews

In groups, have children write questions for an interview. Each child then conducts the interview with several people, recording the results on each occasion.

13. Learning Journals

Children can detail their reading experiences by: recording opinions of books they have read, observations they or the author made, experiments related to topics in a book, new facts they have learned, and problems they have experienced while reading.

14. Graphs

Children graph the results of the interviews.

15. Charts

In response to a nonfiction book, have children organize their ideas under headings related to the topic of the book.

16. Reports

Children, in small groups, choose a topic they wish to explore and develop questions they would like answered. They investigate the topic and prepare a short report that details their findings.

17. Advertisements

Have children create posters or pamphlets advertising an issue they feel strongly about or a presentation (e.g., play, poetry reading) they are planning to make to the rest of the class or another class in the school.

18. Newspaper Articles

Share several newspaper editorials with the children. Ask them to choose one editorial and write an opinion in support of, or against, the editorial. Children can find a partner who shares the same opinion. In turn, they find two children who have written an opposing viewpoint. Partners read the opposing point of view, sharing with the writers parts they found convincing.

19. Letters

Children can write letters to one another in which they ask questions of the recipient. Children write back, answering the first child's questions.

53: Stories

Story does not necessarily mean fiction. Since children appear to write more readily when they work from life experiences, teachers can help them shape their ideas, recollections, and inventories in a variety of ways. Young authors can:

- draw the characters they will be writing about, building a "life map" in pictures.
- create a story map as a plan for writing, listing the problems, the events, the interactions, and the conclusion. As they discuss their story maps with the teacher and a peer group, they can begin to organize their ideas and focus their narratives before writing.
- select an observation or a recollection from their notebooks or journals, and begin to turn it into a story.
- pattern a story they have enjoyed by changing its frame, setting, time, plot, or ending.
- use the format of a story, a fable, a poem, a picture book, or a pop-up book to structure the telling of their story.
- write a story for a particular audience – a younger child, a child who moved away, a child ill at home.
- transcribe a story they have heard or seen, carefully restructuring the incidents.
- work with a partner – one partner writes a page and passes it to his or her partner who writes the next page, passes it back to the first partner and so on.

Story Forms	
adventures	sequels
life stories	legends
parodies	fables
quests	science fiction
historical fiction	comedies
retellings	choose-your-own
tall tales	endings

54: Poems

How to Write a Poem
1. Choose a topic that is important to you.
2. Organize your thoughts about the topic.
3. Select a form of poetry (e.g., rhyme, haiku).
4. Brainstorm and record words and phrases that relate to the topic. Do not stop writing until you run out of ideas.
5. Arrange and organize ideas that work. Delete phrases that have no power or are repetitive.
6. Write your first draft.
7. Revise and publish your poem.

Types of Poems

Free Verse
This type of poem has few restrictions. There is no set line length, no rhythm patterns, and little rhyming. On the other hand, these poems do suggest rhythmical units.

Narrative Poem
A narrative poem tells a story, such as in a ballad, folk song, or rock song. It is usually organized in stanzas that include rhyme and rhythm.

Lyric Poetry
This type of poem conveys strong emotions and impressions. Although we tend to associate lyrics with music or songs, a lyric poem does not have to be set to music.

Formula Poem
This type of poem should be written with specific patterns in mind because it focuses on writing skills related to control of words, structure, and content. It can be structured using limericks or haiku.

Cinquain Poetry
This five-line poem with syllable restrictions can be used as an introduction to haiku. The first line has two syllables, the second line four, the third line six, the fourth eight, and the last line two. The line and syllable restriction requires that words be chosen with care.

Haiku Poetry

Haiku is a restrictive form of poetry — three lines with seventeen syllables. The first line has five syllables, the second line seven, and the last line five. Haiku must refer to nature in some way.

Acrostic Poetry

Writing this type of poetry is like creating a cross-word puzzle. The first step is to choose a word that represents a theme or idea. Once the theme is selected, a word or group of words must be created for each letter in the main word. Each new word or group of words must be descriptive so that it remains within the theme.

Rhymes

These poems, written in short stanzas, are filled with fun, rhythmic words or phrases. Children can clap, march, or tap their feet to set a rhythm. It is often helpful to follow a pattern.

5. Advertising

The children form small groups of four or five. Each group can pick a product and compose a rhyming commercial that tells of its benefits. Groups can share their advertisement with the rest of the class.

6. Erase and Replace

Read the children a poem. Using its rhythm and pattern, they can create their own poem, replacing words in the original poem with those of their choice.

7. Nature Exploration

Take the children on a hike or field trip. When they return to the class, they can write a poem about their favorite moment of the trip from their observations in their notebooks – items they have noticed, unusual comparisons, strange terms, questions, and puzzles.

55: Ideas for Poems

1. Concrete Poems

This type of poem involves arranging words in a shape that will describe the theme chosen. Children can choose a theme from a unit of study and write a concrete poem.

2. Theme Poems (Food)

Each child can select a food and think of different words that describe it. The child then arranges the words to make the shape of the food.

3. Sounds of Music

Have the children close their eyes and listen to a piece of music. Once the music finishes, they can write a list of words that describe how the music made them feel. They can then find a published poem that contains these words or reflects the mood of words on their list.

4. Cut and Paste

Give the children a variety of magazines and have them cut out pictures and make a collage. They can then use their collage as a source for a poem.

56: Modes of Print

Transforming modes of print involves taking the essence of a text (e.g., story, poem, novel) and transforming it into another form of writing or another medium (e.g., video). Such rethinking and reworking of a text, which necessitates shifting the point of view, often leads to a deeper comprehension of the material. Transforming a text is not only a follow-up activity to reading, but can also motivate children to read. (Primary/junior children are more likely to read a story that has been read aloud to them than one they have not experienced.) Assessment is made easier because transforming modes of print makes explicit a child's understanding of the material.

Retelling/Storytelling

Retelling is one way of transforming print. Both oral and written retellings should be encouraged because they allow children to reveal their ideas about what the story means to them. Fidelity to the original version should not be stressed; rather, encourage imaginative and personalized recreations of the story. Retelling is beneficial to both the teller and the listener because it deepens the exploration of the text for both.

Illustrating

Children generally enjoy drawing or painting pictures to illustrate stories they've read, heard, or written. Since this is a nonverbal form of expression, it has a wider appeal to younger children and is a useful tool for reluctant writers and ESL children. Expressing what the story means to them in this form will not be hindered by their lack of language skills. In the primary grades, illustrating could take the form of drawing a character or setting. In junior grades, children could make a diorama of a scene or draw a series of key settings and characters. Even a photo essay is possible, perhaps using fellow children to act out key scenes in similar settings. Of course, text can be added easily to any illustration, or the art can become the starting point for a story.

Other Media

Children in junior grades could film a version of a story. They could act it out or use animation (e.g., dolls, clay, illustrations). In addition, a text could be reworked into an audio play, a choral reading, a reading to a musical accompaniment, or transformed into a musical script at advanced levels. Many computer programs give children the option of making their own slide shows, complete with narration.

The Three Little Pigs

This page and the next comprise several examples of the ways in which children can transform modes of print. Transforming can be done as a group activity in which each group uses a different genre to tell the same story, or it can be done by children working on their own. Before beginning, it might be helpful to show children samples of writing in other forms (a newspaper or magazine would be a great place to start). The possibilities are endless.

Recipe

Mr. Wolf's Award Winning Roast Pig in Orange Sauce
60 mL (1/4) cup flour
5 mL (1/2 tsp.) each salt, pepper, paprika
45 mL (3 tbsp.) cooking oil
2 onions, chopped
60 mL (1/4 cup) vegetable broth
juice of 5 oranges
125 mL (1/2 cup) sour cream
1 little pig

Start a fire using sticks. Combine the first five ingredients in a pot...

News Report

"Good evening, here is the six o'clock news. In our top story, police have revealed that the wolf who has been terrorizing the neighborhood is near capture. Police detective Hunter O'Lupus is on the scene where the wolf is making desperate attempts to blow down a house..."

Advertisement

Open House:
Saturday, June 19 10:00 A.M – 4:00 P.M.
Phone # 555-5555
Affordable, wolf-free area
Luxury three-bedroom home
Solid brick construction

Diary Entry

Dear Diary,
I just got news of what happened to my brother and I'm so upset I can hardly write. I sure hope that mean old wolf doesn't come around here looking for a meal. They say the house came down with just one huff and one puff. I think I'll run and put shutters on all the windows right away.

Directions

Go north on Main Street, through the intersection, past the pile of straw on the right and the pile of sticks on the left. Turn left and drive until...

Den Drive
Woods Edge

Letter of Application

Dear Ms. Boss,

I am writing in response to the ad in the newspaper for bricklayers. I am a pig with a solid background in bricklaying. I once made my own house that withstood all the wolf's huffing and puffing. Please find my résumé enclosed.

Sincerely,
Pig

Invitation

You are cordially invited to attend a black-tie dinner in honor of Pig, who has graciously opened his lovely brick house to guests for the occasion.

Please R.S.V.P. by Saturday.

Letter

Dear Pig,
I will be visiting your home soon to eat you. I suggest you make it easy on yourself and just surrender to me now. There's no reason to ruin a perfectly nice brick house.

See You Soon,
Wolf

Autobiography

I was born in a small den near the city. My childhood was a happy one. I still remember sitting by the fire, listening to my mother tell wonderful wolf stories while my father was out hunting. It was always such a fine feast when he brought home a pig. I've never lost that taste for a fine little pig, with just a hint of garlic and a touch of thyme.

Poster

One Night Only
Come See the Spectacle
Wolf vs. Pig

Also Appearing
The Troll vs. The Three Billy Goats Gruff

57: Assessing Young Writers' Work

Children's writing provides teachers with abundant material to use for assessment purposes. Pieces can be assessed individually or comparatively (e.g., a revised version with the original). Another model includes choosing a piece a child has written earlier in the year. While the teacher dictates, the child rewrites the piece.

Strategies

1. Self-Assessment Criteria
Children will need instruction on how to select criteria, which can be based on the authors and works they enjoy reading. For younger grades, try modeling (talking out loud) your thought process through demonstrations, and provide self-evaluation checklists. At the beginning of each semester or month, consider asking the children:
1. What skills are you trying to learn?
2. What are your best writing skills?
3. What type of writing do you most enjoy?

The children can write their responses in their journal. Now and then, you can ask:
1. What was the hardest part about writing today?
2. What did you do today that was better than yesterday?

One child wrote, "One thing I need to improve on is my handwriting. I also need to improve on what I write about, where to put punctuations, and on spelling." For older children, consider discussing and recording the elements of a good story, posting them in the classroom for reference.

2. Constructive Feedback
When assessing work, avoid simple judgments, (e.g., I liked your story). Instead, look for a piece's strengths and weaknesses, and provide balanced, constructive advice that relates directly to aspects of children's writing. This provides them with feedback that is useful and that reinforces their knowledge of the writing craft.

3. Writing Conferences

Conduct frequent writing conferences with each child in your class. As well, stress the importance in growing as a writer and offer specific strategies that will assist the child in understanding the craft.

4. Writing Workshops

Participating in creative writing workshops can supply you with new ideas to help your writing. Discussing and sharing these ideas with fellow teachers and writers can cast attention of aspects of writing that require examination. Back in the class, share these new focuses with the children.

5. Teacher Self-Assessment

Reading, writing, and reflecting on your work may enable you to better teach children about writing styles and techniques. When you share your experiences with the class, and allow children to evaluate your writing, children better understand the concept that teachers, like themselves, are learners.

6. Flexible Assessment

When examining early drafts, try to look beyond spelling and grammar errors. Children need to be encouraged to use new words to develop their reading and writing vocabulary. Using only words a child already knows will make his or her writing, while error-free, dull and lacking invention. Once a child decides that a particular piece will be published, work with him or her to emphasize the importance of correct spelling and word usage.

Part D: Learning About Language

58: How Language Works

Grammar, usage, punctuation, capitalization, handwriting, and spelling, when used effectively, help writers to make meaning and intent clear to the reader. Like other elements of writing, they should be treated in the context of the children's writing experience as often as possible. Demonstrations and mini-lessons are effective in highlighting specific aspects that arise.

- Language learning programs need to include:
- a focus on the many forms of writing for different purposes and audiences,
- opportunities for constructing text, individually and in groups,
- opportunities for deconstructing text, and analyzing and examining how language works.
- Children's attention can be directed to the many forms of writing:
- for different purposes,
- for different audiences.
- We can help the children to create longer, more complex sentences:
- using conjunctions,
- using clauses.
- Children can add to sentences:
- words,
- phrases,
- clauses.
- Children can analyze the structure of different writing forms:
- factual writing such as reports, explanations,
- fiction writing such as narrative, poetry.
- Children can create sentences for specific purposes:
- opening sentences,
- lead sentences of paragraphs,
- concluding sentences.
- Children can talk about parts of speech and their functions in the text:
- nouns, pronouns, collective nouns, etc.,
- verbs, adverbs,
- comparative and superlative adjectives,
- idioms and expressions.
- Children can rework sentences:
- substituting,
- deleting,
- adding.

- Children can rearrange parts of a sentence to create a more interesting sentence:
- rearrange words and phrases,
- rearrange parts of a sentence such as subject and predicate.
- Children can use different forms of speech:
- direct and indirect,
- first- and third-person voice.
- Children can compare a variety of usages when problems arise in language use.
- Children can discuss appropriate and inappropriate language usage by characters in books and stories.
- Children can submit examples of their writing to be used in mini-lessons or demonstrations to examine alternative usages and structures.
- Teachers can demonstrate interesting differences in language, from both oral and print contexts.
- Teachers can organize investigations by having the children experiment with word order or compare kinds of words that normally occur in the same place in a sentence.
- Teachers can help the children to observe the ways in which a change in sentence structure affects the meaning of the sentence.
- Teachers can give children practice in changing tense, using synonyms, and observing idioms in language (e.g., advertisements).
- Teachers can conduct a survey of the particular jargon of a group (e.g., teens, teachers).
- Teachers can gather a collection of "sentence misfits," examples of ineffective or incorrect language usage from newspapers or television, and create a "What's in a Word" bulletin board.
- Classes can play a variety of games, including computer games, that heighten everyone's awareness of language usage.

59: Grammar and Usage

For many years, teaching specific grammar lessons to the whole class was thought to have an impact on the children's writing. Research today tells us that children learn about language by using it and then by noticing how it was used. Learning when to use standard and nonstandard English depends on the context of the situation, requiring appropriate usage rather than correct usage. We speak the way our community speaks, and to alter language patterns requires creating a positive community environment and encouraging frequent interaction with significant models: speakers, coaches, peers, and, of course, stories – listening to stories, joining in patterns and poems, storytelling, and writing.

However, it is useful for children to examine language, detecting differences in their own oral and written language forms, as well as observing the language used by authors. Children may benefit from knowing common terms, such as "verbs," when discussing how language works so that they can add knowledge about English to their language repertoire. It is important that children have common terms for shared discussion about how our language works.

Discovering How Grammar Works

Grammar can be taught as other elements of writing – in relation to children's own reading and writing experiences. Certainly, the editing process is a natural occasion to discuss grammatical structures. Other occasions can include mini-lessons and child-teacher conferences. Puzzles and games draw attention to syntactic patterns. The following strategies span a range of age levels and grammar concepts.

1. Add-a-Bit Board

This activity can increase children's knowledge of parts of speech and vocabulary and help them to use more interesting words in their writing. Begin by writing a noun on the board, for example, "snake." Ask children to describe what snakes do, for example, they hiss, slither, and slide (verbs), or how they look, for example, they are wriggly, scaly, and long (adjectives). Write each sugges-

tion in a list. Children can record new words and their meanings, and use them in future writing activities.

2. Mix and Match Grammar Books

To make these books, children will need heavy paper, markers, a three-hole punch, and string. On strips of paper, they write sentences that include a noun, verb, adjective, and adverb. Children cut out the parts of sentences and group them with others from sentences they have written. They jumble the sentence parts then organize them by placing them in a pile and using a three-hole punch. They bind each section and then bind the four sections to make a book. Children can mix and match sentences by flipping various sentence parts. An extension is to cut sentences into phrases, bind them, and flip the book to make bizarre sentences.

3. Parts of Speech Books

Children can make personal parts of speech books. As they discover the function of words, they can list them in the appropriate section with a sample sentence. For younger children, focus on nouns and verbs. Older children may also incorporate sections on other parts of speech, for example, adjectives, adverbs, and prepositions.

4. Keep It Going

The object of this game is to create a long, interesting sentence that relies only marginally on the use of "and." One child begins by giving the first word of the sentence. The next child adds a word and so on until a sentence is formed that cannot be continued. As children become familiar with this activity, add further limitations, for example: only three adjectives per noun, or only two adverbs per verb. This activity provides a starting point for discussion on the parts of speech and can take an oral or written form.

5. Sentence Sense

Make numerous sets of the sixteen words shown on the next page. Ask children to arrange as many of the words as they can in a sentence that sounds like English. When they finish, ask them to explain the rationale behind their word order. Take a class census to determine what percentage of children used various words as nouns, verbs, pronouns, and so on.

plomy	when	up	felmed
the	had	the	baslurker
morked	his	lampix	the
ciptally	and	coofed	biffles

6. Corandic

Corandic is an enurient grof with many fribs. It granks from corite, an olg that cargs like lange. Corite grinkles several other tarances, which garkers excarp by glarking the corite and starping it in tranker-clarped storbs.

This passage makes more sense than meets the eye – the grammar can be examined. Explore the sentence by asking children questions like:
1. What is corandic?
2. From what does corandic grank?
3. What are the nouns in this sentence? the verbs? the pronouns? and so on.

Ask the children to translate these sentences into English, substituting words where necessary. Also, they can prepare a similar exercise using their knowledge of parts of speech and word inflections. Children make up a grammatically correct sentence filled with nonsense words then trade sentences with a partner who identifies the various parts of speech.

7. Parts of Speech Cloze

Copy a passage of text that would interest most children in the class. Delete words in the passage that are the same part of speech, for example, nouns, verbs, adjectives, adverbs, or conjunctions. Ask children to form small groups, and give each group a copy of the modified passage. In their groups, they brainstorm words for each blank before deciding on the best word. They rewrite the passage with their choice of words and identify the part of speech the missing words represent. When everyone has finished, a spokesperson from each group reads aloud the new passage. How similar were the group's choices? Children can debate their choices before comparing their passage with the original.

8. MacLibs©

This program is patterned on Mad Libs©, a word game where parts of speech are suggested and then implanted in a prepared text to provide incongruities when read aloud.

60: How Sentences Work

The Four Types of Sentences

No matter what form it takes, a sentence expresses a complete thought, includes a capitalized initial letter, and has a form of punctuation at its end. Although sentences may vary in complexity, they are one of four types:
1. Declarative sentences make a statement.
   The cat waited at the door.
2. Imperative sentences express a command.
   Get the cat inside.
3. Interrogative sentences ask a question.
   Who let the cat out?
4. Exclamatory sentences make an exclamation.
   The cat is terrified!

Building Sentences

Children learn about sentence structure by writing, reading, and discussing the language that they have constructed and read. By creating activities that promote examination of real language in context, young readers and writers can add to their storehouse of literacy knowledge.

1. Describe that Object

Ask children to name something that interests them, for example, dinosaurs. Now ask them to describe dinosaurs – how they look, what they do, and so on.

Dinosaurs are big.

Dinosaurs are scary.

Dinosaurs are loud.

Dinosaurs eat meat.

As children offer descriptions, list them on the board. The activity helps them to see that sentences can be made with three words. They can also see that changing a sentence can be done by altering one word.

2. Purple Cows

Children may feel more comfortable working with sentences when they know that there are numerous ways to write them. Awareness of these options frees the child to take chances. Here is one example:

I never saw a purple cow.

Select one or more words and discuss what they mean and how they could be replaced. For example, "Purple is a color. Can we think of other colors?"

I	never	saw	a	purple	cow.
I	never	ate	a	green	dog.
I	never	kissed	a	red	mouse.

As in the previous activity list the words children offer. This reinforces the concept of changing sentences.

3. Expanding Sentences
Give the children a basic sentence: "I saw a caterpillar." They can add on to the sentence, for example, "I saw a green caterpillar" and continue until the sentence can no longer be expanded. You can have group contests to see who can create the longest sentence.

4. Word by Word
Children, in small groups of three, can write a collaborative story. They can contribute one word at a time, or adding an element of chance, roll a die and contribute the same number of words as dots showing. One group member records the story as it develops. However groups decide to write their stories, members must abide by the rules – they cannot add extra words or take a turn out of order. This may be difficult as children's creative ideas are rarely confined to one word. Completed collaborative stories can be showcased in the classroom.

Working with More Complex Sentences

For older children, run-on sentences, overuse of one sentence type, and punctuation problems can be difficult. Teachers can help children to advance their writing abilities by making them aware of areas that need to be improved.

1. The Three-Sentence Challenge
Children can work with a partner for this activity. Provide each pair of children with a list of four items. The items can be related (e.g., four kinds of animals), or they can be disparate (e.g., coins, trees, sports, holidays). Each partner picks one item and writes three sentences about it without mentioning the item by name. His or her partner reads the sentences and identifies the item.

2. Let's Argue
For the learner who dislikes writing, debating on paper might be somewhat more palatable since it involves defending one's position. Before the activity, prepare debating questions, for example, "Which sport is more fun – hockey or baseball?" "Should the school week remain at five days or be shortened to four and the days made longer to make up the missing time?" Fold the questions and place them in a container. Children find a partner and take a question. Partners pick their side of the debate (possibly a debate in itself) and begin. One partner writes his or her response to the question. The partner reads the response and prepares a countering argument. Partners continue until they have exhausted their arguments, or one partner is swayed to accept the other's point of view.

3. Schedules
Have each child plan and write down the itinerary for a perfect day. The day should last from 9:00 A.M. until 8:00 P.M. The only stipulation is that the child must choose not less than five activities to do on that day. (This prevents the child from only choosing to play a computer game.) This activity encourages the child to talk and write about the things she or he likes to do.

4. Is It True?
Most children enjoy trying to trick an adult. Ask each child to make a list of five statements about himself or herself, some of which may be true. The adult or peer must then guess which, if any, of the statements are fabrications. Switch places so that the child can get a chance to call your bluff.

5. Mixed Up and Missing
Write down a sentence on a strip of paper. Cut out the words, mix them up, and then ask a child to unscramble the strips to make a sentence. To take the pressure off, you may suggest to the child that she or he put the words in the order that makes the most sense while insisting that no answer is wrong. Vary the length of the sentences according to ability and grade level.

6. Reducing Sentences

Some may argue that taking a sentence and reducing it goes against the creative process. What this exercise does, however, is show if a child understands the point of one sentence. It also helps the child understand the difference between flowery language and precise writing, and recognize when each style is more appropriate.

7. Sentence Rearrangement

Give the children a sentence and have them rewrite it in as many ways as possible. The one criterion is that the meaning of the sentence remain unchanged.

8. Sorting Sentences

Provide the child with a number of sentences, some of which have the same meaning. They can sort the sentences according to categories of meaning.

9. Story Tapes and Sentence Structure

Select a short story for which you have the tape and a copy of the book. Prepare a copy of the text with no punctuation marks, and give one copy to each child. Have the children listen to the story on tape. As they listen, they punctuate the text.

10. Who Said That?

Play a taped story for the children. Before you begin, ask them to note how the listener needs to know who is speaking and how this is achieved. Replay the tape, but this time have transcribed sections available. Stop the tape and have the children help you to place punctuation marks to indicate dialogue.

11. Comic Strip Conversation

Give pairs of children a comic strip that has at least four panels. They convert words in the bubbles to dialogue, using appropriate quotation marks. Children add lines to "flesh out" the action of the comic strip, and include the names of characters. To help them with this activity, display a piece of text that features extensive dialogue that they can use as a model.

61: Handwriting

Handwriting used to be a component of the elementary school curriculum, but in recent years, teachers have realized that children need to focus on what they are trying to say, rather than on the shape of their letters. Using a computer, we can select fonts that amaze the eye and strengthen the words. However, handwriting can help the child to notice words and letters – their shape and size, their uniformity and design. Children's writing can become more sophisticated as they develop control and esthetic awareness. Often art activities enable them to notice how cursive writing can help communication.

It is important that teachers not dwell excessively on the quality of the children's handwriting, but that they encourage children to focus on cursive writing as they revise their ideas and feelings. Handwriting should be readable, uniform, and esthetically pleasing. Style grows over time with each child, but it is important to demonstrate the formation and flow of letters with mini-lessons when necessary. Practising handwriting should be kept to a minimum, but careful handwriting should be a part of each writing revision.

Tips for Teaching Handwriting

1. Use challenging, varied activities that motivate children.
2. Supply grips for children who have difficulty holding pencils.
3. Make transcription meaningful (e.g., writing invitations, creating scripts).
4. Models for transcription should be the same size as normal handwriting, and placed where the child can see the letters easily.
5. Various styles of handwriting are acceptable, as long as they are uniform, readable, and esthetically pleasing.
6. Help children to become familiar with a handwriting repertoire where one style is appropriate to a particular task (e.g., calligraphy for invitations, clear writing for instructions).
7. Make available at a writing center a selection of utensils, including pencils, markers (fine and coarse nibs), pen and ink, fine-tipped brushes, pastels, and charcoal. Children can use scrap paper for practising their writing activities.

Beginning to Print

1. Write Away
Children should begin encoding ideas on paper as early as possible. Freed from restrictive letter formation, they will begin to notice the shape, size, and flow of writing. You can rewrite the work or use a word processor, and the children can see their writing honored and yet written in a standard fashion.

2. Erasable Writing
Young children enjoy working with materials such as sand, cornmeal, and flour. If possible, set up an area of the room that contains boxes of one of these materials (sand is the most inexpensive). Children can practise their handwriting skills at the center at various times of the day.

3. Watching the Grass Grow
This activity is best done in two parts. As a large group, discuss a theme or topic you have treated in class. Decide on one theme. In small groups, children will discuss and select one word that describes their feelings about that theme (e.g., holidays – happy). Each group writes its word on paper, checking to see that it is spelled correctly. Give each group a shallow pan, earth, and grass seeds. Children can take turns writing letters of the word in the earth using the end of a pencil. When they are satisfied with the writing, they plant the seeds in the groove of the letters. Over the next few weeks, children can water their word and watch the grass grow!

4. Signature Creatures
Ask children to fold a piece of letter-sized paper lengthwise. Using a pencil, they write their name on one side of the paper, using the space as much as possible. When they are satisfied with their writing, they outline their name with a colored marker of their choice. Children then cut along the edges of the outline. When they unfold their signature, their name looks like an insect. After viewing all of the names, children identify which letters make the most interesting cutouts.

5. Pretzel Letters
This baking activity allows children to eat their work. Purchase refrigerated French bread dough. Give a piece sufficient for each child in the class to shape his or her initials in a cursive fashion. Bake according to instructions and hold a class snack of initials. (Before you begin, ensure that no children have allergies that could prevent them from participating.)

Mastering Writing

As children mature, their ease with language enables them to concentrate on the mechanics of writing, of which handwriting is a component. As with younger children, teachers need to provide activities that are enjoyable and that help them master such elements of handwriting as spaces, margins, and general legibility.

1. A Survey of Handwriting
Children can explore styles of handwriting by conducting an informal survey of friends, family, and schoolmates. They can ask each respondent to sign his or her name and write a sample sentence that includes a number of letters, including ascenders and descenders. When completed, the children can compare the handwriting by charting how each letter is written.

2. Graffiti Writing
A large board and several water-soluble felt pens can serve as a class sign-in center. At the beginning of each day, children sign in and write how they feel. When they leave, they can change their message to better reflect their feelings or leave their message as is.

3. Handwriting Analysis
Some children may be interested in discovering how people analyze handwriting. They can check the local library for information. Ask them to apply what they have learned to samples collected in the survey above, or have them conduct their own survey. Can they tell something of each respondent by his or her handwriting?

4. The Writing Is on the Wall
Challenge children to come up with sayings that refer to writing. Examples include:
- written in stone,
- as it was written,
- written all over her (his) face,
- who wrote the book.

5. Practice Makes Perfect

Older children, like younger children, may want to practise their handwriting. They can place lined paper under acetate and use water-soluble markers. To make the activity more interesting, have on hand calligraphy books. Children can practise calligraphy by placing the acetate on top of the book and tracing the letters.

6. Designing a Letterhead

Children can use a computer to design personalized letterhead. Discuss with them serif and sans serif fonts and the issue of legibility. Children can pick a font that they think would work well in a letterhead. They design their letterhead, using techniques of centering, bold, italic, and so on. You can display examples of each child's letterhead in the classroom.

7. Invisible Messages

When used as "ink," both lemon juice and iodine are invisible unless the paper on which the words are written is held to the light. Children can work with a partner to write secret messages. To give context to the activity, have them write messages regarding a story you are reading aloud to the class. They can predict the story's plot and comment on its events and characters.

8. Reading About Other "Writers"

Beverly Cleary's *Muggie Maggie* is the story of a grade three student who is not confident in her handwriting skills. She refuses to do cursive writing until her teacher and principal come up with a solution. Children who are experiencing frustration with their handwriting abilities may enjoy reading the story or hearing it read aloud.

62: Handwriting as Art

Some children may be interested in researching handwriting as an art form, or in turning their handwriting into art. The following suggestions offer starting points for additional handwriting activities.

1. Writing from Around the World

If possible, display samples of writing from around the world. Of particular interest are samples from countries such as Japan, where subtle differences in brush stroke or length will alter the meaning of a figure. (The book *Mieko and the Fifth Treasure* by Eleanor Coerr is a good introduction to the art of Japanese writing.) Children can pursue their interest in a particular style of writing by conducting independent research.

2. Writing Through History

The discovery of ancient scrolls and records offers children a fascinating glimpse into history. They can conduct research on ancient methods of writing and what we have learned from these writings. Of a more recent nature, some children may be interested in reading more about monks and clerks who spent their entire lives serving as scribes.

3. Shape Poems

Children can record their favorite poem so that it reflects its theme. Completed shape poems can be shared with others in the class. Can they identify the theme of the poem based on its shape?

4. I've Been Framed

Children can create a frame for a piece of handwriting of which they are particularly proud. Suitable materials for framing include shaped poems, calligraphy, and invitations. Framed writing can be displayed for others to view.

5. Handwritten Mobiles

This activity can be tied into a theme, perhaps a topic the class is studying or a book children are reading. Each child can choose favorite words in relation to the theme. Words can be decorated with found materials, paper scraps, and markers. Each word is then attached to a coat-hanger mobile. Encourage children to use bold colors in their work to make the words more visible.

6. Fabric Fun

Using fabric pens, children can write their favorite words, poems, and/or expressions on a blank, white T-shirt. An alternative to this activity is to create a class banner on which each child in the class writes his or her name and favorite saying.

7. Calligraphy

Children can begin by practising basic calligraphy (see Practice Makes Perfect) before moving to free-hand calligraphy. When ready, they can use their calligraphic skills to promote special events such as school concerts. For small-scale work (e.g., invitations), children can use calligraphy markers. For large-scale work (e.g., posters), they can use foam brushes and paint.

8. Advertisements

Advertisements in magazines and newspapers often include handwritten examples. Children can create a "handwriting samples" bulletin board.

63: Spelling

A Brief History of Spelling

English, like any language, is not static. The language we speak today is the result of ongoing countless changes and evolutionary processes. Consider the number of words that we have added to our vocabulary in the last century that relate to technological advances. It is doubtful that our ancestors would have been impressed by hard drives, gigabytes, and web sites, yet these are now a part of everyday language. Here are a few facts about the English language:

- Early duplications of Shakespeare's work contained as many as five spellings of the same word.
- The first English-language dictionary was published in England in 1755 by Samuel Johnson.
- Thirty years later, Noah Webster published an American version of the dictionary, which included adapted spellings (e.g., theater, color).
- Canada, as a British colony and neighbor of the United States, adopted parts of each spelling system.
- Since English is derived from a number of languages, it does not always follow a consistent order. In one computer-assisted investigation, approximately fifty percent of words did not follow a recognizable pattern.
- Until the twentieth century, teaching methods for spelling were not rigorously investigated or tested. Teachers derived word lists for oral drills based on words considered important for use in adult life regardless of whether they would be used or understood. It was not whether, why, or how it should be taught, only that it *should* be taught!
- Today's teachers of English share one complaint with their eighteenth- and nineteenth-century counterparts – spelling!

Developmental Stages of Spelling

Children progress through the following spelling stages, but not at the same chronological age. Some words, of course, are spelled automatically from the first meeting with print (e.g., familiar names, dinosaur names).

1. Prephonetic

Children use letters and sometimes numbers to represent words. They may write and ask for help in decoding what they have written.

2. Early Phonetic

Children use some letters, usually those representing initial and final consonants. Some letters are omitted from a word, often vowels.

3. Phonetic

Children use more consonants, and use vowel sounds without markers (e.g., cak=cake).

4. Structural

Children are aware of vowel sounds, but position markers in a different place (e.g., maik=make).

5. Meaning/Derivational

Children use the correct form of a word, but revert to phonetic spelling for word derivations (e.g., nation, but nashunal). They recognize some word roots.

6. Correct Spelling

Children use resources to find unknown words and patterns to help them remember exceptions.

Helping Children Become Better Spellers

The more exposure children have to reading and writing, to noticing the strategies of spelling, and to a variety of spelling resources, the more they will reinforce and strengthen their mastery of spelling patterns. Research has shown that spelling is developmental and increases and improves over time. Teachers need to keep the requirements of standard spelling in perspective, and assist children in learning to spell with a variety of strategies. Each new piece of information gained about how words work alters the children's existing perception of the whole system of spelling in English. Sometimes, children may appear to regress as they misspell words they previously knew, but they are integrating new information about words into their language competence.

Points to Consider

- Children need to attend to the appearance of words and to check their encoding attempts.
- As children try to spell words, they discover the underlying rules of the spelling system.
- Learning to spell is clearly related to children's general language development.
- Children go through developmental stages in learning to spell, but not necessarily sequentially or at the same rate.
- Spelling is not just memorization; it involves discovery, categorization, and generalization. Spelling is a thinking process.
- Children learn the patterns, regularities, and unique features of spelling as they read, write, play with, and attend to words.
- Writing is the best way to learn about spelling.
- We can draw children's attention to specific patterns or groups of words to help them see a rule or generalization.
- Struggling spellers need to focus on a small amount of information at one time, especially in examining connections among words and word families.
- We need to help struggling spellers with particular strategies for learning and remembering words – patterns, families, mnemonic tricks, word walls, personal lists, computers.
- Children need to develop mechanisms for identifying and correcting errors in revisions.

Spelling Strategies

Everyone, children and adults alike, uses one or more of these three major spelling strategies.

1. Visual Memory of Spelling Patterns
Writers visualize a word in their head or write it down and judge if it "looks" correct.

2. Graphophonic or Sound-Symbol Knowledge
Writers listen to the sounds in words and then write letter patterns for those sounds based on prior knowledge.

3. Morphemic or Word Knowledge
Writers use knowledge of basic words, or parts of words, to help spell related words.

Dictionary Skills

Dictionaries are valuable resources for literacy, especially for expanding vocabulary, but only if they are used as aids in authentic language events (e.g., checking the spelling of a word in a report, usage of a word in a poem). Many kinds of dictionaries can be found in a literacy-centered classroom (e.g., picture, primary, computer, etymological, slang, proverb dictionaries). Multiple copies of different dictionaries are useful for children looking up word information, noting differences in style, content, mode of recording, and so on. Games and cooperative activities can help children to see the many uses of dictionaries in supporting their literacy learning. For example, teams can find the meaning of unknown words, or give definitions that must be matched to an unknown word.

A Common Word Bank								
the	I	you	and	of	said	brother	or	
a	to	he	it	was	in	sister	Ms.	
his	go	my	your	away	two	school	friend	
that	we	would	time	man	or	still	next	
she	one	me	from	old	head	much	open	
for	then	will	good	by	door	keep	has	
on	little	big	any	their	before	children	hard	
they	down	mother	about	here	more	give	enough	
but	do	went	Mr.	saw	eat	work	wait	
had	can	are	father	call	oh	king	Mrs.	
at	could	come	around	turn	again	first	morning	
him	when	back	want	after	play	even	find	
with	did	if	don't	well	who	cry	only	
up	what	now	how	think	been	try	us	
all	thing	other	know	ran	may	new	three	
look	so	long	right	let	stop	must	our	
is	see	no	put	help	odd	grand	found	
her	not	came	too	side	never	start	why	
there	were	ask	got	house	eye	soon	girl	
some	get	day	take	home	took	made	place	
out	them	very	where	thought	people	run	under	
as	like	boy	every	make	say	hand	while	
be	just	an	dog	walk	tree	began	told	
have	this	over	way	water	tell	gave	than	

1. Make words available and accessible to children by supplying resources of correctly spelled words around the classroom:
- labels and signs,
- class word banks,
- word walls,
- personal dictionaries in their writing folders,
- references (e.g., dictionaries, atlases, thesauruses),
- word charts of common errors, theme words, and puzzles,
- key vocabulary from a story,
- content words,
- family words,
- common word patterns.

2. Encourage children to write down their ideas before they stop to locate particular words, using invented spelling or initial letters, and underlining the attempt for later revision.

3. Use misspellings from a first draft to help children understand patterns and their exceptions. Dealing with a few errors at a time can help a child note a misspelling and develop appropriate strategies.

4. Organize mini-lessons and demonstrations, incorporating a wall chart or an overhead projector and calling attention to spelling problems children are experiencing (e.g., doubling final consonants, adding "ing"). Approaches to solving a problem can be verbalized and visualized, and children can learn how an effective speller uses words. Puzzles and games can be incorporated to demonstrate a pattern or an exception. Theme words are not useful for teaching patterns, but are helpful when posted around the room.

5. A brief conference can help a child come to grips with a troublesome word or pattern. Peers or volunteers can assist with spelling revision.

6. Set aside a spelling time each week when children focus on learning to spell particular words and patterns chosen from their writing, or from words they need help with. These should be significant words they will need to learn to use. Children can focus on about five words during each session.

7. Revise the types and use of spelling tests so that children can learn from the experience. They can choose the words they want to be tested on, older students can volunteer to assist in testing difficult words, and children can discuss their problems in finding strategies for coping with misspelled words. Effective spellers learn techniques for coping through successful and helpful activities.

Potential Problem Areas

1. Vowel Sounds/Combinations
* short and long sounds
* combined vowel sounds
  (e.g., **ai-ay, au, ea, ei, ee, ie, oa, oe, ou, oo, ue, ui**)

2. Sounds
* **tion, sion, cian, cean**
* **k, c, ck, cc, ch, que**
* **air, are, ear, ere, eir, aer**

3. Combinations
* **gh** – tough
* **dge** – dredge
* **qu** – queen
* **tch** – watch

4. Suffixes
* **ous** – glamour/glamorous, labor/laborious, grief/grievous
* **y** – burying/buried, lay/laid, luxury/luxurious

5. IE or EI
* "i" before "e" except after "c," etc.

6. Double Letters
* occur/occurring but offer/offering

7. Forming Plurals
* **s, es, ies, ves**
* irregular plurals (e.g., mouse/mice, sheep/sheep, larva/larvae)

8. Silent Letters
* **b** – climb, **k** – knife, **g** – sign, **h** – ghost, **l** – walk, **n** – hymn, **w** – wreck, **p** – psyche, **s** – aisle

9. Prefixes
* **all**+ways=always
* **well**+fare=welfare, but well+made=well-made

10. Endings
* **able/ible, ence/ance, ise/ize**
* **cul** – medical, pickle, circle

11. Soft and Hard C and G
* crack/center, gentle/get
* endings – courageous, peaceable, gracious, staging

12. Odds and Ends
* **c** or **s** – advice/advise
* homophones – there/their/they're, past/passed, no/know
* **ph** – **f** sounds

65: Twenty-One Ways to Become a Better Speller

The following activities focus on a variety of areas that help children to learn about spelling, including letter combinations and clusters and word structures and origins.

1. A Class Mailbox
Make a mailbox and encourage children to write to one another. To prevent situations where some children receive less mail, have each child write in turn to another child in the class. As well, children can write to you.

2. Shape Words/Shape Poems
These words and poems, written to make a specific shape, encourage children to connect the visual image with the written word. Making their own shape words and poems is an ideal way to encourage children to focus on spelling.

3. Inventory Time
Ask the children to list all objects in one area of the room by alphabetical order. When finished, they can compare their list with those completed by their classmates. An extension is to ask children to find a partner. Together, they list all objects in the class by alphabetical order. Completed "inventory" lists can be posted in the classroom.

4. Personal Word Dictionaries

Children can make their own dictionaries using loose-leaf paper and a binder. They can also create another classification system in their dictionary by making theme sections, for example: funny words, big words, and animal words.

5. Alliterative Headlines

Give a letter to a group of children. Together, they come up with words beginning with that letter and which make a newspaper headline, for example: "Cranky Cats Cruise Cabbagetown." They can write a short article to accompany the headline, using as many words as possible that start with the same initial letter as those in the headline. Newspaper headlines and articles can be displayed in the classroom for others to read.

6. Shape Letters

Children fill large letter shapes with words that begin with the same letter. A class alphabet of shape letters can be posted along the bottom of the board.

7. Vanishing Vowels

Write a sentence, then remove the vowels by leaving a line for each letter or joining the consonants. Have the children decode the message.

e.g., Good luck with your new dog.

    G _ _ d l _ck w _th y _ _ r n _w d _g.
                    or
    Gd lck wth yr nw dg.

8. What Word Am I?

Think of a word, write one letter, and draw lines for each remaining letter. Have the children guess the word by calling out letters. For each correct guess, record the letter. In instances where there is more than one of the same letter, record only one. Children can call out the letter again.

9. Find the Word

Children can work on their own or with a partner. They choose a "big" word, perhaps by using a dictionary, and list as many new words as possible using the same letters. They can chart new words by the number of letters each contains, make theme words (e.g., nouns), or retain the original letter order to make words.

10. Concentration

On cards, write beginnings and endings of words. Children can match the cards to make words. Older children can make their own cards using words from their reading and writing before inviting a classmate to match the pieces.

11. Scrambled Words

Use words from the children's reading or writing activities. Scramble the letters and ask them to reorder the letters to make a word. To begin, use simple words. As children become more proficient, you can scramble more difficult words. Children can also make scrambled words from their own writing for a peer to solve.

12. Mnemonic Devices

Mnemonic devices are word associations that we use to help us spell difficult words, homonyms, and so on. Children can make their own mnemonic devices by writing poems or sayings. To get them started, provide them with the following sayings:

- a friend to the end
- a beach is by the sea; a beech is a tree
- from there to here, now where?
- I hear with my ear when it's clear.

13. Scrabble®

This commercial game can be useful as a classroom resource. Set up a quiet area of the room as a game center.

14. Crosswords

You can add crosswords to your game center. To provide variety, make available crosswords that:
- give clues about word meaning,
- give clues about spelling,
- are theme-related,
- are child-made,
- are part of a computer program and that use a child's own words, perhaps related to a topic she or he is exploring.

15. Where In the World?

Post a large map of the world in the class. Children can list and number in sequence interesting or difficult words they have met. They place a marker with the corresponding number on the country where the word originated.

16. A Dictionary for this Century

Ask the children to make a dictionary that contains only words that have developed since the turn of the century. Many of these words describe technological discoveries. Can they determine how the words were formed?

17. A Dictionary for Past Centuries

As children read, ask them to look out for words that are no longer in common use (e.g., thou, thee, doth). They can include a short definition of each word and where they read the word.

18. New Words from Old

Portmanteau words are a combination of two words. One example is motel, which is made up of the words motor and hotel. Ask children to record portmanteau words as they read. When they have recorded five or more words, they can make a quiz for a classmate by illustrating the two original words in each portmanteau word. Classmates look at the illustrations and supply the missing word.

19. Spell a Category

- Select a theme or subject.
- Children form groups of four to six players. Each player draws a letter from a bag or box, and spells a word that starts with that letter and fits the theme.
- One point is awarded for each word that is spelled correctly and fits the theme.
- The opposing team is awarded a point if a player misspells a word or gives a word that does not fit the theme.

20. Telegrams

In small groups of four, each child takes two turns to say a letter. One group member records the letters that have been called out. The group then organizes the letters so that they represent a coded sentence or message, for example: T S W E D V C A. This could stand for "To Spell Well, Examine Different Vowel and Consonant Arrangements."

21. Word Lists

Children can make lists of words in a variety of ways. As examples, they can classify by:
- letter clusters (**ae, oo, ou, ight, tch**),
- compound words (rainstorm, snowball),
- portmanteau words,
- suffixes and prefixes,
- number of letters,
- number of syllables,
- homographs (words that are spelled the same, but sound different),
- homophones (words that sound the same, but differ in meaning),
- silent letters,
- rhyming words,
- plurals (ways of forming),
- contractions (can't, shouldn't),
- abbreviations (i.e., e.g., etc.),
- word families,
- anagrams (rearranged to make other words (wasp/paws),
- palindromes (same both ways – level, did, madam),
- semordnilap (palindromes backwards – yam/may, evil/live).

66: Computers

Computers, in one form or another, are a part of our daily lives. Predicting their potential, *Time* Magazine devoted its 1983 version of "Man of the Year" to "Machine of the Year: The Computer Moves In." Since then, we have seen the power and application of computers evolve at a rate comparable to their ever-increasing role in our professional and private lives.

Computers in the Writing Program

Computers can be used as effective tools for writing in the classroom. They enable children to focus more on content, since the physical constraints of manual writing are reduced. They assist in the construction of substantive knowledge by helping children develop self-evaluative and meaning-level precision skills, as well as a procedural knowledge for writing (aimed at mechanics and syntax). This frees them to devote more time to generating ideas.

A primary challenge for the educational system is to determine how to take advantage of this technology. Sections that follow provide some background information on computers and their potential classroom usage, and can be helpful when assessing computer literacy instruction in a classroom.

Benefits of Using Computers in the Writing Program

- The quality and fluency of writing is increased. Children provide more details and revise more. As well, they confer with teachers more frequently, thus becoming more involved in the writing process.
- The amount of talk about text meaning is increased as well as error detection in peers' writing. This encourages self-monitoring and introduces children to collaborative writing.
- The concept of publishing motivates children to write, in part to receive audience reaction to their work.
- Some programs are specifically designed to help children develop planning processes in writing, narrative writing skills, expressive writing, and revision and editing skills.
- Computers can be used for a variety of writing activities, including: letters, stories, poems, messages, mail, newspapers, banners, book logs, and journals.
- Along with a modem, computers can provide an authentic and interactive means for having children write to one another. Some classrooms have begun sharing journals with classes in other towns and cities, and even in other countries.
- Teachers, like the children they teach, are discovering the usefulness of computers to share ideas and teaching tips with colleagues.

Software Packages

A growing number of software packages offer children a range of literacy experiences. These packages have become increasingly sophisticated through the years, moving from simple story retellings through programs that demand interaction on the part of the user. The following software packages are listed only as examples of the material available and their applicability to classroom use. The producer, computer compatibility, and an overview of its intended use are given for each package.

Amazing Animation (Claris Clear Choice – Macintosh)
Children write a script for a movie they have created.

The Comic Book Maker (Pelican – Macintosh)
A creative writing program, "The Comic Book Maker" helps children to create their own comic, including speech bubbles and sound effects.

Hyperstudio (Robert Wagner – Macintosh)
Children create multiple endings to fairy tales, tell a fairy tale in their own words, write an original fairy tale, and write a letter to a favorite fairy tale character.

Kidwriter (Spinnaker – Macintosh)
Using this program, children can write a story, narrate it, and design colorful pictures to accompany their narration. Pages can be linked together and printed to create a storybook.

Living Books (Bröderbund – Macintosh, PC)
This is a series of interactive storybooks. In "The Living Book of Poetry," for example, children can click on poetry verses to view its animated version. They can also write their own verses.

Super Print (Scholastic – Macintosh, PC)
This package helps children to design posters, banners, cards, calendars, and big books.

CD ROMs

As more computers come equipped with CD-ROM drives, users are discovering the convenience of CDs in learning situations. Replacing the need for full sets of encyclopedias, dictionaries, and other reference materials, users can place a CD in their computer and research a topic at their desk.

Educational CDs are now available for virtually every field of study and every age group – from preschool through university. The following CDs are listed only as examples of the types available and their applicability to classroom use.

Canadian Encyclopedia, Multimedia Edition (McClelland & Stewart – Macintosh, PC)
Comprising the hardcover edition of the encyclopedia, this version includes 600 maps, photos, and sound effects.

Developing Writing Skills (Queue – Macintosh)
Interactive lessons help learners of all levels – preschool, elementary, high school, university. Level-appropriate lessons cover a range of topics including learning to write, English composition, writing skills, and conducting research.

The Greatest Children's Stories Ever Told (Queue – Macintosh, PC)
This collection of classic children's stories includes interactive capabilities that allow children to create and print their own storybooks and posters.

Grolier Encyclopedia Americana (Grolier – Macintosh, PC)
This CD contains the thirty volumes that make up the hardcover encyclopedia and comprises more than thirty million words.

Kid Pix Studio (Bröderbund – Macintosh, PC)
A variation of a previous package, Kid Pix Studio asks children to create a story. They read aloud the story in role and play back their read aloud on the computer.

Kid Works 2 (Davidson – Macintosh, PC - WIN)
Children can write stories and have the computer read them aloud.

The Magic School Bus Explores the Human Body and *The Magic School Bus Explores the Solar System* (Scholastic, Microsoft – PC WIN)
Children travel through the human body and the solar system in these interactive CDs.

67: The Internet

Programs such as the Schoolnet project illustrate how the Internet can be used to access thousands of libraries and databases worldwide. Schoolnet allows you to take part in such diverse activities as exploring libraries in Europe through viewing satellite pictures from space. The service links schools to the Internet, and has helped to foster a worldwide community of readers and writers. Users of the service can "visit" the sites of experts in any number of fields, innovative teacher-de-signed networking projects, and interactive question and answer databases.

Many children are motivated to improve their reading and writing skills when they discover they can send messages to other countries. They are encouraged to use formal language with clarity and accuracy, and want to present themselves in the best possible light.

Classroom Experiences with the Internet

The following examples illustrate projects children have participated in as a result of Schoolnet:
- pairing up with children in Bologna, Italy to compare the quality of local drinking water.
- corresponding with children at Koutokuji Elementary School in Kagoshima, Japan. Once a week, the two sets of children exchanged letters about activities, games, weather, aspects of daily life, and special events (e.g., a volcanic eruption in Japan).
- taking part in a study concerning children's television habits (for information on similar projects, find web sites such as FAX – Friendships Are Exciting – that supply addresses of schools interested in partnership activities).
- communicating with explorers as they trekked across an ice field in a polar expedition, thereby taking part in history as it was made.
- contacting NASA to learn more about space. Kindergarten children had the opportunity to experience a virtual reality space shuttle trip.
- connecting with a distant school to compare experiences of urban living, sharing a Native Studies unit, and discussing world issues such as the environment, child rights, hunger, and poverty. One school created a rap to introduce itself to the partner school.
- writing to national leaders with questions and possible solutions for world problems.

The Internet and Other Learning Opportunities

In addition to school partnerships and databases related to school curriculum, the Internet offers a number of sites that are relevant to children at primary through senior levels. As the number of subscribers to the Internet increases so too does the number of web sites relevant to educational endeavors. The following sites are representative of projects that make children enthusiastic about learning, and make concrete the concept of the world as a global village.

Educational Electronic Mail (FrEdMail)
In this site, groups of children can assume the personalities of historical figures. In role, they take turns interviewing one another.

One Book List
Children can select a book they particularly enjoyed and share their views with others.

Global Village News
This site offers children the chance to contribute to a worldwide newspaper.

I*EARN (International Education and Resource Network)
Children can work together to make a difference in the world. Recent efforts include writing and preparing news magazines, journals, and environmental and human-rights newsletters, as well as offering emotional support to children in Bosnia and Somalia.

WIER (Writers in Electronic Residence)
Children can connect with an author on the Internet. They can submit their creative writing and receive feedback, allowing them to feel like real writers.

Electronic Innovators
Children can link up with a scientist in a mentoring arrangement through this site. They can compare samples of local rainwater with that of another school to examine causes and effects of acid rain.

Part E: Organizing a Literacy Classroom

68: Timetabling

Questions to Consider

1. What types of activities will best suit the concepts that will be learned in the time period?
2. What are the timing and resource requirements for activities in the unit? How much time will be needed for
   - preparation,
   - completion of activities,
   - clean up,
   - follow-up activities and discussions,
   - reflection,
   - evaluation?
3. Will children have the opportunity to work as part of a whole-class group, a small group, and on their own in order to complete activities?
4. Is there a good balance between activities that are mandatory and those that are free choice?
5. Which aspects of the curriculum are not integrated? Have appropriate amounts of time and effort been allocated to non-unit related activities?
6. Have timing, transitions, and pacing been considered from the child's perspective?
7. Do activities address a range of learning styles, needs, and interests? Will all children be challenged by the activities? Will all children be included in the teaching and activities?
8. Does the unit allow children to take responsibility for their learning, or is it primarily teacher driven?
9. How will reflective assessment be carried out?

Components for Building a Literacy Program

Each teacher will need to design a literacy timetable for the reading workshop and the writing workshop that suits the particular needs of a classroom. In some cases, the teacher will combine the two areas and create an integrated literacy program. This list of components should be seen as suggestions for developing a timetable that allows for maximum literacy growth for each child.

A. The Reading Workshop

Meeting Time
- set the agenda for the day's reading events
- summarize previous day's events
- read aloud to the class
  - book talks, poems, folk tales, personal letters
- shared reading
  - big books, overhead transparencies, charts
- demonstrations
  - word charts, prepared children's oral reading
  - add to community knowledge

Group Time
- silent reading
- literature circles, response activities, literature journals (self-directed, teacher selected)
- guided reading and/or peer directed
- organized by theme, author, or genre

Mini-Lessons
- how words work, word recognition, word games
- word histories, word sorting
- how sentences work
- how stories work

Independent Reading
- self-selected, library supported
- connect to literature circles
- assess individuals (miscue analysis, comprehension tests, inventories)

Sharing Time
- discuss responses
- raise questions
- connect various book sets
- read aloud responses by children

B. The Writing Workshop

Meeting Time
- shared writing
  - morning messages
  - observations of class research projects
  - rules and regulations
  - experience charts
  - book evaluations
  - newsletters
  - cooperative poems
- write aloud
  - the teacher writes and talks as she or he writes, demonstrating how writers compose and modeling the phases of writing
- publish completed drafts
  - number of times children complete a project for publishing
  - resources and materials available to children (in library, in publishing center)

Guided Writing
- self-selected topics for process writing
- opportunities for mini-lessons on a variety of issues
  - choice of topic, generate ideas, plan the work
- format, revision, audience
- assist children in learning to use the revision and editing strategies through proofreading
- place the emphasis on clear, effective writing before stressing editing
- ongoing assessment with the children, believing that we learn as we experiment with becoming writers

Independent Writing
- personal journals, letters, projects children choose to write on their own in writing centers

Sharing Time
- volunteers read drafts and completed works aloud
- children read published books by young authors
- group talks about issues that have been investigated and resolved (e.g., computer skills)

C. Curriculum Connected Reading and Writing

- notebooks for social studies, health, etc.
- projects for individuals and groups in subject areas
- celebrations where the whole class is involved, such as writing in role in a drama unit
- publishing techniques demonstrated in visual arts periods
- recording observations in science and mathematics

69: Conferences

Conferences enhance literacy growth, and are essential in developing "a community of readers and writers." They provide opportunities for making reading and writing development a natural part of the school day. There are several types of reading and writing conferences: child-teacher, peer, and parent-child-teacher conference. While each has its own structure and purpose, the following general points outline reasons for holding conferences:
- to relate language learning to the child's life experiences,
- to improve the child's attitude toward reading and writing,
- to assess a child's reading and writing privately and to offer assistance,
- to share personal interests in reading materials,
- to build strategies for word recognition and comprehension,
- to develop oral reading competence,
- to talk about new books to groups of children,
- to help a child build understanding through conversation,
- to deepen a reading experience with extending discussion,
- to provide a forum for questioning,
- to help the child venture forth into new learning with more complex materials,
- to build a literacy community incorporating children at all levels of development.

Elements of Conferences

1. Comfort Level
Making a child feel comfortable is of utmost importance. She or he should feel at ease and understand and appreciate the input that the teacher has to make, realizing that his or her ideas will be respected and considered at all times.

2. Positive Relationships
When creating a positive relationship, a relaxed atmosphere is necessary. The teacher can establish an area where both are comfortable. This could be a space on the rug designated for conferences that has been made cozy with pillows and functional with papers and pens.

3. Recording Conferences
Children should have the opportunity to record elements of the conference (e.g., a tip or saying they want to remember, a change in conference time). They can record notes on special conference sheets or use a "conference" pen (a pen used only for conferences). Conferences can be recorded (video or audio), primarily for the teacher's benefit, but also for the child's. If recording is not an option, the teacher should make jot notes that can be transcribed and added to when time allows.

4. Open-Ended Conversations
Once a positive relationship and relaxed atmosphere has been established, work on writing can begin. Open-ended questions, as opposed to specific comments, are more helpful to the children's work and self-esteem, and lead to more reflective self-assessment. The teacher can begin by asking open-ended questions, such as:
- Tell me about your subject. Tell me about what you are writing.
- How does the piece sound when read aloud?
- Could we compare the story/writing style with another piece?
- Are you happy with the ending? the beginning? a certain word?
- What is your favorite part? best line? funniest part? saddest part?
- How does the title fit the story? What title would work well with the story?
- What do you like or dislike about your story?

- Are there any problems you would like help with? Do you have any questions?
- Does this book remind you of your family?

5. Developing Confidence
Descriptive, nonjudgmental phrases, suggestions, and praise are necessary for the confidence that each child needs in order to develop his or her writing. Some phrases and praise that are nonjudgmental may begin:
- Show me how...
- Tell me how...
- I like the way...
- The ending/the beginning/the middle...
- The colors...
- The characters...
- The story...

6. Numerous Conferences
The teacher can hold conferences with each child throughout the writing process. A sign-up sheet listing stages and children's names can be completed by children so that the teacher and child meet at least several times throughout the project.

7. Attentive Listening
Teachers need to remember that the main point of a conference is to allow children the chance to talk – to retell their reading experiences, to describe writing difficulties, to problem solve, and to celebrate. While a teacher's input is valuable in a conference, it should not dominate it.

8. Teacher Improvements
In order to improve a conference, teachers can ask themselves these questions: How am I benefiting or learning from this conference? How can I improve? What new or different resources might be helpful? What new book can I read now? Will taping and analyzing a conference help me improve? When is a good opportunity to do this? Such questions result in the growth of the teacher, which in turn results in the growth of a child.

9. Flexibility
It is not always possible to have long conferences with everyone. Teachers should mix short and long conferences. Some children may be at a stage when more discussion is necessary, others may not. Conference length can be changed according to time, stages, and children.

10. Acceptance

A child who is looking for attention or unable to focus on his or her own work may accompany the teacher on different conferences to take minutes of the meeting. The recording aspect makes him or her feel worthwhile at the same time that the child may gain from repeated exposures to conferences and the teacher's attitude toward reading and writing.

70: Types of Conferences

Child-Teacher Conferences

Child-teacher conferences are a vital link in promoting a lifelong passion for reading and literature. Teachers must model for children a love of reading that is nurtured on a daily basis so that they can see the value of reading and the importance it can play in their life.

Through the use of child-teacher conferences, children are encouraged to extend their exploration of a text, and teachers can assess and evaluate their progress. In addition, the accepting attitude of the teacher during the conference does much to promote the sharing aspect of reading, encouraging the children to become part of a "community of readers."

These conferences give children varied and frequent opportunities to talk about books they have read. The conferences should always occur in a relaxed atmosphere where the children feel secure and comfortable in expressing their feelings about what they have read. During these conferences, teachers can:

- listen to children talk about their personal interests, attitudes, and purposes for reading,
- ask questions to promote the children's exploration of the text,
- identify reading strategies the children use,
- determine the children's comprehension of what they have read,
- expand on children's oral reading competence,
- activate the children's thinking,
- foster the use of more efficient reading strategies,
- recommend other books of a similar theme,
- draw children's attention to books that present contrasting themes or views,

- recommend other books by the same author,
- promote related forms of writing,
- suggest further response activities (e.g., drama),
- advocate further research,
- encourage the children's own writing,
- assess children's reading competence.

Peer Conferences

This form of conference requires a learning climate that is friendly and open, and that emphasizes the importance of peer reading. In such an environment, freedom to learn builds responsibility and success. For the teacher, it offers a way to integrate learning with assessment. In this conference, the teacher needs to:

- organize small groups,
- begin lists of questions children can refer to as needed,
- encourage children to tell and retell,
- promote relating and reflecting as part of the group's experiences,
- help children obtain feedback on their progress.

This is a time for book talk – responses and stories that increase children's interest and understanding of a text. They employ models of writing and speaking that reflect their knowledge and ownership of their learning.

Parent-Child-Teacher Conferences

While child-teacher and peer conferences promote children's reading in class, the third type of conference – parent-child-teacher – promotes children's reading at home. Each party has responsibilities in this conference.

Parents can:
- encourage reading at home,
- share reading and understanding of books they have read,
- promote reading growth through praise,
- offer helpful suggestions.

Children can:
- read a selection of their choice,
- share their response to the book, ask questions, and demonstrate understanding,
- read out loud or retell parts of the book to their teacher and parents.

Teachers can:
- encourage reading at home,
- maintain teacher-parent communication,
- extend the community of readers by sharing a book with parents and family,
- show that evaluation is an integral part of learning.

Sharing a book helps to broaden the reading experience. It allows children to be responsible for their learning, lays the groundwork for successful reading experiences, fosters independent learning, and increases children's confidence so they will want to further their literacy knowledge. In addition, an important part of the conference is collaboration – between the teacher and parents, between the teacher and child, and between the parents and child. Each form of collaboration involves a unique form of sharing learning.

71: Teacher Demonstrations

Demonstrations, which can happen at any time during the school day, are conscious, explicit attempts to show children how something is done. Demonstrations can have a powerful and lasting effect on the learner, but it is the implicit aspect that explains their richness and importance. Teachers can unknowingly give negative demonstrations to children in a variety of ways: reading is a serious business; there is one interpretation – the teacher's; children are not smart enough to choose their own texts; reading is always followed by a test; teachers talk a lot about literature, but they don't read much of it; reading is a waste of class time. In contrast, how often do children see their teacher captivated by what they are reading? Classrooms need to be filled with relevant and functional literary demonstrations.

Ideas for Demonstrations

The following suggestions for demonstrations supply children with a raft of letter-writing ideas:
- letters to friends,
- letters to pen pals,
- letters to the editor,
- complaints or requests to corporations,
- thank you letters,
- fan letters to heroes, villains, famous people,
- memos to teachers, staff, or parents,
- letters to or from favorite characters in books, videos, or films.

Elements of Successful Demonstrations

- Explicit demonstrations need to be demonstrations of language "wholes" (i.e., all the pieces must fit) rather than isolated, unrelated bits of language.
- Demonstrations need to be continually repeated. Since demonstrations are larger, more general, and more contextual than mini-lessons, children can learn something new again and again from the same demonstration.
- There is no set length for a demonstration. Children will generally take from a demonstration whatever they find interesting or relevant to their learning needs.
- Demonstrations should be contextually relevant and therefore appropriate to the literary task the child is trying to complete. Children will engage with a demonstration if they have a need for what you are showing them.
- Part of an ongoing series of demonstrations are the reading expectations you have of your students. Expect them to read, discover books they love, find satisfaction in books, and learn.
- Know enough about reading literacy to be able to present a range and variety of demonstrations that will enable learners to get all the pieces they need to become fully literate.
- Demonstrations are more effective when delivered to smaller groups.
- A good form of demonstration is the think-aloud. Reading the text and then reflecting out loud on what you have read shows children that adults also need support and time to reflect. This is a good way to give children a variety of strategies and ways to approach a text. The goal is to develop in children the methods and habits used by good readers to become self-monitoring and independent, and able to read with depth and meaning.
- Following a demonstration, give children the opportunity to model the behavior.

72: Mini-Lessons

A mini-lesson is a brief, focused lesson that allows teachers to demonstrate or teach a specific skill or idea in a short, purposeful way. Reading, writing, or thinking strategies can all be demonstrated using mini-lessons, which are often generated by the needs of the children. As well, mini-lessons can be used to review classroom procedures, to show ways to think about what one has read, and to teach specific reading skills.

A good, powerful mini-lesson should be short, specific, and relevant to what children are doing so that it will "stick" (particularly if they can put to use immediately the skill or strategy). The question-answer method should be avoided when giving mini-lessons as it can slow the lesson and detract from the teaching of the skill or concept. Instead, children can save their questions for the end where questions asked and participation levels can be indicators of children's depth of understanding of the concept.

Introduce the concept of mini-lessons early in the year by letting the children know the behavior expected of them (e.g., where do they meet for mini-lessons?). Keep in mind that content mini-lessons are most effective when delivered to small groups of children or an individual child. For mini-lessons dealing with topics that children will refer to repeatedly (e.g., punctuation), teach the mini-lesson using chart paper. When completed, it can be hung together with related charts and displayed on the walls for children's reference.

Mini-lessons can be conducted on any number of topics:
- an author,
- a genre,
- a poem,
- a short story,
- an opening chapter or an opening sentence,
- writing styles,
- reading aloud, reading for speed, skimming, or scanning,
- rereading, abandoning a book,
- reading workshops,
- favorite authors, favorite books,
- finding good books,
- keeping a reading journal,
- how to talk about what you read,
- using a library,
- characters, plot, theme, time, or setting,
- point of view,
- narrative voice, dialogue,
- prologues, epilogues, sequels,
- how books are published, copyright,
- screenplays adapted from a book, "novelization" of screenplays,
- rhythm/sound, rhyme, imagery, or sequence.

73: Reading in Groups

Reading in groups promotes cooperation and co-operative learning. Children learn from each other, share, discuss, and make meaning. Group reading situations include a large group (whole class) or small groups using a reading series or a core book. Group reading can be organized in one of two ways.

1. Homogeneous Groups
All students in the group have similar reading ability. At the early primary level, it is important that children be taught at their instructional level. Small groups of children who have similar reading abilities can meet for twenty minutes a day to develop specific strategies and reading fluency. Further support should be given to children who, unable to read, need to learn strategies to apply to their reading efforts. Once they have mastered these skills, children should become part of a new group, which will change repeatedly throughout the year. Reforming groups eliminates the stigma associated with belonging to a lower-level group, and provides children with more interesting and positive learning experiences.

2. Heterogeneous Groups
These groups comprise students with different reading abilities and are appropriate for older grades. In heterogeneous groups, all children benefit in some way. Those who are limited readers improve their reading skills, participate more, and develop self-esteem. Advanced readers become involved in peer tutoring, which extends their own thinking and learning.

- The main purpose for working in small groups is to have children engage in high-level discussions as they respond to a story, a novel, a poem, or a curriculum-related text.
- Children will meet a variety of literature, authors, and formats that they might not choose independently.
- Children are supported in thinking critically about what they are reading or what they have read.
- Small groups allow all children to participate and be heard.
- Responses should be open-ended, conversational, and connected to the children's personal experiences.
- The group's focus should be on a reason for reading, learning how and why readers read in real-life situations — satisfaction and appreciation, information, to support personal views, to share, to expand language use.
- Teachers can help the children relate and connect books and authors to their lives.
- Group members discuss their questions and insights into an author's ideas and style.
- Children can read aloud (but not one after the other) descriptive passages that they enjoyed, statements that back up a point made in a discussion, excerpts that seem confusing, or dialogue that comes to life when read orally.
- Groups are generally heterogeneous, but there may be times when a teacher will want to use a particular technique only with children who share a similar developmental stage.
- Teachers can meet with heterogeneous groups two or three times a week.
- Teachers can confer with individuals two days a week or daily.
- Teachers need to work with small groups of children who are experiencing difficulty, working on sight words, attacking new words, or reading for fluency.
- A group of children can complete an anthology story or a book in about a week. Selections may be grouped around a theme.
- Children can work independently on activities, some where participation is required and others where it is up to the child to decide. A scheduling chart may help children organize activities, and a log can keep a child on track.

74: Individualized Reading

Individualized reading helps children to develop unique interests and an appreciation of the variety of literature. Focused, independent reading programs require planning and commitment on the teacher's part. When individualized reading is scheduled, the child can prepare by finding material of significant interest.

A reading corner provides a focus for reading, but teachers need to be aware that choice and self-directed reading cannot be isolated in a particular context. Independent selection depends on an environment that allows for opportunities of choice to be present in varied and enriched contexts. The opportunity to read is also extended through tapes children can listen to, both at home and school. Choice of texts can be personalized when tapes of books that have interested the children are made available. Of prime importance is building pleasurable experience through modeling by the teacher, as well as through personal and private reading times.

Sustained Silent Reading

A child's concentration can be extended over time, as can the level and range of reading material. When a child's sustained silent reading demonstrates developed interest in reading, the teacher has been successful in guiding the reader toward independence. To achieve this, it is important to match the child and the book in reading instruction. Reading at a level of proficiency encourages the development of positive attitudes and confidence. Many basal-reader manuals provide information on how to determine a child's reading level. It is important to teach skills at a level that permits independence and success.

Initially, short daily sustained silent reading periods are best. A quiet time without interruption can be extended from five minutes at the kindergarten-grade 1 level to thirty minutes at the grade 6 level. The children should be encouraged to read books that are enjoyable and not overly difficult. If they are aware of their responsibilities during these periods, such as choosing appropriate materials, they are more likely to persevere with their reading. When they run into difficulty, children will benefit from help in selecting an appropriate text. That said, it is not appropriate that they run to a teacher each time they meet an unknown word. Instead, the teacher can discuss with them strategies such as skipping the word or thinking about what word would make sense. Modeling procedures of skill development, especially in a one-on-one context when a problem arises, is particularly beneficial.

When Young Children Read Alone

Kindergarten and first grade teachers need to modify their programs by distributing picture books and books children have heard read aloud. These children like to share books they are reading so they will need to learn how to read books silently and independently. Initially, children cannot be expected to read independently – they need encouragement and practice in class routines that will require the teacher to work with both groups and individuals. When the children have internalized criteria for independent work and classroom control has been achieved, a successful sustained silent reading program has been put in place.

Demonstrations

The independent reader becomes the owner of his or her reading and learning experience, and will be stimulated and rewarded by owning and selecting books for personal reading. A teacher needs to explain, demonstrate, and have children practise the skill of selecting books that are of an appropriate reading level and genre. Older children can be taught the "five-finger" technique that involves reading a passage of 100 words and learning how to estimate this amount. Each time the child makes an error in reading the passage, she or he curls one finger into the palm. If, at the end of the passage, she or he has curled five or fewer fingers the book is approximately the correct reading level. However, the child should not be forbidden to read a book that is too difficult. Some may persevere – and triumph!

Teachers can demonstrate to children the various levels of reading comprehension so that they will have a greater awareness of what to expect from themselves. Young children can also be made aware of the deceptive level of some books.

Text, and not illustrations, is the major criterion in determining reading difficulty. High-interest, easy-reading books may be pitched at a lower level than what children can read, but they may be attracted by their content. These books are particularly appropriate for independent reading by children who have experienced difficulty – the books appeal to their interests and provide them with opportunities for successful reading experiences. Teachers must watch that children do not make a habit of choosing overly difficult books since their amount of reading will suffer, as will their self-concept and dedication to reading.

The importance of children selecting appropriate books needs to be emphasized. The independent reader may read in his or her spare time in the classroom, go to the library voluntarily, talk about books with other children, complete reading assignments promptly, and order books from paperback book clubs, but unless the child is owner of his or her learning experience, independence as a reader remains to be developed.

Tracking Independent Readers

Independent readers can keep track of their reading, encouraging comparison and the development of focused reading habits. Reading diaries, reading records, and book reports offer formal techniques for tracking children's reading experiences. Through diaries, private or public, children develop personal response to reading and develop a sense of pride and accomplishment in reading skills by making visible the amount of reading they have completed. Reporting on books may be accomplished creatively, either through oral or written forms, when presented in a context in which children's ideas about the book take precedence over its content. In reporting, the children are encouraged to form opinions about the book – discussions may encourage such a response by eliciting from the audience interactions through questioning and sharing.

Teaching situations may occur whenever the opportunity or occasion arises, but may be especially focused in individualized reading conferences. The conference represents an opportunity for the teacher to assess the child's learning process, and to participate in a shared activity in which assessment of the book, opinions, and perceptions serve as the topics from which evaluation is made. As in a child's oral reading, when the focus of the activity is directed to a response that is stimulating, the response and growth of the child is encouraged.

75: Tutoring a Troubled Reader

A troubled reader requires teachers who are aware of and sensitive to the many possible causes of troubled reading, who recognize characteristics and behavior typical of such a reader, and who modify the literacy program to assist each child at risk.

The job of the teacher is to try to make the child want to read. There are many ways to accomplish this, but first the problems must be identified. Above all, teachers must try to improve the child's self-concept: she or he may not be able to recognize his or her own success.

Teachers can work with an individual or a small group to directly or indirectly influence the literacy development of the emerging reader:
- to create a library habit,
- to allow children time to browse,
- to allow children time to prepare before sharing a book,
- to develop fluency through rereading,
- to establish confidence,
- to present and reinforce strategies,
- to focus on word skills (phonics, sight words),
- to connect reading and writing.

Characteristics and Behavior of a Troubled Reader

The personality of the troubled reader may be a problem because of several factors, including age level and maturity. Children delight and learn quickly at young ages, swimming, bike riding, and climbing, but will become easily frustrated with activities that require time to focus on small detail. This is what sets apart the troubled readers who have a greater sense of frustration that may be combined with external pressures. Some are fearful and lack confidence, some are highly self-conscious, many are action-oriented. Regardless of the frustration, children need to learn to read and teachers can help.

Teachers ca
identify chara
reading style.
"Reading is fu
purpose, it is
job, reading i
something el
of the teache
strate an en
apprenticesh
see that teac
a reading e
dren to give
to reading.

Classroom Activities

Teachers need to spe
vidually. They can
to the child, rea
to the child re
giving the
identify
throu
me

Identifying the Troubled Reader

Typically, it is the behavior of a child that can help us to identify possible causes of troubled reading:
- an unwillingness to try reading due to unsuccessful past experiences,
- lack of motivation to read,
- unable to read,
- low self-esteem,
- feeling of failure around the issue of reading,
- lack of purpose in reading,
- inexperienced with the structures of literature,
- limited background experience and an underdeveloped sight-word vocabulary,
- insufficient print problem-solving tools to support progress,
- poor record of attendance.

Reading Styles

A child's reading style can help teachers identify troubled reading. Many clues are evident:
- eye movements are erratic – they have trouble focusing, they skip up/down lines, they read several words beyond the next one,
- reversals continue longer than usual,
- unusual visual processing style – "global processing" – children see detail in three-dimensional ways rather than ordered (e.g., buttons),
- poor accuracy,
- inconsistent fluency,
- sketchy comprehension,
- overuse of personal interpretation,
- overuse of a single strategy (e.g., decoding),
- poor substitutions,
- difficulty with sentence length.

...nd time with children indi-
...share a book by reading aloud
...ing with the child, and listening
...ad. Teachers should help readers by
... quiet reading time. In class, they can
...the purpose for reading and input it
...gh other activities to make the purpose
...ningful and real. Peer reading is a successful
...ay of engaging troubled readers.

Making meaning from print is essential. Pronunciation, phonics, and spelling by themselves will not make children "readers." Teachers need to bring words into context, supply unknown words through flashcards or sight-word recognition. They can help children to connect words/print to a whole context. Fluent reading requires the automatic knowledge of many words. Teachers can help children to connect words by integrating background knowledge, using their experiences, feelings, interests, and questions triggered by the text. This is also a source of developing personal growth in expression and interaction with the reading material.

Broadening vocabulary is key to expanding the reader's world, through writing personal stories or journals where children search for words for the purpose of writing. Teachers can apply reading to a song. They open the door to history, social studies, and reading more about a preferred topic. This will also improve knowledge of punctuation and expression. Children will learn to read sentences with exclamations and quotations. Scripting also encourages troubled readers to improve structure and syntax.

While reading with troubled readers, teachers should give plenty of reinforcement. For example, they can run a finger along a line or let the child do the same so that they track the teacher's reading progress. Teachers can keep records of children's reading patterns, such as skipping words, reversals, and decoding. They can encourage creative thinking on several levels as the reader improves, moving from a literal level to higher thinking skills such as interpretation, (with teacher guidance), comparison/contrast, anticipation, inference, and finally application. Children then apply these components in stimulating, encouraging experiences.

Teachers can implement various strategies according to the needs of a child. However, with any troubled reader they must develop reading through interest.

1. A teacher can introduce new books (of high interest) and at appropriate reading levels.
2. A teacher can explore the book before reading, familiarizing the children with content and style, building personal connections, introducing one or two significant words, encouraging prediction from the cover and title and/or from several illustrations, the setting, and the purpose for the reading.
3. At times, as in shared reading, the teacher can read the story aloud as the child follows along, preparing the new reader with a general understanding of the text.
4. Beginning readers may need to read or reread the text aloud as the teacher observes the strategies the child uses and offers support through comments and questions. She or he can offer prompts for helping the child with structural words like "they," "where," and "when" in sentences that emphasize the difficult word – When did that happen? What did they do? The goal is to help the child discover particular words using all the techniques available to him or her.

The teacher can demonstrate self-monitoring strategies that good readers use: thinking, predicting, sampling, confirming, self-correcting.

- Does that word sound right?
- Does it make sense in the story?
- Skip the word and go on.
- Does it fit in the sentence?
- Put in a word that makes sense.
- Where have you seen that word before?
- Do you know a word with the same sound in it?
- Now what do you think it is?
- What is the first letter? Does it help you? How will the word begin?
- Check the word with the picture.

Children should be given enough time to figure out the word. The teacher can point out word patterns that will help them figure out a word from knowledge they already possess and write a pattern for the word on the chart, present a rhyming word, or draw the child's attention to the word on an existing label or word wall. The context of the story can be used to promote word identification, calling attention to incidents and events that incorporate the word, to predictable and recurring patterns.

5. Independent reading can be fostered through meaning-based strategies since the eventual goal is to help the child figure out the word independently. There are several ways to do this:

- The teacher can promote discussion about what the children have read before narrowing in on a skill follow-up.
- The teacher can encourage sight-word recognition in context by writing high-frequency words from the text on cards so that the child can match them with the text, using context, patterns, and pictures.
- The teacher can create an innovation from the text where the children determine the pattern of the "new" text and the words it will contain. Record their text on a chart for rereading. Later, the children can record the words in individual booklets that they can also illustrate.
- The teacher can use an unfamiliar text to observe how children apply strategies they use for daily reading and writing behaviors.

6. Focusing on phonics with a particular word can help the children to examine it carefully, notice how it works, make generalizations, and then restore it to the context of the text. The teacher can follow up with related response activities that draw the children back to the text, extending their understanding, increasing their word recognition, and fostering their knowledge of how readers and writers work.

77: Tracking Reading Progress

Teachers can use literacy record-keeping techniques to track the reading abilities of children. The main purpose of these techniques, which can be modified to suit the particular needs of each teacher and his or her students, is to identify the strengths of each child's performance so that decisions about appropriate expectations for subsequent learning and assessment can be made.

1. Anecdotal Records
One easy recording device is to divide a file folder into 3.5 x 3.5 inch squares. Allocate one square for each child in your class, using Post-it notes to track daily progress. Attach the notes to the appropriate box in the folder. At the end of each week, transfer the notes to individual student summary sheets.

Another method of recording individual reading development is to record each child's progress on a 3 x 5 index card – cards can be placed one on top of the other on an open file with only the child's name, recorded at the bottom of the card, visible. Divide the class list into even groups and assign each group a shape. (Label index cards with the appropriate shape.) Select a group to monitor and track the progress of the children in that group during specific activities.

Formulate a checklist to identify children's weaknesses and strengths in specific areas. Examples of areas checklists can focus on are: enjoyment of books, shared reading, retelling, recalling main ideas, positive attitudes toward reading, and meaningful participation in independent reading.

2. Reading Logs
Children can list the titles and authors of books they have read and the dates on which they finished reading them. As well, they provide a comment about the book, perhaps a constructive criticism or an endorsement. At the end of the year, children can put stars next to their ten favorite books. Each child contributes his or her three most favorite books to a class recommended book list to be used by next year's children.

3. Genre Chart

Children can keep a genre chart to track the types of books they have read and when they read them. The children make their own reading choices. Some genres they may include are: poetry, picture books, fairy tales, folk tales, novels (e.g., adventure, fantasy, historical, mystery, science fiction), nonfiction, magazines, and comic books. This chart not only helps the children learn more about their reading interest, it also directs them to genres they might like to try.

4. Reading Response Journals

Once a week, regardless of how much they have read, ask children to write in their reading journals. These responses can take the form of letters to the teacher or other children, in which they outline their thoughts on the book they are reading. Decide, as a class, whether to respond to the letters.

5. Written Reports

After completing a book, ask children to write a brief description about it. Their description can take the form of "What I Have Learned," "What I Want to Learn about Now," and "Why this Book Was Unique." Encourage the children to veer away from writing a synopsis, instead concentrating on one aspect of the book.

6. Reading Evaluation Sheet

Have children evaluate their reading abilities at the end of each grading period. Sample questions you can include are:
- What do you have to do to be a good reader?
- What is the best book you have read this term? What makes it the best?
- What did you learn from this book or from the characters?

End-of-the-year reading self-evaluation encourages children to think about their progress and helps them to identify their success as a reader. Questions for them to think about include:
- How have you grown or changed as a reader?
- What have you discovered about yourself as a reader?

7. Contracts

Establish reading contracts with children to have a set number of books read by a specific date.

Depending on the age level, books may be distinguished between fiction, nonfiction, picture books, and poetry. The contract may also include specific activities to be completed, for example, drawing a story map, drawing the main character, writing character descriptions, writing newspaper headlines, and writing a letter. As with any contract, signatures of the child, parent, and teacher are required to make it valid. Often parent involvement encourages children to work harder.

8. Reading Portfolio Conferences

Children bring to the conference a reading evaluation sheet and several journal entries to discuss with you how they have grown as readers. For example, children may make connections between characters in a book. Informal discussion questions may include: How many books have you read? How many books did you begin, but not finish? Why did you not complete these books? Use the conference time to set teacher-student goals (e.g., select new authors, read more books, choose a variety of books), and work together to evaluate reading progress – is meaning brought to and taken from the written text, and is the child reading with interest?

78: Miscue Analysis

Miscue analysis is founded on the concept that while all readers make "errors" when they read, the errors are of different kinds. The term "miscue" is used because it implies that cues are used to derive meaning from what is being read. Using miscue analysis allows a teacher to observe and evaluate a reader's oral reading. From such an analysis, the teacher is able to understand whether a reader is making sense of a passage. Teachers will be more aware of children's failed attempts to make meaning out of print, and can assist those who experience difficulty.

How to Conduct a Miscue Analysis

The first step in conducting a miscue analysis is to find an appropriate passage for the child to read: for example, a short story or a nonfiction account. While the passage should be brief, it should also be somewhat difficult for the child to read. Children should understand that they will read the passage aloud and that the teacher will not help him or her. They should also understand that the reading will not be graded. If the child agrees, miscue sessions can be tape recorded. As the child reads, the teacher identifies the miscues. When finished, the child retells to him or her what was read with as few interruptions on the part of the teacher as possible. At the end of the retelling, the teacher can ask open-ended questions regarding areas omitted in the retelling.

When summarizing a child's reading performance, the teacher should understand that a miscue analysis does not reflect a child's ability to comprehend a text, nor can it accurately portray reading strategies the child employs. Reading is a matter of constructing meaning, more than of identifying words. Many readers who are not good at oral reading comprehend well.

Types of Miscues

Substitution:	substitutes a word or non-word for the word in print
Insertion:	inserts something that is not in the print
Omission:	leaves out a portion of the text already read
Repetition:	repeats a portion of the text already read
Correction:	goes back to try to correct a section of text already read
Reversal:	reverses the order of a portion of the print, such as letters, words, or phrases

---

A miscue analysis is diagnostic because it is an evaluation designed to determine a reader's attitude, skills, or knowledge in order to identify his or her specific needs. It may be used as a formal strategy of assessment at the beginning of the school year to determine a child's reading level – the child can then be given a program appropriate to his or her ability. As well, the miscue analysis can be conducted halfway through the school year to understand a child's reading progress and to decide on changes to his or her reading program. At the end of the year, a final analysis can be done to see how far a child has progressed in reading and to determine the recommendations for the following year.

79: Teaching Thematically

A thematic approach to learning combines structured, sequential, and well-organized strategies, activities, children's literature, and responses to expand a particular concept. A thematic unit is multidisciplinary and multidimensional, responsive to the interests, abilities, and needs of children, and respectful of their developing aptitudes and attitudes. In essence, a thematic approach to learning offers children a realistic arena in which they can pursue learning, using a number of contexts and a range of materials.

Advantages of Thematic Learning

1. Connections or relationships that exist between subjects, topics, and themes can be developed naturally to extend learning opportunities across the curriculum and throughout the day.
2. Learning can be a continuous and natural activity. It is not restricted to textbooks, curriculum guidelines, or time constraints.
3. A thematic unit allows a teacher to initiate a supportive and encouraging environment that emphasizes collaboration, cooperation, and process – not product.
4. Children's literature becomes an integral part of the curriculum.
5. Children understand that the focus of their work should be on individual problem solving, creative thinking, and critical thinking processes.
6. The class, including the teacher, becomes a "community of learners."
7. Units allow for relevant, accurate assessment.
8. Through self-initiated learning activities and experiences, children have realistic, first-hand opportunities to initiate risk taking.
9. Children become active learners: they inquire and investigate connections between ideas and concepts, and reflect on their inquiries.

Steps to Developing and Implementing Thematic Units

1. Selecting the Theme
When selecting a theme, teachers can consider:
• the curriculum,

- the children's interests,
- relevant issues,
- inclusion of related events (e.g., field trips).

The theme should be broad enough to allow for a range of research and response but not so broad that children will have difficulty linking concepts that are related to the theme.

2. Learning Outcomes and Curricular Area
Teachers can list the attitudes, skills, and knowledge that children will gain and develop through participating in the unit, and the areas that they will work in (e.g., language arts, social studies, science, math, art, music, drama). They can decide on the most effective learning environment for the children (e.g., small groups, whole-class discussion, independent learning).

3. Resource Availability
The teacher will need to be familiar with resources (print, visual, human) that relate to the unit. Information sources include parents, people in the community, libraries, and resource centers.

4. Organizing the Theme
The teacher can list and plan activities through theme webbing.

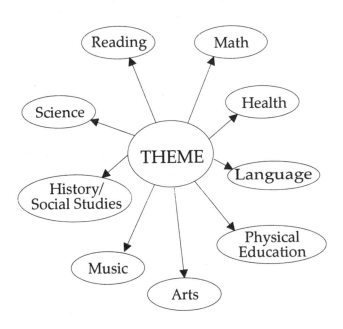

5. Brainstorming with the Class
Teachers can introduce the theme and share unit plans, discussing with the children their level of previous knowledge, their interests, their attitudes, and their responses to the theme.

6. Selecting Resources
The teacher can tailor the focus of the unit, based on class response to the brainstorming session.

7. Organizing the Classroom
The classroom will need to be organized to accommodate the unit – its activities, centers, and resources. Aids such as bulletin boards can support theme teaching by including related materials that stimulate and motivate the children.

8. Implementing the Thematic Unit
The length of the unit will depend on its scope, the level of interest it creates, availability of resources, and the teacher's comfort level. Daily or weekly schedules of activities and outcomes can be posted that reflect each teacher's style and personal experience, and the needs of his or her students. The following represent only a sampling of schedules for themes:
- for the entire day and then for several days in succession,
- for several half-days,
- integrated into two or more subject areas (e.g., math, science) for several days,
- intermittently over the span of several weeks.

9. Monitoring the Thematic Unit
Sharing projects and activities helps children to construct meaning, build a sense of community, and take ownership for their learning. The teacher, through circulating and monitoring children's work, can facilitate problem-solving, exploration, discovery, and investigative skills. Children can be encouraged to discuss their findings, pose and answer questions about their learning, and reflect on skills. As well, teachers can help children to make a connection between background and new knowledge, and reflect on their progress in relation to theme goals.

10. Evaluating and Reflecting
Discussions with children provide feedback for the unit. Was there sufficient time given? Was the topic too broad? Too narrow? How did it help the children grow? Feedback can be reflected on and incorporated when planning another unit study.

80: An Author Unit

An author unit involves the close study of a number of texts written and/or illustrated by one author. A collection of a specific author's work is experienced, discussed, and written about. In addition, children learn of the interests, experiences, and styles of authors and gain an awareness and appreciation of authors as people. As an example, an investigation of Steven Kellogg's more than 100 books allows a teacher to choose from simple texts such as those found in the *Pinkerton* series, pattern books like *There Was An Old Woman*, and color-oriented stories like *The Mystery of the Flying Orange Pumpkin* to detailed recountings of the tales of Pecos Bill, Paul Bunyan, and Johnny Appleseed. An author study of Steven Kellogg, then, would provide a rich source of literature and an even more spectacular visual display of illustrative technique.

Materials

- a collection of books by the same author,
- biographical information or reviews about the author,
- films, tapes, cassettes, filmstrips, and records of his or her work, if available.

Procedures

- the teacher and/or children make a book display of the author's work in the classroom,
- the teacher displays biographical material about the author – articles, posters, or other suitable objects.
- the teacher reads the author's work to the children, or the children read on their own or as part of a small group.

Learning About an Author

1. Discussing the Author's Work
With the children, discuss the author's work, including common patterns or themes it contains, comparisons with the work of another author, the author's culture and language and the influence of these factors on the work, and the children's personal responses to the books.

2. Responding Through Art
Children can respond to the author and his or her work through art activities. They can create murals, book jackets, bookmarks, posters, and mobiles that feature the author's work and their response to it. They can work in the style of the artist as they create their own published writings.

3. Responding Through Drama
Ask children to form small groups of four or five members. They discuss the books and decide on one of their favorite scenes. Together, they plan how to dramatize the scene through tableaux, mime, or role play. They practise their scene several times before presenting to another group.

4. Responding Through Writing
Children can respond to the author's work by writing to him or her in care of the publisher, writing about the author and his or her works in their journal, or employing some of the author's devices in a piece of their writing or illustrating.

5. Picking a Favorite
When all the children in the class have read the author's work, they can form small groups based on their favorite book. They can discuss reasons why the book is their favorite and record their comments to celebrate the book. Completed projects can be displayed together.

6. Making a Historic Time Line
Children can create a decorative, historic time line that tells of an author's life. They can include events they know of his or her personal life (e.g., date and place of birth, schooling) and the dates when the author's books were published.

7. Inviting an Author to Visit
Local authors or authors visiting the area can be invited to the class or school to give readings. In advance of his or her visit, children can take part in an author study, familiarizing themselves with the author's books and style. As follow-up to the author visit, children can write thank-you letters and share their response to the reading.

Extension Ideas

1. Study more than one author at the same time, especially if the themes of their books can be linked.

2. Study authors who write in more than one genre (e.g., Eloise Greenfield).

3. Examine the relationship of an author to his or her illustrator (e.g., Robert Munsch uses different illustrators for his picture books while Paulette Bourgeois uses the same illustrator).

4. Celebrate the authors in your class – the children.

81: Genre Study

Each genre of writing (e.g., narrative, biography, poetry, research, persuasive writing, informative) follows rules governing the format, the language patterns, and the effect on the reader.

Using a genre study in the classroom is similar to studying a theme or doing an author study. However, a genre study has many other benefits. Instead of focusing on only one concept or on a limited selection of books from one author, children will explore a type of writing, understanding the nature of the medium on the message.

Genre reading can be a helpful tool for children to explore, compare, describe, and assess types of books and various forms of writing. Understanding genre may eventually help children to explore and experiment with their own writing styles and formats.

Getting Started

Teachers can begin by choosing a genre that is appropriate to a theme children are working with, or that is of interest to the class. Similar to choosing a topic for a thematic unit, the choice of a genre may arise from observations of the children's choices of books from the library. Teachers can choose a few books from this genre and read them aloud to the class, or discuss with the children titles from a genre that all have read. Together, they can generate a list of similar characteristics or patterns that are found in these books. This list and the follow-up activities will motivate children to think, read critically, and become more aware of their own writing.

Teachers can set up a class library with books in the genre. Children can be encouraged to select books from this library and to bring in books of their own or from another library that they think complement the study. Teachers can discuss with the children characteristics or rules of the genre in question, comparing these characteristics with other genres studied and charting similarities and differences.

Advantages of Genre Study

1. Similar to a thematic study or an author study, a genre study can be used as an organizational frame.
2. Genre study allows the teacher to explore many topics, themes, and authors.
3. Genre study incorporates a large selection of books to work with, and is therefore able to accommodate the interests, preferences, capabilities, and needs of all children in the class.
4. Children are stimulated to read other books in the same genre or by the same author.
5. Children gain appropriate language to describe, compare, and talk about books, and are more comfortable sharing their reading experiences with peers.
6. Children will be able to relate books to other books (and to other genres).
7. Understanding print structures not only helps children understand what they read, but it also helps them to organize and to think creatively about their own writing.
8. Genre study provides a meaningful context for reading and writing.

A Genre Study: Folk Tales and Fairy Tales

1. Defining the Genre
In small or large groups, children can work to define folk tales and fairy tales. Among characteristics they may mention are:
- stories were passed down orally, then written,
- time is not specific – Long time ago..., Once upon a time...,
- show conflict between good and evil,
- involve an adventure, a journey, a quest, magic,
- setting is often a forest or a castle,
- end happily.

2. Looking at Variations in Fairy Tales

Discuss how many cultures tell the same tale with only slight variations. Ask children to look at Cinderella and Yeh-hsien, the Chinese version of the tale. Can they spot the similarities and differences? Children can find other example of similar tales told by several cultures. Can they explain their development and reasons for such strong similarities?

3. Exploring Stereotyping

Ask children to keep a record of stereotypical characters they meet in folk tales and fairy tales, for example, the helpless girl, the brave man, and the wicked stepmother. Next, do a survey of class members, noting characteristics such as eye color, hair color, height, hobbies, family size, number of hours spent watching television, and number of hours spent doing homework. Chart the results and describe the average – stereotypical – child in the class. Children will realize that few, if any, fit the stereotype. The activity helps them to understand that while statistics can give a general picture of the group, they cannot be applied to describe an individual.

4. Reversing Stereotypes

Discuss with the children how some authors have changed or reversed certain stereotypes in folk tales and fairy tales. Good examples are *The Paperbag Princess* by Robert Munsch or *The Politically Correct Fairy Tales* by J. F. Garner. Others have been retold with a new, fresh slant, for example, *Snow White in New York* by Fiona French and *The True Story of the Three Little Pigs by A. Wolf* by Jon Scieszka. Children can compare these newer versions with the traditional tales. What changes has the author made? Children can then retell or rewrite one of their favorite tales by reversing a stereotype, thus changing its plot, characters, or ending. If desired, some children can present their retelling in a puppet play and present it to younger classes.

Ideas for General Genre Study

1. Mapping

Have the children make a map that shows the locations of adventures depicted in one genre (e.g., tall tales, historic fiction, short story).

2. Improvisation

Have the children form small groups. Give each group a genre. Group members can brainstorm all the characteristics of their genre before creating an oral story. They retell their story several times before making a tape. In addition to the story, members can provide a soundtrack through the use of instruments and noisemakers.

3. True or False?

Is the story real? Did it really take place? Did the characters exist? Encourage the children to explore and research the places and events that are documented in a story (e.g., historical fiction, biography, science fiction, tall tales, and folklore).

4. Time Line

Children can create time lines to plot inventions, technological breakthroughs, and historical events detailed in science fiction, biography, and historical fiction books.

5. Fantasy World

After a fantasy or science fiction genre, ask children to create and describe a world that they imagine. They can outline how its inhabitants live, what they look like, their culture, and their value system. Children illustrate their world through pictures or models, and display them with a written explanation.

6. The Future

Following a science fiction genre, ask the children to predict the future. What technological and ecological advances and changes do they think will take place? For each prediction, ask them to also predict the consequences of these changes.

7. Biography and Autobiography

When children have completed a biographical or autobiographical genre study, ask them choose one person – a family member, friend, or person they know in the community – that they would like to research in order to write a biography. Children can interview the person, and talk to others who know him or her. With their findings, they write a biographical sketch of the person that they present to the class.

82: Literacy and the Curriculum

Writing and literacy are important in all areas of the curriculum, from music and drama through social studies, math, and science. The following activities extend children's knowledge of the curriculum at the same time that they further their reading and writing development.

Social Studies/History

History is important to our identity – who we are and where we have come from. It is through written words and symbols that we know what has gone before us.

1. Origin of the Alphabet

Children can explore the history of writing, the origin of our alphabet, and differences that exist between our alphabet and those of the Middle and Far East, for example. Children can create their own alphabet, and use it to write a message or a story that a peer tries to decipher (children will need to provide a key to help their peers).

2. Writing in Role

Children can select a famous historical figure and research his or her life. When they have completed their research, they take on the role of the person in writing activities, for example writing to his or her friend or another historical figure. They can write about incidents that took place during the person's lifetime, or write entries they think that person might have written to a friend or family member.

3. Writing to Peers

If possible, arrange for a pen pal program with a class in another province, state, or country. Children, through writing letters to pen pals, can learn about regional and cultural differences that exist in our country and around the world.

Music/Drama

For most, music in one form or another is a part of our daily lives. Whether one prefers classical or rock, music can evoke a range of responses.

1. Stories

Select a piece of music that most children will not have heard (e.g., instrumental). Play the music for the children and ask them to write the feelings and images they experience as they listen to the selection. When the music finishes, have the children pick a theme from their notes, and develop it in a poem or another form of written reflection.

2. Script Writing

Have children form small groups of four or five members. In their groups, they review favorite stories, rhymes, and folk and fairy tales. They select one text and write a script to transform it from story to play. Children will need several periods to polish their script and rehearse it. When all groups are ready, they can take turns presenting their drama.

Math

Math, like music, is an inherent part of our daily lives. We use math when we buy a bus ticket, when we make a transaction at a banking machine, and when we purchase food for dinner. Teachers can be helped to see the link between math and living through the provision of activities that call literacy skills into play.

1. Problem Solving

Write a math equation children are working with on the board. Ask them to help you write out each step needed to solve the problem – children may be surprised to see the lengthy description at the end of the activity. Working with a partner, children choose another math problem and write out the steps. When finished, they can compare their work. If pairs described a similar problem, they can compare their outlines for similarities and differences.

2. Free Writing

During a math lesson, ask children to take a few minutes to reflect on what they are learning, how they like math lessons, what factors they would like changed or added, and personal successes or problems with math. They can write their thoughts and choose whether they want to sign their letters. When done periodically through the year, the letters can be helpful in providing feedback on the math program.

Science

Writing, reading, and record keeping are important components of science. The children, through literacy exercises, can be made aware of the need for precise language use in this area.

1. Following Instructions

Set up simple experiments or demonstrations that the children can do on their own or with a partner. As they conduct the experiment, children make notes of their observations. When finished, discuss with the children the necessity of precise, correct instructions when carrying out a science exploration and, similarly, the need for concise observations of phenomena that result from the exploration.

2. Learning Log

Children can record, on a daily basis, what they learned or questioned in science. In addition, they can write about how they feel about a particular concept and what they would like to research further.

83: Multiculturalism

Multiculturalism is an important part of an inclusive curriculum that also includes sensitivity to gender and socioeconomic class.

Categories of Culturally Based Literature

Multicultural literature features people with a wide variety of racial characteristics, ethnic backgrounds, gender roles, and home circumstances. Multicultural literature can feature the following categories of books for young readers:
- books that introduce readers to other nations, or that focus on a group within a nation,
- nonfiction books, such as biographies, for specific group study,
- authors and illustrators of an "other" culture (e.g., Dionne Brand, Virginia Hamilton, Lawrence Yep),
- genres, such as folk tales, immigrant experience stories, pourquoi stories,
- theme books that show how common themes are interpreted across many cultures.

Advantages for Teachers

Teachers will:
- develop in children a respect, rather than a fear, of differences among the ways people think and live,
- discover diversity in the classroom,
- make clear similarities as well as differences,
- explore two basic complementary concepts:
  - all people are similar because they have the same basic needs,
  - different groups fulfill some of these needs in different ways,
- seek to meet the needs of all children – cultural literature is inclusive,
- create high expectations for children that allow them to reach their fullest potential.

Advantages for Children

Children will:
- develop an awareness of cultural practices,
- increase understanding and an appreciation of different points of view,
- promote acceptance,
- treat others with respect,
- encourage discriminating and critical thinking,
- communicate through understanding and knowledge,
- develop an increase in cultural pride.

A Teacher's Resource of Activities

1. Time Capsule/Museum – Defining Culture and its Components

With the children, gather materials and items from various sources that reflect culture. Together, classify them under four headings: food, festivals, folklore, and fun. Children can compare these items with their counterparts in other lands and other times. How many were in existence twenty years ago? Fifty years ago? One hundred years ago? Children pick selected items that they think will interest people in the future. For each item, they research its origin, if possible, and write a brief description. Completed descriptions and examples of items can be displayed in a class "museum."

2. Elements of Culture – How Stories Bring Us Culture

Children, with a partner, read a story about another culture. When they have finished, they list the story's components and arrange their answers under the following headings:

- content, subject, or theme,
- language patterns, and unique words, phrases, chants, and names,
- skills of each character,
- roles and occupations,
- personal information, such as dress, costume, jewelry, food,
- story type,
- story pattern,
- setting, unique landmarks, typical buildings, houses, markets.

Each pair of children shares their response with a pair of children who read a book focusing on another culture. Together, they look for similarities and differences.

3. Culture and the Individual – Ascribing Value to Cultural Items

Ask children to imagine that they are moving to an island. They are allowed only one large suitcase so they will need to pack carefully. Give children a few minutes to reflect on what they value most. These will be the items they take with them. When children have completed their list, ask them to form a group with four or five of their classmates and pool their lists to determine what they have. Do their lists contain similar ideas, values, attitudes, and beliefs? Will items on the list meet their needs and wants? As a group, children make a final list of items they will take.

Have children remain in their groups and ask them to imagine that they have arrived on the island. It is deserted – they are the first humans to have walked its shores. Group members list their ideas for building a new society on the island. They outline:

- needs (e.g., shelter, food, clothing),
- expectations of good conduct,
- roles of group members,
- laws to govern the island including those relating to health, education, and social assistance.

Children need to come to an agreement regarding their society, a harder activity than it appears at first glance since even those of us who have lived in the same culture can hold values that differ greatly from one person to the next. When children have finished, they review the list of items they brought with them. As a group, they discuss the usefulness of each. Given their experience in planning a society, what other items would they have packed?

4. Holidays and Celebrations

These occasions provide ideal opportunities to teach about history and cultural diversity. Each child in the class can research special days in his or her culture. Together, as a class, draw up a yearly calendar to mark the days. Children can research the occasions, including their origin, evolvement, special foods, and costumes. On the day of each occasion, the child can present his or her research. In some cases, the class can make simple recipes that are a hallmark of this day.

5. Research a Culture

Children, working with new group members, pick a culture they would like to research. Headings for their research could include:

- festivals, foods, dances,
- profiles of prominent members of that culture,
- interviews with members,
- traditional art forms,
- recommended reading (e.g., other stories related to the culture).

Children can choose a method of presentation and report on their findings to the rest of the class.

6. Language – An Important Component of a Culture

Language often indicates what is important to a culture. As examples, the Inuit language includes many words for snow while the Arabic language includes many words for camel. In our culture, "time" is important – we have a past, present, future tense – and a number of sayings related to time (e.g., "time marches on," "be on time," "in the nick of time," "running out of time"). In Hopi or Chinese, there is only one tense for time so people do not specify when an event took place.

84: Involving Libraries

A school library functions like a hub, providing a center for resource-based learning to children, parents, and school staff. Its design, organization, and utility reflect the philosophy and collaborative efforts of a school's professional core – teacher-librarians, teachers, and the principal. While a principal works primarily behind the scenes, teachers and teacher-librarians work together in the forefront, designing and implementing an integrated curriculum that promotes the literacy development and independent learning of each child.

Children are active learners with diverse learning styles that need to be stimulated and motivated with interesting and relevant resources. The role of libraries is ultimately for the benefit and development of the child and therefore must provide and utilize the most effective human, material, and physical resources possible.

Teacher-librarians maximize the library's potential effectiveness by enlisting the human resources available within the community. Through communication and interaction with consultants, social agencies, and arts organizations, teacher-librarians develop a sense of how to help teachers meet the needs of children.

Material Resources

A library must have a wide range of print material (books, magazines, periodicals, brochures, kits), media (audiotapes, videos, computer software, CD-ROMs, video discs), and equipment (computers, television monitors, tape recorders, modems, printers, camcorders, cameras, VCRs, film projectors) available to children, school staff, and parents. The effectiveness of these material resources is determined by how they are integrated into the curriculum by teachers and teacher-librarians.

Physical Resources

The library is designed to be an inviting, safe, and exciting place in which to work and learn. When designing the library's physical space to maximize its use, the teacher-librarian needs to take into account learning and teaching styles, traffic patterns, and the number and variety of work areas needed. Consideration is also given to the availability and utility of the school's gymnasium, auditorium, playgrounds, and computer labs. Further consideration is given to integrating available physical resources beyond the school, such as public libraries, planetariums, museums, outdoor education centers, parks, community recreational facilities, and government agencies. Also, field-trip sites offer facilities, personnel, or material resources beyond the scope of the individual school.

Information-Based Learning

The role of school libraries is changing. With the development of digital technology, libraries are increasingly described as centers that provide and coordinate the sharing of all kinds of information.

The rapid changes that are taking place in information technology greatly affect the responsibilities of the teacher-librarian. The present technology provides more resources for children and enables them to acquire information from a much wider field. The teacher-librarian will need to learn how to integrate effectively and efficiently all new technology into the information center, and encourage children to become independent learners who can move freely from books to CD-ROMs, from card catalogues to the Internet, from letters to e-mail.

Literacy in the Library: Ideas

1. Book Sharing
Teacher-librarians utilize their expertise in children's literature to bring a child and a selection of books together with the intent of expanding the child's interest in, and enjoyment of, reading books. Communication with teachers and parents regarding a child's reading experience aids the teacher-librarian in bringing the most relevant and exciting reading material to the child.

2. Book Study
Teacher-librarians, in collaboration with teachers, can plan ways to expose children to new books by focusing on, for example, the works of one author, the works of one illustrator, or a theme.

Using books that represent a range of genres – fiction, nonfiction, picture books, novels, poetry – increases the potential of a child's interest and involvement in meaningful reading.

3. Promoting Books

A school library uses a variety of strategies and resources to promote books:

- props that bring stories to life,
- computer-integrated book-sharing lists that may include reviews, synopses, "Top Ten," or "Must Read" lists,
- bulletin boards that display book-sharing lists,
- book of the day (or week) chosen by children,
- display of international stories with each story marked by a flag indicating country of origin,
- multimedia displays that relate to a study unit.

85: Assessment and Evaluation

Assessment and evaluation, essential responsibilities of every teacher, are used routinely each day. Teachers assess and evaluate in order to:

- determine what a child or group of children know, how they learn best, and their capabilities and needs,
- maintain records of children's needs, developing and modifying programs to be effective,
- collect a broad variety of indicators that track children's progress and achievement.

Assessment is an ongoing process of gathering and recording information about, and observations of, children's performances. Information gathered through assessment includes:

- anecdotal records (e.g., observations pertaining to children's behavior, notes on their reading),
- tracking records (e.g., children's efforts, needs, improvements, participation),
- process items (e.g., drafts of a written work, conference notes, self-reports of group participation),
- end products (e.g., completed worksheets, stories, research projects).

Assessment involves a number of strategies:

- inquiry: verbal communications with children (e.g., reading interviews, conferencing),
- observation: anecdotal records of children's behaviors, attitudes, comments, and participation,
- analysis: scrutinizing records to identify a child's strengths, needs, and progress,
- testing: intentional situations designed to provide material for evaluation.

Assessment requires:

- teachers as the principal recorders of children's behavior and work,
- children as self-assessors and record keepers (e.g., conference participants, reading logs, portfolios),
- peers as peer editors, conference participants, co-assessors of group processes,
- parents as valuable resources of information, insights, and observations about children.

Though initially focused on children, assessment material also reflects the program's progress and success: assessment should provide feedback for a teacher's program planning and design.

Evaluation is the making of value judgments about children's achievements based on materials gathered through assessment. For example, evaluation involves the grading of submitted or presented products on the basis of a rubric of criteria. Evaluation reflects not only the children's achievements, but also to the degree of success of teaching strategies. As with assessment, evaluation should provide feedback for programming.

Diagnostic assessment and evaluation takes place at the beginning of the year or unit in order to assess children's skills and knowledge. Information will be used to determine a child's or group of children's status regarding a part of the curriculum or placement of individuals in learning groups and programs. Examples of formal diagnostic assessment and evaluation are cloze procedure and miscue analysis; examples of informal diagnostic assessment and evaluation are reading interviews and one-on-one oral reading observations.

Formative assessment and evaluation is ongoing throughout the year or unit. It provides continuous information about learners' development, and can be used as a resource for program planning and modification. Examples of formal formative assessment and evaluation include teacher-made tests; examples of informal formative assessment and evaluation include anecdotal records, inventories, surveys, checklists, observation guides, portfolios, writing folders, conferencing, audio and video recording, and child self-assessment.

Summative assessment and evaluation occurs at the end of the year or unit, and involves conferencing, analysis, grading, and reporting. Results can serve as feedback for program evaluation. Examples of formal summative assessment and evaluation include norm-referenced and criterion-referenced tests; an example of informal summative assessment and evaluation includes feedback to program evaluation.

86: Portfolio Assessment

Portfolio assessment has received growing attention as a powerful means for encouraging children to become aware of their learning. Portfolio programs have been identified with "authentic" assessment since they provide for a fluid, ongoing, and collaborative perspective on children's performance.

A portfolio program can...
• encourage self-directed learning:
  - through ongoing engagement with their portfolios and a teacher's guidance, children can develop self-assessment and goal-setting skills.
• be an authentic source of motivation:
  - the teacher and children can see and appreciate the continuity and growth in their skills over time,
  - be a great motivator when children review their effort, progress, and achievement.
• contribute to children's self-esteem by providing each child with a "self-portrait" of themselves as learners.

• create mor
  - as childr
create their
their ideas, a
• emphasize
  lum:
  - as childr
personal sy:
life experie
• provide in
  - teachers
each child':
grounds, at
• enable an
  reflection,
• be a valuable resource for developing and assessing programs, preparing reports, participating in parent interviews, and taking part in division and school planning.

Setting Up a Portfolio Program

1. Set general parameters on the basis of aims, resources, and age of children.
Portfolios can be...
• assessed and/or evaluated,
• used at any grade level,
• a repository for "best work," or a broader collection of artifacts,
• used in one or more curricular areas (e.g., writing folder, literacy portfolio),
• used for varying lengths of time (e.g., throughout a unit, a year).

For example, a literacy portfolio, consistent with a year-long reading and writing "workshop" program, is:
• a personal collection of diverse materials that reflect an individual's literacy development (i.e., their engagement with language through thinking, reading, and writing over time).
• a child-owned vehicle for pursuing and experimenting with individual interests and expression.
• a "record of process" (i.e., a work-in-progress, not just finished, "best" work).
• a performance assessment tool (not a basis for product evaluation):

...r collaborate in confer-
...ss strengths and needs,
...s for the learner and the
...ing.

...tive portfolio assessment (child,
...r) develops children's abilities to criti-
...ct on their reading and writing habits,
...nd goals.

... List items children will include in their portfolios and provide examples of optional items.

Portfolios can contain ...

- drawings, pictures, photos and/or descriptions of favorite things, places, people,
- letters (e.g., to authors, people in books, heroes),
- reading responses (assigned work, journal entries, notes made outside the classroom),
- drafts and final versions of writing (both assigned and free writing),
- unfinished writing,
- journal entries (e.g., "What I think," personal, reading journals),
- notes on ideas, observations, experiences, interests, sources to look for,
- audiotapes and videotapes, computer disks,
- a table of contents (encourages children to organize their entries),
- captions on each entry describing why the child selected it,
- reading and writing logs, including the title, author, date, and the child's comments,
- memorable quotes from reading,
- an "I want to read" list of books to access,
- a list of interesting words encountered in reading, other media, conversation,
- an "About the Author" piece (consider as a preliminary portfolio activity),
- comments from peers, the teacher, and conference notes,
- anything that the child wants to share from school, home, or elsewhere and that reflects him or her as a speaker, listener, reader, writer, storyteller, actor, poet, person!

3. Design or acquire necessary standard forms.

Portfolios require a number of forms, for teacher and child use, including a reading log form, conference reflection form, self-assessment form, and a peer evaluation form.

4. Schedule ample time for all to benefit from the program.

Portfolio assessment is labor- and time-intensive. Once a teacher has invested time in design and implementation, she or he must provide time for maintenance to reap returns. Teachers will need to allot time for:

- independent child interaction with portfolios;
  - organizing materials, keeping records (e.g., reading logs), selecting and captioning entries, reviewing contents.
- peer interaction:
  - formal, informal sharing of portfolios.
- child-teacher conferencing:
  - ideally, the teacher will conference with each child at least four times during the year to review portfolio contents, discuss growth, and set goals for further development.

5. Prepare a model portfolio to share with children.

When teachers provide a concrete example for children, they help them to embark confidently and enthusiastically on a portfolio program. A teacher who uses his or her material and models reflecting on and sharing a portfolio's contents shows children how their portfolios will be used.

6. Encourage children's ownership of portfolios.

Teachers can provide a variety of examples of what portfolio holders can look like and encourage children to be creative when decorating them (consider storage options when modeling sizes). How the children organize the portfolio, however, must be their choice. While they will need some guidelines and input from the teacher regarding content, children will control the selection of items to be included in their portfolio.

7. Integrate portfolios in the instructional program.

Portfolios are a rich resource that teachers can use as references for activities and lessons (e.g., "Look in your portfolio to see if you have an example of..."). As a program evolves, teachers can address common needs among children that have been identified when discussing their portfolios or through lessons or activities, and can continue to provide models for objectives (e.g. "Here's what a peer-edited piece might look like").

8. Portfolio conferences can take place between the teacher, peers, parents, and children.

Portfolio conferencing can take place between a teacher and child, between peers, or between a parent and child. Of these, teacher-child conferences are essential, peer conferences are desirable (depending on the age of the children), and child-led parent conferences are recommended. A teacher's one-on-one conferencing with children is essential for the development of self-assessment skills and should precede (i.e., provide a basis for) peer and parent conferencing. When a teacher has conferenced once with every child, the class may be ready to begin peer conferencing. Ongoing child-teacher conferences and peer conferences may culminate in child-led parent conferences at the end of the year.

Parents must be prepared so that they can participate in, and respond meaningfully to, their child's presentation. To facilitate this, teachers can send home a letter with guidelines or, better yet, discuss the process with parents in advance (e.g., at the previous reporting interview). During the child-led parent conference, the teacher serves as a "resource person": she or he observes and supplies input only when requested to do so. Teachers who have experience in holding child-parent conferences have found that they need a time period of at least twenty minutes to a half-hour, and that up to four child-led parent conferences can be held at the same time.

87: Literacy Snapshots

An effective classroom will be captured throughout the year in a variety of snapshots revealing the reading, writing, and thinking experiences that lead toward success in literacy:

- listening to a taped book and following along with the text,
- discussing a novel read by the group,
- reading all together with a big book,
- self-evaluating each member's participation in a completed unit,
- writing a report in groups about a school trip,
- reading independently in the library,
- retelling a story from a different point of view,
- revising a poem using the computer,
- working with a group on a spelling pattern, listening to the teacher read stories aloud, innovating on a patterned picture book,
- reading a revised draft aloud to a partner,
- recording observations in a journal,
- reading aloud chorally a poem on the overhead projector,
- organizing a classroom poetry anthology,
- reading with a buddy, taking turns to read aloud,
- writing captions on a photography collage,
- working with a teacher in a one-on-one conference,
- brainstorming a list of editing suggestions,
- attending to a mini-lesson conducted by the teacher,
- examining a series of magazine ads for puns and word play,
- writing a response to the teacher in a dialogue journal,
- reading aloud to a parent a book prepared at school,
- singing a song with actions,
- creating a mobile of a word family,
- role playing, as a class, a village that is faced with a problem,
- recording notes from a science experiment,
- illustrating events from a novel,
- creating lists of favorite books,
- participating in a mini-lesson on a phonic pattern,
- reading a letter from a pen pal,
- reading silently books published by classmates,
- conducting a survey of favorite books,
- using a reference book to prove a point with another class,
- comparing two versions of a folk tale.

Part F: How to Choose Books

88: Organizing Class Collections

Teachers need to consider choosing and organizing reading resources for classroom collections. Once they have these resources in place and understand how to use them, teachers need strategies that will enable them to prepare lessons for different types of reading groups and independent reading times. They also need to be aware of troubled readers in hopes of involving them in an effective reading program. Once teachers have a basis for collecting materials and are knowledgeable about the types of reading programs that they can implement, they need to be aware of concurrent methods of teaching reading and keeping detailed anecdotal records.

Five Ways to Organize Classroom Book Collections

1. Multiple Copies of Collections of Stories in an Anthology or Reader

Anthologies contain a number of pieces of literature that are housed together based on their shared reading level and/or theme. Those published for the educational market can be used for individual and group work, and can provide a good opportunity for reinforcing stage-appropriate or level-appropriate reading skills. Typically, these anthologies will consist of five to ten copies of books at each level, making it possible for groups of children to have a shared reading experience that the teacher can monitor.

2. Multiple Copies of a Single Story

These can range in length from the shortest short story to a longer novel form. Many teachers include multiple copies of novels in class sets in order to accommodate the excitement of young children. Often they want, and need, to talk to peers about books that they are reading – a resourceful teacher will be able to provide those books on demand as the need arises. Many schools find that five to ten copies of single works can be shared among classes.

3. A Collection of Many Works Written and/or Illustrated by One Author

Collections often take the form of an organized author study – an investigation of authoring skills and styles by one author and/or illustrator. Some popular authors write for a range of age and interest levels – the study of such an author will give the teacher the opportunity to provide literature for all levels of reader in his or her program.

4. A Collection of Disparate Literature Pieces

Many of today's classroom libraries include a number of books that do not share a common theme. Such a collection helps to create a good environment for a "pick and read" program, a necessary part of an individualized reading program.

5. A Collection of Literature Pieces that Share a Common Theme

By considering differences and similarities in books that share a common theme, children can investigate aspects of culture, social science topics, countries of origin, or other universal themes. A good story can cross the curriculum – a "set of books" can launch an investigation that will result in children introducing additional resources into the classroom to share with classmates. If children are given opportunities to assume ownership of the learning process by finding and bringing material to class, the reading program will grow and flourish.

How Using the Same Text Can Be Beneficial

- In the primary grades, an important teaching objective is to create a community of readers. Assisting the children with selecting good reading materials that can be shared is crucial as they develop as readers, thinkers, and explorers.

- In most patterned or repetitive texts, the stories lend themselves to patterning. The text then becomes a skeleton or taking-off point for additional learning by the children.

- Reading the same text helps to set the stage for young readers to achieve the skills they will require in becoming independent readers.

How Using Different Texts Can Be Beneficial

- An environment that includes a variety of texts, authors, and writing styles creates an atmosphere where, as a community of readers, we share information in a meaningful way.

- Using a variety of texts encourages children to explore, in cooperative groups settings, the many elements of a theme.

- Exposure to a number of texts enables children to connect literature to their lives, and provides opportunities for critical thinking.

- Reading a variety of texts gives children the chance to learn and teach others.

- During silent reading times, sometimes referred to as DEAR (drop everything and read), children are encouraged to read for enjoyment and satisfaction, exploring books individually.

89: How Books Work

Children need to be immersed in books of all kinds in order to become readers and writers. As well, they need to receive demonstrations of how books are constructed and used, since books vary in their purpose, audience, format, and organization, as well as in the publishing devices and designs they employ. The type of book may influence the language it uses and the way in which information is presented. This, in turn, will influence how the book will be read. Consider how dictionaries, novels, poetry anthologies, diaries, and picture books differ. Through familiarity with types of books and through discussion about what readers do with them, children develop an understanding of how different kinds of books can be used. Some books can be read from beginning to end; others will require the reader to:

- scan a book for a particular item of information,
- read part or all of a book to better understand a concept,
- read part or all of a book to follow directions,
- read only a portion of a book,
- refer to a book over and over again.

Awareness of how books work, and an understanding of book and print conventions, can be developed through activities that help children explore the components of print.

1. What Is a Book?

Consider, as a class, the question, "What is a book?" before developing a reference chart of types of books (e.g., poetry, picture, narrative). Give the children opportunities to classify books according to this chart.

2. What We Find in a Book

Make available a variety of types of books. The children may come up with a list such as this:

- both pictures and text have meaning,
- text is usually written from left to right,
- text is usually written from top to bottom,
- words are represented by a letter or a combination of letters,
- there are two forms of letters – upper-case letters and lower-case letters,
- words can be highlighted by writing in different graphic forms,
- print can be presented in lists,
- words can be used as labels,
- words can be enclosed in speech or thought balloons,
- punctuation illustrates how to read a text,
- some words begin with capital letters, depending on their meaning or their position in a sentence,
- different forms of writing have different print conventions.

3. Parts of a Book

As you use books in class, you can draw the children's attention to the parts of books and the names of these parts:

cover	copyright	preface
chapters	contents	epilogue

index   title page   dedication
glossary   spine   bibliography

With the children, develop a large diagram and label the components.

4. What's in a Title?

The children can discuss the importance of a book's title. To facilitate this, display, compare, and discuss various titles and their effectiveness. Can children identify the importance of an effective title? Can readers rely on a title to tell them about a book?

- Children can use the title of a book and its front cover to make predictions about what the story will be about. Record their predictions on a chart and post it for easy reference. After reading, they compare what they have read with their earlier predictions.
- Children can read or listen to a nonfiction book then create a web of information.
- Cover the title and author of a book and give it to a pair of children. After reading the book, they decide on an appropriate title. They share their suggestions and justify their choice of title with another pair of children before reading the original title.

5. Endpapers

Have children examine and discuss endpapers, which appear at the front and back of some books. Illustrators such as Steven Kellogg and Susan Jeffers use endpapers to create a mood, set a scene, and support the story. In *Hey Al*, endpapers change from a dull beige at the beginning of the book to a bright yellow at its end. Discuss with the children possible reasons for this and what it might signify.

The Language of Literature

Classrooms should contain a range of book types, including narrative fiction (e.g., fairy tales, folk tales, realistic fiction, novels, legends, mysteries, fantasy, adventure), nonfiction books (e.g., diaries, biographies, encyclopedias, atlases, memoirs), poetry, picture books, and alphabet books. Housing such reading material is not enough, of course. Teachers must then find the time to talk about books.

Exposure to a wide range of books offers children the opportunity to learn how authors use language since the language of literature differs from the language of daily conversations. It uses a richer vocabulary, more complex sentence structure, imagery, and phrasing. The rhythms, cadences, and organizational and structural characteristics of literature differ from those found in our speech.

By reading to children and having children read in the class, teachers can change their linguistic knowledge/metacognitive structure. Authors use features to achieve particular effects – teachers can talk about what is said and how it is said. They need to help children discover how a writer's use of details paints a character, sets a scene, and achieves authenticity of dialogue and language. Children can practise specific techniques in their writing.

Participating in a variety of reading experiences helps children to learn how print functions from the inside out. They develop a sense of story, increase their understanding of words, and develop a sense of the predictability of language that will help them as independent readers. When teachers talk about literature, they help children develop an understanding of the nature of written language and how people read. Teachers must develop in children a language that relates to print and the reading process.

1. AARGH!

Authors make use of a number of typographical conventions in their texts that give information to the reader about meaning and suggest how a particular word or sentence is to be read. Draw children's attention to sentences within a text in which words are presented in different forms (e.g., all capitals), and ask them to think about why it was written this way. How would they read the sentence?

2. Once Upon a Time

Discuss the role of an opening sentence in a book like *Charlotte's Web* by E.B. White. Such a sentence often draws the reader into the story by its sense of immediacy. Children can think about and discuss other opening paragraphs and chapters and their effect on readers.

3. In My Own Words

Have children examine how the form of a story influences its content. As an example, a story told through dialogue between two characters would be different had the author written minimal dialogue and events were reported by a third person.

4. Modeling Published Books
Children can use published books as a model to create their own book. They can include components such as a dedication and a contents page, and can organize the content in chapters, modeling how authors chunk text, first in paragraphs and later in chapters.

5. Exploring Picture Books
Picture books, once the domain of prereaders, now span a range of topics and reading abilities that appeal to a broad spectrum of readers. Whatever their level or subject matter, picture books exemplify the use of illustrations to enhance text and convey information.

- Have children choose their favorite illustration from a picture book. They explain their preference for the illustration and describe its importance to the story.
- In a book like John Birmingham's *Oi! Get Off Our Train*, illustrations carry the main burden of the narrative. The written text consists of dialogue with much of the action implied. Mask the text in this book (or a similar picture book), and ask children to create a story that matches the illustrations.
- Have children consider how the text in a book is presented and reasons why the author may have chosen this format. A good example of this is *Where the Wild Things Are* by Maurice Sendak. As the text progresses, the illustrations increase in import.
- Ask children to look at the book *Bird's Eye* by Judy Graham and Michael Ansell. The print follows the pattern of a bird's flight and the illustrations are from the perspective of a bird.

90: Reading Novels

Novels allow children to step outside of their own lives to identify and reflect on human behaviors, emotions, values, and conflicts. The reader becomes the participant and is drawn into the story, experiencing the lives of the characters involved.

As children develop their reading skills, they come to appreciate a story, not only by identifying with the characters but also by seeing the story through the eyes of the author. By reading and responding to novels, children are able to see how authors use their talents to create stories. Children also come to understand and appreciate the style, language, plot, and characters that make up a novel.

How Readers Make Sense of What They Read

Before reading, readers:
- think about the text,
- prepare themselves for reading by drawing on prior knowledge.

As readers read, they build a coherent, personal interpretation of both the selection and its real-world connections by:
- looking for important ideas,
- paraphrasing,
- predicting,
- anticipating,
- reading ahead for additional context,
- rereading to clarify a confusing part, or to relate new knowledge to existing knowledge,
- testing hypotheses and understandings,
- creating mental images to visualize description,
- looking for interconnecting details,
- monitoring reading to ensure comprehension (if the material is too difficult, the reader stops reading).

After reading, readers:
- reflect on what they have read,
- relate what they can to their experience,
- respond in a variety of modes to enrich and extend the meaning-making process.

Plot Activities

1. Writing a Newspaper Article
Children can write a newspaper article about an exciting event they read in a novel. They follow the journalist's motto by answering the questions – who, what, where, when, why, how. When finished, a partner can help the child edit the piece. Completed articles can be displayed for others to read.

2. Playing a Part

Children can pick one chapter from a novel they are reading. They make notes of important events that took place in the chapter, as well as entertaining situations and conversations. Children present the information from the chapter in one of several ways:

- becoming storytellers by retelling the story in their own words,
- telling the story in role, playing one or more of the characters,
- creating an improvisation based on one scene.

Character Activities

1. The Press Conference

This activity requires children to work in a group of three. One child will role play a character from a novel; the second, a reporter; and the third, a director. The reporter interviews the character while the director analyzes the filming of the conference, examining the quality of the questions asked and the responses given by the character. Children switch roles. When finished, they choose which situation best represented the character and present it to others in the class.

2. Character Wall Charts

Groups of three or four children can create wall charts comprising short quotations or key descriptive words a character has said that capture the essence of his or her personality. Children can keep track of developments in the novel by adding to their charts during the reading of the novel, providing material for reflection of a character's growth from the beginning of a novel to its end.

3. Family Trees

Often children "tune out" from stories when they are confused about the relationships between characters. Working as a group to create a family tree that visually depicts these relationships helps children to understand them. As they continue to read the novel, they can refer to the family tree when necessary.

Language Activities

1. Writing to an Author

On their own or with a partner, children can write to the author of a novel they enjoyed reading.

Some ideas they could write about include:

- comments about how they felt about the novel,
- why they would recommend it to a friend,
- how they identified with the characters,
- their opinion of the ending,
- what they learned from the novel and how they connected it to their own life,
- questions they would like the author to answer.

2. Word Play

Reading is a fun way to learn new words. Often, readers can guess the meaning of new words from their context. Children can revisit a novel they have read recently and record ten new words they met. They then write a brief description of each word, using clues from the novel or by looking the word up in a dictionary. Children use the new words in a word-search puzzle that they create.

Tips for Promoting Novels

1. Give children several books to choose from.
2. Be aware of children's interests and needs.
3. Encourage the use of the library and the librarian as a resource.
4. Talk with children about what they have read.
5. Survey children to discover current favorites.
6. Share with the children opinions of peers, librarians, and reviewers.

91: Recommended Novels

Avi. *Nothing But the Truth*. New York, NY: Avon, 1993.

Babbitt, Natalie. *Tuck Everlasting*. New York, NY: Farrar, Straus, Giroux, 1975.

Blume, Judy. *Tales of a Fourth Grade Nothing*. New York, NY: Dell, 1976.

Burnett, Frances. *The Secret Garden*. New York, NY: Dell, 1989.

Byars, Betsy. *The Eighteenth Emergency*. New York, NY: Puffin, 1981.

Cleary, Beverly. *Dear Mr. Henshaw*. New York, NY: Morrow, 1984.

Cooper, Susan. *Dawn of Fear*. New York, NY: Simon & Schuster, 1989.

Dahl, Roald. *James and the Giant Peach*. New York, NY: Puffin, 1988.

De Felice, Cynthia. *Weasel*. New York, NY: Avon, 1991.

Doyle, Brian. *Angel Square*. Toronto, ON: Groundwood, 1995.

Fitzhugh, Louise. *Harriet the Spy*. New York, NY: HarperCollins, 1990.

George, Jean Craighead. *Julie of the Wolves*. New York, NY: HarperCollins, 1974.

Hughes, Monica. *My Name Is Paula Popowich!* Toronto, ON: Lorimer, 1983.

Katz, Welwyn. *Out of the Dark*. Toronto, ON: Groundwood, 1995.

Konigsburg, E.L. *From the Mixed-Up Files of Mrs. Basil E. Frankweiler*. New York, NY: Simon & Schuster, 1987.

L'Engle, Madelaine. *A Wrinkle in Time*. New York, NY: Dell, 1976.

Lewis, C.S. *The Lion, the Witch and the Wardrobe*. New York, NY: HarperCollins, 1994.

Little, Jean. *From Anna*. Markham, ON: Fitzhenry & Whiteside, 1977.

Lowry, Lois. *The Giver*. Boston, MA: Houghton Mifflin, 1993.

Lunn, Janet. *The Root Cellar*. Toronto, ON: Penguin, 1986.

MacLachlan, Patricia. *Journey*. New York, NY: Dell, 1993.

Major, Kevin. *Dear Bruce Springsteen*. Toronto, ON: Doubleday, 1994.

Naylor, Phyllis Reynolds. *Shiloh*. New York, NY: Dell, 1992.

O'Brien, Robert C. *Mrs. Frisby and the Rats of NIMH*. New York, NY: Simon & Schuster, 1986.

Paterson, Katherine. *Bridge to Terabithia*. New York, NY: HarperCollins, 1987.

Paulsen, Gary. *Dogsong*. New York, NY: Puffin, 1987.

Pearce, Philippa. *Tom's Midnight Garden*. New York, NY: HarperCollins, 1992.

Spinelli, Jerry. *Maniac Magee*. Boston, MA: Little, Brown, 1990.

White, E.B. *Charlotte's Web*. New York, NY: HarperCollins, 1990.

Wilder, Laura Ingalls. *Little House on the Prairie*. New York, NY: HarperCollins, 1990.

92: Picture Books

Five Reasons to Use Picture Books

1. Picture books combine art and words as material for the children's meaning making.
2. Picture books allow children to experience environments unlike their own, to travel to another time, to confront novel situations, and to empathize with characters who share their problems.
3. Picture books can help children develop competencies in language as they acquire skills in reading, talking, listening, and writing.
4. Picture books can be used to teach the sensory, formal, and technical properties of art and literature.
5. Picture books can contribute to children's social experience. They are inherently sociable and provide opportunities for interaction.

Connecting Prior Background Knowledge

1. Prediction Chart

Prepare a chart with two columns at the top, "What I Think Will Happen" and "What Actually Happened." Before reading, ask the children to call out major events that they predict will occur. List their responses. After the reading, ask them to call out actual events. As a large group, compare and discuss the predictions and the events. Was there overlap between the columns, or were children's predictions largely unrealized? If yes, can children give reasons for this discrepancy?

2. Storytelling Bone (or Stick, Stone)

This prop is used to encourage storytelling among the children. Build a papier mâché bone using a wire base that has been shaped to resemble a large bone. Children hold the bone while they tell a section of story. When finished, they pass it to the next person who continues to tell the story or begins a new story.

Constructing Intellectual and Creative Insights

1. Character Webs

Write the name of a character in the middle of a large piece of paper and draw a circle around his or her name. Ask children to call out information about the character (e.g., age, family members, place of birth). Record and circle these facts on the page and connect them to the character's name to make a web. Secondary information can also be webbed.

2. Cause and Effect

Explain, in simple terms, cause and effect in a book by providing the children with several examples. As a large group, prepare a cause/effect chart for a story you have experienced together.

Creating Literary Responses

1. Dear Abby

Children choose a character from the story. They can select a problem the character has experienced or invent a new problem. In role, they write a Dear Abby letter that explains his or her dilemma and asks for advice.

2. Following a Character

Just as children have favorite picture books so too do they have favorite characters. In their logs, children can follow the progress and events their favorite character experiences in each book.

3. Wall Mural

Children often have a favorite picture book that they can hear many times over. An activity that capitalizes on this interest is to have them work in small or large groups to make a wall mural or collage containing scenes from the story.

4. Making a Wordless Book

These picture books rely solely on illustrations to tell the story. Readers "read" the visuals to follow the story's plot. When children have experienced a number of these books, they can work with a partner to "write" their own. Completed wordless books can be shared with others in the class.

5. A Lift-the-Flap Card

Children choose a scene from a favorite picture book and recreate it in a lift-the-flap format. They can send the card to a friend or family member.

6. Picture Story Circle

Read a picture book several times to develop a sense of the main events of the story. Number and list these events with a brief description, then divide the class into the same number of groups. Give each group one event. They read it and create a collaborative picture that tells of the event. At the bottom of the page, they include the description of the event. When all groups are finished, they put their pictures in sequence to tell the story. The pictures can make an effective display, or can be stapled to make a book.

7. Compare and Contrast

The goal of this activity is to develop discussions that delve into the strengths and limitations of art style, technique, and medium. With the children, compare and contrast illustrations in terms of line, color, theme, and medium. When finished, ask them to identify differences between illustrations and photographs. Do they prefer one medium, or does their preference vary from book to book? Volunteers can explain their reasons for their preferences.

8. Comparing Authors

Children, with a partner or as part of a small group, can compare how various authors treat characters, settings, or themes. They use examples from the books to support their comparisons.

9. Video Commentary

Children can make a segment of a radio or television program that incorporates the reading of an extract from a review or article about a picture book, an interview with a child who has read the book, and discussions involving two or more people who have differing opinions of the book.

10. What If? Incidents

Children can replace an important event in a plot with one that they have devised and which is compatible with the original event. In groups or in pairs, children can discuss the effect this replacement would have on the story. How would it be different? How would it remain the same?

93: Recommended Picture Books

General Interest

Ahlberg, Janet and Allan. *The Jolly Postman.* New York, NY: Little, Brown, 1991.

Blades, Ann. *A Boy of Taché.* Montreal, PQ: Tundra, 1984.

Booth, David. *The Dust Bowl.* Toronto, ON: Kids Can, 1996.

Bourgeois, Paulette. *Franklin's Blanket.* Toronto, ON: Kids Can, 1995.

---. *Grandma's Secret.* Toronto, ON: Kids Can, 1991.

Brown, Margaret Wise. *Goodnight Moon.* New York, NY: HarperCollins, 1947.

Browne, Anthony. *Gorilla.* New York, NY: Knopf, 1985.

Bruchac, Joseph. *Fox Song.* New York, NY: Putnam, 1993.

Bunting, Eve. *Smoky Night.* Orlando, FL: Harcourt Brace, 1994.

Carle, Eric. *The Grouchy Ladybug.* New York, NY: HarperCollins, 1986.

Carrick, Carol. *Patrick's Dinosaurs.* Boston, MA: Houghton Mifflin, 1983.

Carrier, Roch. *The Hockey Sweater.* Montreal, PQ: Tundra, 1984.

Chase, Edith Newlin. *The New Baby Calf.* Richmond Hill, ON: Scholastic, 1984.

De Paola, Tomie. *Strega Nona.* New York, NY: Scholastic, 1992.

Heide, Florence Parry, and Judith Heide Gilliland. *The Day of Ahmed's Secret.* New York, NY: Morrow, 1995.

Jonas, Arn. *Round Trip.* New York, NY: Greenwillow, 1983.

Khalsa, Dayal Kaur. *Tales of a Gambling Grandma.* Montreal, PQ: Tundra, 1986.

Martin Jr., Bill, and John Archambault. *The Ghost-Eye Tree.* New York, NY: Henry Holt, 1988.

Meddaugh, Susan. *Martha Speaks.* Boston, MA: Houghton Mifflin, 1992.

Mollel, Tololwa. *Big Boy.* Toronto, ON: Stoddart, 1995.

Munsch, Robert. *The Paperbag Princess.* Toronto, ON: Annick, 1981.

Polacco, Patricia. *Chicken Sunday.* New York, NY: Putnam, 1992.

Raschka, Chris. *Yo! Yes?* New York, NY: Orchard, 1993.

Sendak, Maurice. *Where the Wild Things Are.* New York, NY: HarperCollins, 1992.

Steig, William. *Rotten Island.* Lincoln, MA: Godine, 1985.

Van Allsburg, Chris. *Jumanji.* Boston, MA: Houghton Mifflin, 1981.

Viorst, Judith. *Alexander and the Terrible, Horrible, No Good Very Bad Day.* New York, NY: Simon & Schuster, 1987.

Wildsmith, Brian. *What the Moon Saw.* New York, NY: Oxford University Press, 1987.

Alphabet Books

Anno, Mitsumasa. *Anno's Alphabet.* New York, NY: HarperCollins, 1988.

Dodson, Peter. *An Alphabet of Dinosaurs.* New York, NY: Scholastic, 1995.

Elting, Mary, and Michael Folsom. *Q Is for Duck.* Boston, MA: Houghton Mifflin, 1980.

Hague, Kathleen. *Alphabears: An ABC Book.* New York, NY: Henry Holt, 1984.

Harrison, Ted. *A Northern Alphabet.* Montreal, PQ: Tundra, 1989.

Hoban, Tana. *Twenty-Six Letters and Ninety-Nine Cents.* New York, NY: Greenwillow Books, 1987.

Jonas, Ann. *Aardvarks, Disembark!* New York, NY: Greenwillow, 1990.

Lessac, Frane. *Caribbean Alphabet.* New York, NY: Morrow, 1994.

Lobel, Anita. *Alison's Zinnia.* New York, NY: Greenwillow, 1990.

MacDonald, Susie. *Alphabatics.* New York, NY: Simon & Schuster, 1986.

Marshall, Janet. *Look Once, Look Twice.* New York, NY: Ticknor & Fields, 1995.

Martin Jr., Bill, and John Archambault. *Chicka Chicka Boom Boom.* New York, NY: Simon & Schuster, 1989.

McPhail, David. *David McPhail's Animals A-Z.* New York, NY: Scholastic, 1993.

Mullins, Patricia. *V for Vanishing: An Alphabet of Endangered Animals.* New York, NY: HarperCollins, 1994.

Musgrove, Margaret. *Ashanti to Zulu: African Traditions.* New York, NY: Puffin, 1992.

Owens, Mary Beth. *A Caribou Alphabet.* Willowdale, ON: Firefly, 1990.

Redhawk, Richard. *Grandfather Origin Story: The Navajo Indian Beginning*. Newcastle, CA: Sierra Oaks, 1988.

Van Allsburg, Chris. *The Z Was Zapped*. Boston, MA: Houghton Mifflin, 1987.

Counting Books

Garne, S.T. *One White Sail*. New York, NY: Simon & Schuster, 1992.

Lottridge, Celia. *One Watermelon Seed*. Toronto, ON: Stoddart, 1990.

McMillan, Bruce. *Counting Wildflowers*. New York, NY: Morrow, 1995.

Shwartz, David. *How Much Is a Million?* New York, NY: Morrow, 1994.

Sloat, Teri. *From One to One Hundred*. New York, NY: Dutton, 1991.

Beginning Books for Readers

Ahlberg, Janet and Allan. *Each Peach Pear Plum*. New York, NY: Viking, 1992.

Brandenberg, Franz. *Leo and Emily*. New York, NY: Greenwillow, 1981.

Brown, Margaret Wise. *The Important Book*. New York, NY: HarperCollins, 1949.

Carle, Eric. *Do You Want to Be My Friend?* New York, NY: HarperCollins, 1971.

---. *The Very Hungry Caterpillar*. New York, NY: Putnam, 1981.

---. *The Very Quiet Cricket*. New York, NY: Putnam, 1990.

Cohen, Miriam. *When Will I Read?* New York, NY: Greenwillow, 1977.

Dragonwagon, Crescent. *This Is the Bread I Baked for Ned*. New York, NY: Simon & Schuster, 1989.

Fox, Mem. *Hattie and the Fox*. New York, NY: Simon & Schuster, 1987.

Ginsburg, Mirra. *Good Morning, Chick*. New York, NY: Greenwillow, 1980.

Guarino, Deborah. *Is Your Mama a Llama?* New York, NY: Scholastic, 1989.

Hill, Eric. *Spot's First Walk*. New York, NY: Putnam, 1981.

Hutchins, Pat. *Rosie's Walk*. New York, NY: Simon & Schuster, 1968.

Jorgensen, Gail. *Crocodile Beat*. New York, NY: Simon & Schuster, 1989.

Kovalski, Maryann. *The Wheels on the Bus*. Toronto, ON: Kids Can, 1987.

Lobel, Arnold. *Days with Frog and Toad*. New York, NY: HarperCollins, 1979.

Marshall, James. *Fox on Stage*. New York, NY: Dial Books, 1983.

Martin Jr., Bill. *Polar Bear, Polar Bear, What Do You Hear?* New York, NY: Henry Holt, 1991.

McKissack, Patricia. *Who Is Coming?* Danbury, CT: Children's Press, 1990.

Minarik, Else. *Little Bear*. New York, NY: HarperCollins, 1978.

nichol, b.p. *Once: A Lullaby*. Windsor, ON: Black Moss Press, 1983.

Parish, Herman. *Good Driving, Amelia Bedelia*. New York, NY: Greenwillow, 1995.

Rees, Mary. *Ten in a Bed*. New York, NY: Little, Brown, 1988.

Robart, Rose. *The Cake that Mack Ate*. New York, NY: Little, Brown, 1986.

Rylant, Cynthia. *Henry & Mudge in Puddle Trouble*. New York, NY: Simon & Schuster, 1987.

Sendak, Maurice. *Chicken Soup with Rice*. New York, NY: Scholastic, 1992.

Serfozo, Mary. *Who Said Red?* New York, NY: Simon & Schuster, 1992.

Seuling, Barbara. *The Teeny Tiny Woman*. New York, NY: Puffin, 1978.

Shaw, Charles G. *It Looked Like Spilt Milk*. New York, NY: HarperCollins, 1988.

Shaw, Nancy. *Sheep in a Jeep*. Boston, MA: Houghton Mifflin, 1986.

Stinson, Kathy. *Red Is Best*. Willowdale, ON: Annick, 1992.

Tafuri, Nancy. *Have You Seen My Duckling?* New York, NY: Morrow, 1991.

Titherington, Jeanne. *Pumpkin, Pumpkin*. New York, NY: Morrow, 1990.

Voake, Charlotte. "The Gingerbread Man" in *Three Little Pigs & Other Favorite Nursery Stories*. Cambridge, MA: Candlewick, 1992.

Wadsworth, Olive. *Over in the Meadow*. New York, NY: Puffin, 1986.

Williams, Linda. *The Little Old Lady Who Was Not Afraid of Anything*. New York, NY: HarperCollins, 1988.

Wood, Audrey. *The Napping House*. Orlando, FL: Harcourt, Brace, 1994.

94: Folk Tales

<table>
<tr><td>

Four Reasons to Read Folk Tales

1. Folk tales enhance children's reading and imagination by connecting to their emotions, knowledge, and previous experience.
2. Folk tales contain simple yet rich expressive and figurative language that children enjoy.
3. Folk tales broaden children's awareness of people from other backgrounds.
4. Folk tales encourage children to use their imagination and problem-solving skills to anticipate and predict the behavior of characters.

</td></tr>
</table>

Before Reading

1. Introduce the Character
Display a picture of a character from a well-known folk tale. Ask the children if they can identify the character, the story to which she or he belongs, and what the character does. If children are not familiar with the character, ask them to brainstorm as a group his or her background and experiences. Record the results of their brainstorming so that it can be referred to as, or after, they read or listen to the folk tale.

2. Make a Prediction Chart
Prepare a chart with two columns at the top, "What We Think Will Happen" and "What Happened." Before reading the folk tale aloud, ask the children to brainstorm as a group major events that they think will occur. As you read the tale, record or have a child record events that took place. How do the lists compare? Were children able to predict major events?

3. Prepare a Three-Stage Chart
Before beginning a folk tale, ask children to list items under the heads, "We Know" and "We Want to Know." When they have experienced the folk tale, they can review the first two columns and complete a third, "We Have Learned."

After Reading

1. Probe and Compare
Elicit children's responses to the story's plot, characters, setting, theme, and literary form. Ask them to compare it to other folk tales they have heard read aloud or read themselves. How does this tale compare to others? Children can discuss similarities and differences, and gain a better understanding of the genre.

2. Character Web
Record the name of the folk tale's main character in the center of a paper. Draw a circle around his or her name and ask children to call out other characters and facts related to the main character. Record their responses to make a character web.

3. Buddy Buzzing
Record the name of each character of a folk tale on a separate card. Ask the children to form a large circle and pass one of the cards to a child in the circle. She or he tells something important about the character before passing the card to a neighbor who repeats the activity. This continues until children have exhausted all information they know about the character. Pass a second character card to another child to continue the activity.

Language Activities

1. What If? Incidents
Children can replace one important event in the plot with one that they have devised and which they think is compatible. With a partner, children take turns retelling the story as it would unfold if their imagined event were a part of the story. Pairs can decide on the most likely "what if?" incident and write up the story to share with classmates.

2. Compare Versions
If possible, have children compare several versions of the same folk tale for similarities and differences in events, characters' behavior, language, setting, and structure. When everyone has finished, conduct a class poll to discover the folk tales children investigated. Together, discuss the lessons taught in each of the folk tales and their relevance to modern life.

3. Research Project
Have children work in small groups or with a partner to research and write their own folk tale. They develop a character and the lesson she or he

will learn. They pick a historical period in which to tell their tale, and research what their character would have experienced if she or he were to have lived during that time. When all groups have finished writing and illustrating their tale, they can share their work with others.

Art and Drama Activities

1. Story Quilt

Cut an old cotton sheet so that each child in the class has a same-sized piece. Children can select their favorite scene from a folk tale and draw and color it on the cloth. Completed scenes could be stitched together to make a class quilt.

2. Literacy Cooperative Groups

Children can find other class members who share their reaction to a folk tale that the class has experienced as a large group. They can choose any method of dramatic response, for example, mime, tableaux, or improvisation. They plan and develop their response and share it with another cooperative group.

3. Modern Adaptation

Children work in small groups of four or five to create a modern adaptation of a folk tale, changing language, setting, and costumes but retaining the essence of the tale. Each child in the group assumes the role of one (or more) character in the folk tale. As a group, they improvise a scene involving the characters and stage it for their classmates. They can use their own words to express the feelings of characters.

4. Experiment with Sounds

Children can form small groups of four or five members. In their groups, they listen to a taped reading of a folk tale. They plan sounds that would enhance the telling of a tale, for example, a tapping noise to represent the sound of footsteps. Using a blank tape, they read aloud the story chorally and include sound effects. The results of their work can be shared with other groups in the class, and the tape can be left at the listening center for independent use.

95: Recommended Folk Tales

Barton, Bob. *The Storm Wife*. Kingston, ON: Quarry, 1993.

Brown, Ruth. *A Dark, Dark Tale*. Toronto, ON: General, 1992.

Bruchac, Joseph. *The Boy Who Lived with the Bears: And Other Iroquois Stories*. New York, NY: HarperCollins, 1995.

Cole, Joanna, ed. *Best-Loved Folk Tales of the World*. New York, NY: Doubleday, 1983.

Davis, Aubrey. *Bone Button Borscht*. Toronto, ON: Kids Can, 1995.

Gilman, Phoebe. *Something from Nothing*. Richmond Hill, ON: Scholastic, 1992.

Grimm, Jacob and Wilhelm. *The Complete Grimm's Fairy Tales*. Ed. James Stern. New York, NY: Pantheon, 1972.

Hamilton, Virginia. *The People Could Fly: American Black Folk Tales*. New York, NY: Knopf, 1992.

Lottridge, Celia. *The Name of the Tree*. Toronto, ON: Groundwood, 1989.

Martin, Rafe. *The Boy Who Lived with the Seals*. New York, NY: Putnam, 1993.

Mollel, Tololwa. *The Orphan Boy*. Toronto, ON: Stoddart, 1995.

San Souci, Robert D. *Short and Shivery*. New York, NY: Doubleday, 1989.

Schwartz, Alvin. *Scary Stories Three*. New York, NY: HarperCollins, 1991.

Scieszka, Jon. *The True Story of the Three Little Pigs*. New York, NY: Viking, 1989.

Wallace, Ian. *Hansel and Gretel*. Toronto, ON: Groundwood, 1994.

Wolkstein, Diane. *The Magic Wings: A Tale from China*. New York, NY: Dutton, 1983.

Yagawa, Sumiko. *The Crane Wife*. New York, NY: Morrow, 1987.

Yee, Paul. *Tales from Gold Mountain*. Toronto, ON: Groundwood, 1989.

Yolen, Jane. *Greyling*. New York, NY: Putnam, 1991.

Zeman, Ludmila. *The Last Quest of Gilgamesh*. Montreal, PQ: Tundra, 1995.

96: Sharing Poetry

Five Ways to Share

1. Choose poetry that you enjoy and that children will find significant.
2. Help children to enjoy the pleasure and satisfaction of poetry.
3. Prepare poetry beforehand, and explore different ways of reading it.
4. Explain poetry when necessary (and when asked), but don't dissect it line by line.
5. Discuss a poem after it has been read. Open-ended questions can lead to discussions:
   - What struck you about the poem?
   - Did any particular words create interesting pictures?
   - Were there any words you liked?

Fifteen Ways to Create a Poetry Environment in Your Classroom

1. A Poem a Day
Each day, you can transcribe a poem on chart paper or on the chalkboard – any surface where the poem will be visible to all children – and take a few minutes to read it to the class. As the children become more familiar with the activity, they may want to read the poem chorally, clap its rhythm, or simply close their eyes to better appreciate its words and cadence as you read it aloud. Recording the poem's title and author on a class calendar provides children with a record of all the poems you have shared.

2. Poem of the Week
Each Friday, children can decide which of the poems presented that week is their favorite and revisit it as a class. This activity can also be done at the end of each month, term, or school year.

3. Favorite Poet of the Week
This activity is a modification of the poem of the week activity. Children can work in pairs to find works of a single poet (anthologies are a good source for this activity). They then choose their favorites, record them on paper, and read them aloud to the rest of the class over the course of the week.

4. Creating a Class Anthology
Children, working as a class, can create a poetry anthology around a theme, topic, poetic form, or author. Each child chooses two or three favorite poems that match the focus of the anthology. Children copy and illustrate their poems before submitting them for publication. The finished collection can be bound and displayed in class, or displayed in the school library so it can be shared with the rest of the school.

5. Experimenting with Readings
On their own or as part of a small group, children can use a tape recorder as they experiment with ways to read a poem. They decide on the most effective method of reading and tape their poem so others may listen to it. Children may also want to incorporate music into their reading.

6. Responding Through Drama
After children have heard a poem read aloud a few times, they can use drama and movement to convey its images or mood.

7. Capturing a Poem on Paper
Children can choose a poem from their anthology, or a favorite poem they have experienced as a class. After reading it aloud chorally, discuss as a group the role of illustrators in conveying an author's characters, mood, and/or setting. Propose to them that they have been hired by the poet to illustrate his or her poem. Before they begin their work, ask them to consider the message the poet is conveying and the medium (e.g., chalk, oil, pastels) that would most effectively express this message. When children have decided on the message and medium, they can work on their own to record and illustrate their poem. You can display completed poems and children can compare their work with that of others in the class. Did the majority of children depict a similar message in a similar medium? If not, discuss as a large group reasons that might explain variations in the children's artwork.

8. Jumbled Lines
Choose a short poem (maximum – fifteen lines) that doesn't rhyme. Cut and jumble the lines before presenting them to the children. In small groups of four or five, they organize the lines in the order they think makes the best poem.

Encourage the children to divide lines, eliminate others, or add new lines that they think would be of benefit. When all groups have completed their work, they take turns sharing their poem with others. At the end of the presentation, read the original poem aloud to the class. Together, you can discuss how the meaning and mood of poems can be changed when their lines are reorganized.

9. "I Wrote the Song"

Children can bring to class copies (e.g., tapes, CDs) of songs they think are poetical, and share them with their classmates by writing the lyrics for others to read, singing the song, and playing the tape or CD. As an extension, children can separate the lyrics from the tune to see if their song can stand alone as a poem, or if it needs to be modified (e.g., adding new words to the refrain).

10. Journal Jottings

As children experience poems, on their own or as part of a group, they can jot down thoughts, images, and feelings the poems elicit, as well as the reflections, associations, and connotations the poems hold for them. This independent activity can help children to understand their response to reading and appreciating poetry, and can provide them with material to discuss in response to the reading of particular poems in class.

11. Questioning the Poem

After reading or listening to a poem, children can take a few minutes to think of questions they have about the poem that they would like to discuss with others. In small-group discussions, children take turns raising their questions with peers.

12. A Poem in Need of a Title

Find a poem that children have not experienced. Before you read it aloud to the children, explain to them that you will read the poem but not its title. Children form small groups, listen to the poem, then brainstorm possible titles. They decide on the best title and share it with other groups. As a large group, children can vote for the title that best suits the poem. You can share the poem's real title after the vote.

13. From a Poem to a Script

Children can select their favorite poems and then translate them into other forms of writing, for example, a monologue, script, advertisement, and so on. Conversely, children may translate an advertisement, synopsis, or photograph into poetic form and shape. Display the children's writing where others can view their work.

14. A Picture Is Worth a Thousand Words

Help children to become more visually aware of poetry by using picture books, films, art books, prints, and filmstrips of poems and poets. As well, children can appreciate poetry in the world around them by examining magazine pictures and advertisements for poetic form and language.

15. Create a Poetic Dictionary

Children can note special phrases, words, or passages they meet in their writing that hold poetic quality or form. Later, they can record them in a personal dictionary to be used when writing poetry.

97: Recommended Poetry Books

Adoff, Arnold. *All the Colors of the Race*. New York, NY: Lothrop, Lee & Shepard, 1982.

---. *Chocolate Dreams*. New York, NY: Lothrop, Lee & Shepard, 1989.

---. *In for Winter, Out for Spring*. Orlando, FL: Harcourt Brace, 1991.

Agard, John, and Grace Nichols, eds. *No Hickory, No Dickory, No Dock*. Cambridge, MA: Candlewick, 1994.

Booth, David, ed. *Doctor Knickerbocker and Other Rhymes*. Toronto, ON: Kids Can, 1993.

---. *Images of Nature: Canadian Poets and the Group of Seven*. Toronto, ON: Kids Can, 1995.

---. *'Til All the Stars Have Fallen*. Toronto, ON: Kids Can, 1989.

Dahl, Roald. *Revolting Rhymes*. New York, NY: Puffin, 1995.

Day, David. *Aska's Animals*. Toronto, ON: Doubleday, 1991.

Dunn, Sonja. *Primary Rhymerry*. Markham, ON: Pembroke, 1993.

Fitch, Sheree. *There Were Monkeys in My Kitchen*. Toronto, ON: Doubleday, 1992.

Fleischman, Paul. *Joyful Noise: Poems for Two Voices*. New York, NY: HarperCollins, 1988.

Graham, Carolyn. *Fairy Tales*. New York, NY: Oxford University Press, 1988.

Heidbreder, Robert. *Don't Eat Spiders*. Toronto, ON: Stoddart, 1985.

Janeczko, Paul B., ed. *The Place My Words Are Looking For*. New York, NY: Simon & Schuster, 1990.

Lee, Dennis. *The Ice Cream Store*. Toronto, ON: HarperCollins, 1991.

Little, Jean. *Hey World, Here I Am*. Toronto, ON: Kids Can, 1986.

Lobel, Arnold, ed. *The Random House Book of Mother Goose*. New York, NY: Random House, 1986.

Merriam, Eve. *You Be Good & I'll Be Night*. New York, NY: Morrow, 1988.

Nye, Naomi Shihab, ed. *This Same Sky: A Collection of Poems from around the World*. New York, NY: Simon & Schuster, 1992.

o'huigin, s. *A Dozen Million Spills*. Windsor, ON: Black Moss Press, 1993.

---. *Scary Poems for Rotten Kids*. Windsor, ON: Black Moss Press, 1988.

Polacco, Patricia. *Babushka's Mother Goose*. New York, NY: Philomel, 1995.

Prelutsky, Jack. *The New Kid on the Block*. Novato, CA: Living Books, 1994.

Prelutsky, Jack, ed. *The Random House Book of Poetry for Children*. New York, NY: Random House, 1983.

Priest, Robert. *A Terrible Case of the Stars*. Toronto, ON: Penguin, 1994.

Rosen, Michael. *Walking on the Bridge of Your Nose*. London, UK: Kingfisher, 1995.

Rylant, Cynthia. *Waiting to Waltz: A Childhood*. New York, NY: Simon & Schuster, 1984.

Schwartz, Alvin, ed. *And the Green Grass Grew All Around: Folk Poetry from Everyone*. New York, NY: HarperCollins, 1992.

Silverstein, Shel. *Where the Sidewalk Ends*. New York, NY: HarperCollins, 1974.

Yolen, Jane, ed. *Sleep Rhymes around the World*. Honesdale, PA: Boyds Mill, 1994.

98: Reading Nonfiction

For a time, nonfiction could not compete with the enchantment and fascination of appealing picture books, folk tales, and novels. Nonfiction appeared only utilitarian, and was used by teachers in preparing lessons and by children who sought answers to questions. Today, nonfiction is colorful and exciting, and the children who read these books are intrigued with the factual information they contain.

A successful nonfiction book should...
• animate its subject by bringing it to life,
• create a vivid and believable world,
• like a good storybook, be a pleasure to read,
• encourage further discovery and reading,
• make the reader feel that the search for answers was as rewarding as the facts themselves.

When choosing nonfiction...
• be selective; skim the book by reading a page or two to assess the reading level, tone, and style,
• study the illustrations – are they appealing?
• ask, "Is this a good read?" "Will children argue over who reads it first?"
• confirm accuracy of facts.

Activities to Explore Nonfiction Books

1. Comparing Fact to Fiction
Children can read two or three nonfiction books (e.g., books on dinosaurs) and then read storybooks on the same topic. The children can compare similarities and differences that exist between books from the two genres.

2. Comparing Biographies to Fiction
Children can read a biography and respond to its narrative structure. Does the book read like fiction? Are real events fictionalized? How and why does the author use this technique?

3. Keeping a Journal or a Log
Children can respond to nonfiction in a journal, allowing them the freedom to:
• speculate on the facts that will in turn encourage further research and discovery,

- write about what they want to know about a particular topic (drawing from their experiences), then adding what they have learned,
- comment on the way the author presented information – chronologically, spatially, logically.

4. Becoming a Book Detective
This activity provides children with the opportunity to share their knowledge about a favorite nonfiction book. In groups of two, they examine the books for:
- illustrations,
- photographs,
- title,
- print size, font,
- price,
- table of contents,
- chapters,
- diagrams or charts,
- glossary,
- author information,
- jacket or cover.

Children can determine if these items were included and if so, if they were appropriate and helpful.

5. The Making of Nonfiction
In small groups, children research various topics, gathering enough information to write their own nonfiction books. Here, children will gain an appreciation for the amount of research that goes into writing nonfiction and the importance of including correct information.

Help children use nonfiction books by:
- giving them structured opportunities to reflect personally on the information they collect.
- encouraging them to consult books only to answer questions that arise from interviews and direct experiences with the topic.
- giving them opportunities to teach one another about their topics, and encourage listeners to insist that they be given a sensible understanding of what the writer is trying to explain.
- having them write weekly memos to report on their learning.
- asking them to write a draft before they feel they have "enough material" so that they focus on the quality of writing rather than including excess data.

99: Recommended Nonfiction Books

Aliki. *A Medieval Feast*. New York, NY: HarperCollins, 1983.

Bondar, Barbara. *On the Shuttle: Eight Days in Space*. Toronto, ON: Greey de Pencier, 1993.

Bouchard, David. *If You're Not From the Prairie*. Vancouver, BC: Raincoast, 1994.

Cherry, Lynne. *The Great Kapok Tree: A Tale of the Amazon Rain Forest*. Orlando, FL: Harcourt Brace, 1990.

Cole, Joanna. *The Magic School Bus Series*. New York, NY: Scholastic.

Donnelly, Judy. *The Titanic Lost... & Found*. New York, NY: Random House, 1987.

Granfield, Linda. *Cowboy, A Kid's Album*. Vancouver, BC: Douglas & McIntyre, 1993.

Greenwood, Barbara. *Pioneer Story*. Toronto, ON: Kids Can, 1994.

Ingram, Jay. *Real Live Science*. Toronto, ON: Greey de Pencier, 1992.

Leigh, Nila K. *Learning to Swim in Swaziland*. New York, NY: Scholastic, 1993.

Macaulay, David. *Ship*. Boston, MA: Houghton Mifflin, 1993.

Morimoto, Junko. *My Hiroshima*. New York, NY: Viking, 1990.

Oppenheim, Joanne. *Have You Seen Birds?* Richmond Hill, ON: Scholastic, 1986.

Petry, Ann. *Harriet Tubman: Conductor on the Underground Railway*. New York, NY: Simon & Schuster, 1990.

Wild, Margaret. *A Time for Toys*. Toronto, ON: Kids Can, 1991.

100: Newspapers and Magazines

Newspapers and magazines of all types can and should be brought into the classroom by the teacher and children. Of particular interest will be material children read on their own. They can discuss favorite sections and issues that attract their attention. Eventually, in any long-term, comprehensive media literacy unit, children will learn how to become discriminating readers of newspaper and magazine articles, and will realize the importance of this type of reading.

The first step in this process is to help children reflect on the content of what they read and their reasons for reading it. Teachers can make available a variety of newspapers and magazines, which children can flip through in order to find articles they want to read. The variety should be diverse in order to capture the interests of all children in the classroom. While print media study can be concurrent, some teachers prefer to separate the study of newspapers and magazines.

Learning About Magazines and Newspapers

1. Following a Journalist's Lead
Discuss with the children the questions journalists answer when they write an article – who, what, where, when, why, and how. Provide them with short articles that model this format. For each, children can write short answers to the questions. These short answers should then serve as an outline of the article. Children can practise this journalistic principle by reporting on classroom events.

2. Headline Scrapbook
Children can work on a group project through the year. Each day they cut headlines from the paper that represent the day's news. As well, they can cut headlines that have relevance to the class (e.g., local news). Headlines are pasted in a scrapbook to provide a summary of the year's news. At the same time, children can construct a timeline to serve as another reminder of important news events.

3. Predicting Articles
Display examples of headlines and ask children to brainstorm the contents of the articles in small groups. Give one article to each group. With group members, children read the piece, make notes on the content, and check for predictions. Groups take turns reporting their findings.

4. Matching Headlines and Articles
Cut headlines and articles from newspapers or magazines and paste each on separate pieces of paper. Make copies for five small groups. Children, in their groups, match the articles to the headlines. When all groups have finished, they can compare results. Did all groups come up with the same matches? If not, can children identify what made the task difficult?

5. Read All About It
One of the many ways that newspapers serve as a school resource is their role as models for writing. Familiarity with a paper, its sections, and its features can be increased by organizing a class field trip to the local newspaper where children can learn about the roles of writers, editors, cartoonists, proofreaders, designers, and other personnel. Armed with first-hand exposure to a newspaper and its staff, children can then prepare a class newspaper. Children in the class can volunteer for roles and staff meetings can be held to determine the paper's content.

6. From Reports to Short Stories
This activity provides an opportunity for children to analyze the structure of texts and transform them into other print forms. Before children begin this activity, select several reports from the daily newspaper that would interest them. Post each article on a separate piece of paper. On their own or with a partner, children can rework the article in various forms, for example, a short story or an interview. Similarly, children can rewrite short stories as news reports.

7. A Magazine of Books
These magazines, containing contributions from all class members, can be as long or as short as the children like and can include a number of features (e.g., poems, stories, author biographies, illustrations) that relate to books read in the classroom.

8. Critical Media Analysis

Children need to be able to use a variety of strategies to identify bias and inaccuracy in newspaper and magazine articles. Together, select several newspaper and magazine articles. Read/view the articles and their layouts, and discuss elements that engage an audience. Discuss, as well, the importance of qualifications and/or knowledge needed by a nonfiction writer, and that we, as readers, can't assume that all writers are experts.

9. Product Logos

Children can examine logos featured in magazine and newspaper advertisements. They cut out the logos and make collages by product genre (e.g., sporting goods, foods). When collages are finished, discuss with children differences among logos. Do they differ from genre to genre? Can children explain reasons for these differences?

(*Games Magazine* has logo puzzles children can solve during free time.)

10. Persuasive Messages

Children can write and design an advertisement for print, television, billboard, or radio. Before they begin, they use the class collection of magazines and newspapers to study approaches specific to print mediums, and discuss approaches taken in television and radio commercials and billboards. Children can work with three or four classmates to create an ad. If they choose to prepare a television advertisement, arrange for their use of a video camera. Similarly, children developing a radio advertisement can use a tape recorder. When finished, children can share their work by medium or by product type (e.g., consumer goods, service).

References for Teachers

Atwell, Nancie. *In the Middle: Writing, Reading, and Learning with Adolescents.* Portsmouth, NH: Boynton/Cook, 1987.

Barton, Bob. *Stories to Tell.* Markham, ON: Pembroke, 1992.

---. *Tell Me Another.* Markham, ON/Portsmouth, NH: Pembroke/Heinemann, 1986.

Barton, Bob, and David Booth. *Mother Goose Goes to School.* Markham, ON: Pembroke, 1995.

---. *Stories in the Classroom.* Markham, ON/Portsmouth, NH: Pembroke/Heinemann, 1990.

Baskwill, Jane. *Parents and Teachers: Partners in the Process.* Richmond Hill, ON: Scholastic, 1989.

Beaty, Janice J. *Picture Book Storytelling: Literature Activities for Young Children.* New York, NY: Harcourt Brace, 1993.

Benedict, Susan, and Lenore Carlisle, eds. *Beyond Words: Picture Books for Older Readers and Writers.* Portsmouth, NH: Heinemann, 1992.

Bomer, Randy. *Time for Meaning: Crafting Literate Lives in Middle & High School.* Portsmouth, NH: Heinemann, 1995.

Booth, David. *Classroom Voices: Language-Based Learning in the Elementary School.* Toronto, ON: Harcourt Brace, 1994.

---. *Spelling Links.* Markham, ON: Pembroke, 1991.

---. *Stories to Read Aloud.* Markham, ON: Pembroke, 1992.

---. *Story Drama: Reading, Writing and Role-Playing Across the Curriculum.* Markham, ON: Pembroke, 1994.

Booth, David, and Bill Moore. *Poems Please!* Markham, ON: Pembroke, 1988.

Booth, David, and Larry Swartz. *Novel Sense.* Toronto, ON: MeadowBook Press – Harcourt Brace, 1996.

Booth, David, and Carol Thornley-Hall, eds. *The Talk Curriculum.* Markham, ON/Portsmouth, NH: Pembroke/Heinemann, 1991.

Bos, Candace, and Sharon Vaughan. *Strategies for Teaching Students with Learning and Behavior Problems.* Needham Heights, MA: Allyn & Bacon, 1994.

Brownlie, Faye, Susan Close, and Linda Wingren. *Tomorrow's Classroom Today: Strategies for Creating Active Readers, Writers, and Thinkers.* Markham, ON/Portsmouth, NH: Pembroke/Heinemann, 1990.

Calkins, Lucy. *The Art of Teaching Writing.* New ed. Portsmouth, NH: Heinemann, 1994.

Calkins, Lucy, with Shelley Harwayne. *Living Between the Lines.* Portsmouth, NH: Heinemann, 1990.

Carletti, Silvana, Suzanne Girard, and Kathlene Willing. *The Library/Classroom Connection.* Markham, ON/Portsmouth, NH: Pembroke/Heinemann, 1991.

Chambers, Aidan. *Introducing Books to Children.* Boston, MA: Horn, 1983.

---. *Tell Me: Children Reading and Talk.* York, ME/Markham, ON: Stenhouse/Pembroke, 1996.

---. *The Reading Environment: How Adults Help Children Enjoy Books.* York, ME/Markham, ON: Stenhouse/Pembroke, 1991.

Clay, Marie M. *Reading Recovery Diagnostic Survey.* 3rd ed. Portsmouth, NH: Heinemann, 1985.

Cunningham, Patricia M. *Phonics They Use.* New York, NY: HarperCollins, 1995.

Daniels, Harvey. *Literature Circles.* York, ME/Markham, ON: Stenhouse/Pembroke, 1994.

Davidson, Merilyn, Rita Isherwood, and Ernie Tucker. *Moving on with Big Books.* Richmond Hill, ON: Scholastic, 1991.

Goodman, Kenneth S., ed. *Miscue Analysis: Applications to Reading Instruction.* Urbana, IL: National Council of Teachers of English, 1973.

---. *What's Whole in Whole Language?* Portsmouth, NH: Heinemann, 1986.

Grant, Janet Millar, Barbara Heffler, and Kadri Mereweather. *Student-Led Conferences: Using Portfolios to Share Learning with Parents.* Markham, ON: Pembroke, 1995.

Graves, Donald. *Investigate Nonfiction.* Portsmouth, NH: Heinemann, 1989.

---. *Writing: Teachers and Children at Work.* Portsmouth, NH: Heinemann, 1983.

Greenwood, Bob and Barbara. *Speak Up! Speak Out!: Every Kid's Guide to Planning, Preparing, and Presenting a Speech.* Markham, ON: Pembroke, 1994.

Harste, Jerome, Kathy Short, and Carolyn Burke. *Creating Classrooms for Authors: The Reading-Writing Connection.* Portsmouth, NH: Heinemann, 1989.

Hart-Hewins, Linda, and Jan Wells. *Borrow-a-Book: Your Classroom Library Goes Home.* Richmond Hill, ON: Scholastic, 1988.

---. *Real Books for Reading*. Markham, ON/Portmouth, NH: Pembroke/Heinemann, 1990.

Harwayne, Shelley. *Lasting Impressions*. Portsmouth, NH: Heinemann, 1992.

Heathcoate, Dorothy. *Dorothy Heathcote: Collected Writings on Education and Drama*. Ed. Liz Johnson and Cecily O'Neill. London, UK: Hutchinson, 1984.

Holdaway, Don. *The Foundations of Literacy*. Richmond Hill, ON: Scholastic, 1979.

Jobe, Ron, and Paula Hart. *Cultural Connections: Using Literature to Explore World Cultures*. Markham, ON: Pembroke, 1993.

Lonsdale, Bernard J., and Helen K. Mackintosh. *Children Experience Literature*. New York, NY: Random House, 1973.

McDermid, Terry Z. *A Tapestry of Reading: Introducing Literacy Genres, Grades 4-6*. Glenview, IL: Good Year, 1994.

Meek, Margaret. *On Being Literate*. Portsmouth, NH: Heinemann, 1992.

Moffett, James, and Betty J. Wagner. *Student-Centered Language Arts and Reading, K-12*. Portsmouth, NH: Boynton/Cook, 1991.

Moline, Steve. *I See What You Mean*. York, ME/Markham, ON: Stenhouse/Pembroke, 1995.

Morgan, Norah, and Julianna Saxton. *Asking Better Questions*. Markham, ON: Pembroke, 1994.

Neelands, Jonothan. *Structuring Drama Work*. Cambridge, MA: Cambridge University Press, 1990.

Parsons, Les. *Response Journals*. Markham, ON/Portsmouth, NH: Pembroke/Heinemann, 1990.

Phenix, Jo. *The Spelling Teacher's Book of Lists*. Markham, ON: Pembroke, 1995.

Rasinski, Timothy, and Nancy Padak. *Holistic Reading Strategies*. Englewood Cliffs, NJ: Prentice Hall, 1996.

Rhodes, Lynn, and Curt Dudley-Marling. *Readers and Writers with a Difference: A Holistic Approach to Teaching Learning Disabled and Remedial Students*. Portsmouth, NH: Heinemann, 1988.

Robb, Laura. *Whole Language, Whole Learners – Creating a Literature-Centered Classroom*. New York, NY: Morrow, 1994.

Routman, Regie. *Invitations: Changing as Teachers and Learners, K-12*. Portsmouth, NH: Heinemann, 1994.

Samway Davies, K., G. Whang, & M. Pippitt. *Buddy Reading: Cross-Age Tutoring in a Multicultural School*. Portsmouth, NH: Heinemann, 1995.

Schwartz, Susan, and Maxine Bone. *Retelling, Relating & Reflecting*. Concord, ON: Irwin, 1994.

Swartz, Larry. *Classroom Events through Poetry*. Markham, ON: Pembroke, 1993.

---. *Dramathemes*. Rev. ed. Markham, ON/Portmouth, NH: Pembroke/Heinemann, 1995.

Taylor, Stephen. *Planning and Assessing the Curriculum in English Language Arts*. Alexandria, VA: Association for Supervision and Curriculum Development, 1991.

Tierney, Robert J., Mark Carter, and Laura Desai. *Portfolio Assessment in the Reading-Writing Classroom*. Norwood, MA: Christopher-Gordon, 1991.

Trelease, Jim. *The Read-Aloud Handbook*. 4th. ed. New York, NY: Penguin, 1995.

Wason-Ellam, Linda. *Start with a Story*. Markham, ON/Portsmouth, NH: Pembroke/Heinemann, 1990.

Weaver, Constance. *Reading Process and Practice: From Socio-Psycholinguistics to Whole Language*. Portsmouth, NH: Heinemann, 1988.

Wells, Gordon. *The Meaning Makers: Children Learning Language and Using Language to Learn*. Portsmouth, NH: Heinemann, 1986.

Wells, Jan, and Linda Hart-Hewins. Phonics Too! How to Teach Skills in a Balanced Language Program. Markham, ON: Pembroke, 1994.

Woodward, Virginia, Jerome Harste, and Carolyn Burke. *Language Stories and Literacy Lessons*. Portsmouth, NH: Heinemann, 1984.

Yopp, Ruth and Hallie. *Literature-Based Reading Activities*. Needham Heights, MA: Allyn & Bacon, 1996.